FOLLOW YOUR CAREER STAR

Follow Your CAREER STAR

A
CAREER QUEST
BASED ON
INNER VALUES

Jon Snodgrass, Ph.D.

KENSINGTON BOOKS

KENSINGTON BOOKS are published by

Kensington Publishing Corp.
850 Third Avenue
New York, NY 10022

CAREER STAR SYSTEM

(AT A GLANCE)

CAREER STAR SYSTEM
(IN DETAIL)

DIAGRAM

CHART

MAP

ACKNOWLEDGMENTS

Private clients and college students individually and in groups are the main sources of material for this book. While abstract at times, the work is empirically derived and practically designed. Those who contributed, often unknowingly, probably would not recognize their input. They are, however, the "real stars" of the *Career Star System*. By this acknowledgement they are sincerely thanked.

I would like to thank the following individuals for their special contributions: Margaret Campbell, Patricia Conlee, Julia Crookson, Rosemarie Esposito, Rosemary Gray, June Griffith, Vera Handricks, Liz Hargrove, Naomi Hart, David Scott Kadin, Connie Leonard, Heather Lovasz, Rosalie Ortega, Rob Peeples, Jacqueline Rameriz, B. J. Richter, Judith Stevens-Long, Cynthia Sohaili, Ulysses Serrano, Lisa Spiegel, Karen White, Suzi Wigutow and Gerilynn Wright.

Ben Lizardi and Lisa Lizardi helped produce the original *Career Strategies Map and Guide*. Darcy Tom drew and dyed the *Career Star Map*. Kathryn Kelly and Reiko Irisawa drew and dyed the original *Career Strategies Map*. Lisa Lizardi drew the prototype of the *Career Strategies Map*. Greg Dahl drew the graphic diagrams. Jean-Noel Bassior advised as a publishing consultant, Leslie Keenan served as literary agent, and Tracy Bernstein was executive editor.

In particular, however, I would like to express my deepest appreciation to Greg Marshall who helped continuously with practical and theoretical matters and who always lent steadfast encouragement. Greg became a partner in the editing and production phases of the prepublication edition for which I am very grateful. Through Greg I was also introduced to *A Course in Miracles*.

The metaphor of a star, the "light-motif" of the book, arose through my study of *A Course in Miracles*. This is true generally as in, "The journey that we undertake together is the exchange of dark for light," and true specifically as in, "You find a star; a miracle of grace."

Readers familiar with the *Course* will recognize its influence throughout the work. *A Course in Miracles* helped me find my star. Thank God for *A Course in Miracles*.

My sincerest thanks to everyone who helped all along the way.

DEDICATION

For more than twelve years my calling has been to write this book to you about how to find meaning and fulfillment in your life-work. The project began in 1983 as a two- or three-page handout for a seminar entitled "Finding Your Calling." The manuscript grew erratically over the years as it was revised frequently based on feedback from participants in various workshops, classes, and counseling sessions.

The manuscript became the working papers of a private career counseling center, which I founded. Additional content was derived from notes taken with clients in person or on the telephone during the crisis hours of late night and early morning. Accordingly, the text is almost entirely based on empirical experience.

The metaphor of a star and the *Follow Your Career Star* title were adopted in 1992 when I first began to really believe that my star was also your star, that we are all of one star, not lone stars nor alone stars. Before this time my perspective was more linear, and I called it the *Career Strategies System.* "Star" was as yet an unrecognized word in "*stra*tegies."

When the concept finally broke through, I became obsessed with stars, which will be evident soon enough to the reader. Dante's lines, "If you keep navigating by your star, you will find a glorious port," (Canto XV of the *Inferno*), was discovered long after I was at sea with this book.

Friends and relatives, clients and students often got as carried away as I did and contributed to my "star craziness" by giving me star ornaments, cards, paperweights, and erasers. For a time I thought I might change my name to Jon Stargrass, which *is* the name of a flower. Alas, it is difficult to cast aside something so familiar as your name. I was delighted, pun intended, with all the stars but I warn the reader: *You do not yet realize that you too run the risk of becoming possessed of a star,* a beautiful star with incredible rays.

You may think you can continue to stay in control of ruining your life by not finding your star. Work can be misused to keep you disgruntled and apart from your life-purpose. Everybody is secretly doing what they really want to do even while yearning for an alternative.

You have to let go of being who you are not, to become who you are meant to be. You can or cannot find your calling as you wish upon a star. Your calling is as responsive to your desire as your potentials are unlimited. Probably you have understood too much for your own good already.

The danger lies in your contemplation of a star even for a split second. In this space your star can grab your mind with its powerful rays of light. A twinkling star needs only an instant of your tiniest inkling. From here on, you are grappled by a light that takes hold out of the darkness of your hidden mind. Undimmable, the fireball kindles wide-eyed consciousness. Hereafter, you are always both the object and the subject of a possession.

Read further cautiously! At first you will be seen as "fanatical," accused by others of being "hysterical," in need of rest called a "sabbatical." In time, you will become jovial and lyrical, considered now to be "really farcical," intervention is said to be "medical." But, it is true and simple, you are struck by your Career Star quintessential; you are not in need of a hospital.

Stars are the sparks in the sky that represent higher purpose both in the natural and mental universes. Since ancient times stars have represented purposive life. When we look into the night sky the darkness mirrors our own unknown self and the starlight the potential for self-discovery. Under the starry sky we can see that the limits we perceive and set for ourselves are circumscribed by our mind, not by the universe, for the latter is boundless.

The earth is a planet in orbit around the sun. The earth is less than 8000, while the sun is 864,000, miles in diameter. The sun is only one of a billion stars in the Milky Way Galaxy, a band of blended starlight that stretches in a ring around the earth.

Stars are symbols of higher purpose.

A light year is the distance light travels in one year, or 5,878,000,000,000 miles. The Milky Way is 80,000 light years across at its widest point—and it is only one galaxy in the universe in which there are an estimated 100 million other galaxies.

What all these numbers mean is that the universe is actually infinite. The inner world is not restricted by the outer world and is just as infinite. The truth of personal, unlimited star-potential has been known from time immemorial. It is a truth forgotten and rediscovered time and again by generations who adopt anew the symbol of a star as their own. This causes the symbol to become mythical and endure through cultures and over the ages.

"Among all the strange things that men have forgotten," wrote G. K. Chesterton, an English novelist, "the most universal lapse of memory is that they are living on a star." "And Earth is but a star, that once had shone" is the way the English poet, James Elroy Flecker, put it. It is possible to reverse the perspective and see a star in a grain of sand, a little star cooled by time. We are tiny, nuclear, living sparks of giant stars, great crucibles in the sky.

> **We are tiny living sparks of stars, those great crucibles in the sky.**

A star is a universal symbol of higher purpose. It is not a religious symbol of Christianity although it is a sign for "Christmas" or "Christ Mass" that comes at the end of the calendar year. A star is a part of the symbolism also of Judaism (Star of David), Islam (Star and Half-Moon Crescent) and the Bahā 'ī Faith (a double star in a shield). The wheels in the logo of the various forms of Buddhism also resemble stars.

Stars are also used frequently to designate power and rank. A pentagram or pentacle, a five-pointed star, is an emblem that identifies military equipment in many armed forces. Traditionally, the higher the authority of a military officer, the greater the number of uniform star insignia. Around the world stars are used in thirty-five national flags.

In the flag of our country, stars represent the loyalty of the fifty states to the greater union of the United States of America. Stars, therefore, stand for the idea of devotion to the higher purpose of a greater unified whole, a "more perfect union." Similarly, stars symbolize the loyalty of the individual to a collective cause.

As a light shining in the darkness a star is an image symbolic of spirit. The light of self-knowledge arises from a greater source to illuminate life's purpose in the vast darkness of inner space. It reveals an unbreakable connection between your inner being and your outer origin. Men and women in time, countless as the multitude of stars, have started and ended their historical quests at the crucial point of this eternal juncture.

If you incorporate the vision of inner starlight into consciousness, total darkness does not vanish but the spark of your unique destiny is lit. Once you begin to believe in your precious Career Star, it shines even brighter as proof positive against the black backdrop of the long night of self-doubt. *Star Trek* and *Star Wars* are searches for spiritual meaning in outer space just as Dante, in the *Inferno* and Odysseus in the *Odyssey*, looked in geographical places.

A Career Star is a body of light assigned to guide you in the quest for your purpose. With self-trust, a Career Star bursts forth brilliantly into awareness and stays there radiantly. While the *Career Star System* draws on ancient wisdom and symbolism, it comes full circle as a modern concept designed especially for those looking forward and moving eagerly to create meaning in the twenty-first century.

Because I am a stranger to you, as you may be to yourself, the idea of a Career Star may seem alien and hard to follow. I have also been a starless stranger in my past, stranded by the blackout of my own disbelief. Therefore, I can totally understand being reluctant to find and follow your own star. Rarely have I met anyone who chased his or her destiny readily and easily.

Just as the desert, however, was once the floor of the ocean, you and I and others like us can also change. Usually we become teachers of subjects we need most to learn and I confess that I am a model offender and typical expression of the dilemma. I tell my clients and students what I need most to hear and pay attention to myself about as much as they do.

In this respect, *Follow Your Career Star* is autobiographical, as are most self-help books. For the longest time, I thought perhaps my calling was an echo, until I began to hear clearly that the sound of my calling is calling you to your calling, calling . . . calling . . . calling . . . Are *you* calling *your* calling? Are you straining to hear with ears receptive to a reply?

Questar of a Career Star, I hope this manual helps mend and meld your mind and heart as one. With it in hand, may your Calling Star arise in your psychic and cosmic sky, twinkling undiminished by self-doubt, and may it gleam you vibrantly and steadily into the twenty-first century. In time it can become so luminescent your Career Star is impossible to forget. Ultimately, our collective amnesia will no longer continue to obscure our common vision as a nation of the star.

OVERVIEW

Follow Your Career Star is a comprehensive manual and workbook on the process of career discovery and development. Below is a review of the *Career Star System* for the "Nova Star," the neophyte. A quick "Overview for Career Counseling Professionals" is contained in Appendix 1. The most frequently asked questions about the *Career Star System* are answered in Appendix 2, "Career Star Questions."

Many people today are looking for a departure from the way life has been. Yet they are reluctant to abandon what is traditional and familiar. The *Career Star System* is crafted to help you see a new way, to make a wise choice, and to dedicate your life to purpose.

This manual will teach you how to assess, strengthen, and integrate intuitive and logical styles of thinking so that you can use both forms of intelligence to guide your career quest. You will learn to bridge the two so that you actually enter the process of career discovery and development. Also you will design a rational plan of action based on your intuitively acquired knowledge of yourself to make your new career actually begin to happen.

To find your Career Star you must want to learn to know yourself at least as well as you want to master the outer world. You have an inner-life universe where only you alone can go to discover the value within. In this respect, getting ahead in life really does depend upon who you know. "Networking" begins with *you*.

You honor yourself through the quest for self-knowledge and you uplift society by taking a meaningful stance with your life and serving as a model to others. You can take an extra step and vow to return your gifts once discovered to the human family. The tragedy, however, is often the life not chosen.

The first four chapters are the foundation of the *Career Star System* and present in detail the idea of having a "Career Star." Within each chapter is a practical exercise relevant to the ideas of that chapter. You are encouraged to "work the system" by reading and practicing each exercise. Chapter and exercise numbers coincide.

Chapter 1, "Star Orientation," is an introduction to the basic principles of the *Career Star System*. It contains a "Job Satisfaction Assessment" that covers sixteen major aspects of work to help you determine
the extent of your present discontent. The higher your score the
more you need to adopt the *Career Star System* as your method for finding meaningful work in life.

Because some people believe that the idea of a calling is unrealistic and idealistic, Chapter 1 also contains a discussion of your calling
in the context of the current economic crisis. You may be dissatisfied
with your career because of unemployment or underemployment, or
you may be threatened by a layoff. Another source of recruits to the
Career Star System are individuals caught in organizational conflict and
office politics.

As the economic crisis tightens its hold, competition becomes
stiffer, rewards more meager, and business ethics more flexible. Employees in both large and small companies have always needed to understand organizational behavior but this is true all the more in hard
times. You stay separate from the in-fighting and are able to pursue
your Career Star within and outside the organizational setting with
this knowledge.

Chapter 2, "Star System," outlines the theory and method of the
entire program of study and practice. First the tools of the system
are reviewed: the Career Star Text, the *Career Star Map*, the Career
Star Meditation, and the Career Star Mandala, among other components. This chapter also contains a "Commission" statement to be
signed by the reader affirming a commitment to the quest for a Career Star.

Chapter 3, "Star Storms," examines the turbulence that almost
everyone encounters in the pursuit of a calling. Why resistance usually appears immediately after making a commitment is explained in
this chapter. Most people interpret an emotional backlash to mean
there is a real danger and want to quit their quest. This chapter shows,
however, that resistance is actually like the needle of a compass that
points in the right direction.

What it means to have a "calling" is defined, diagrammed, and illustrated fully in Chapter 4, "Star Mission." Inspirational quotes by several famous artists and leaders are also discussed in the chapter. The
ancient idea that each person has a personal star in the heavens is also
presented.

Chapter 5 contains the *Career Star Map* which is used as an assessment tool to determine the extent to which an individual is a mod-

erate or radical Starphire or Starphade. The reader is carried through a "star-type" assessment process step by step. The results reveal in a visual form the consequences of being a Starphire or a Starphade. How to use the *Career Star Map* is explained fully in this chapter.

"Star Types," Chapter 6, reviews two basic personality types, Starphires and Starphades, who represent the most common ways of getting off the beam of a Calling Star. Starphires are usually angry with themselves for not being able to find their calling through logical means. They are called Starphires because they often burn furiously with frustration from overachievement and overwork.

What color is your Career Star?

"Starphades," the opposite type, are shaded by a cool indigo of self-doubt, and often their star burns too faintly to be tracked or trekked. "Super Stars" follow their Career Star naturally and "Sun Stars" apply the *Career Star System*. The color of Sun and Super Stars is bright white like the most luminous real stars.

The colors of most regular Career Stars are exactly the same as the rainbow, from inky-black Starphades to red hot, molten-orange Starphires. The hue of your Career Star varies, like a mood ring, according to your attitude toward it. A question continuously raised in the *Career Star System,* therefore, is "What Color is Your Career Star?"

Chapter 7, "Star Stories," provides case studies of two wayward types of stars. For example, a successful business woman becomes despondent after abandoning her musical career; an accomplished actor goes on the skids with multiple addictions; a perfectionistic secretary struggles to take the risk of a career transition; a fine artist wrestles with low self-esteem; a medical sales person suffers panic attacks; and a fine artist is so fearful of rejection he can barely present his work. Case histories of two children illustrate the basic Starphade/ Starphire split evident at an early age.

Two important aspects of personality, rationality and creativity, are explored in Chapter 8, "Bright Stars." The reader is shown how these two healthy sides of the personality can be joined to find both fulfillment and prosperity through work. Excluding one or the other results in either too little income on the Starphade side, or too little happiness on the Starphire side of life. This chapter offers a powerful exercise, "Star Self A to Z," that helps readers to actually identify their core creative personality.

Chapter 9, "Dark Stars," introduces the concept of the "Inner Injured Child," a part of the personality that appears in the form of an "internal adversary" who obstructs plans and actions by causing emotional resistance. The reader is taught as an adult to care for this injured part of the self.

Chapter 10, "Star Force," examines extreme Starphires who persistently direct their rational mind and willpower toward successful achievements, but deny both their Creative and Injured Child Selves. In the extreme, Starphires become workaholics who eventually burn out.

Chapter 11, "Star Flowe," deals with the phenomenon of "Flowe," or a way of being that is totally focused on sensuality. An extreme Starphade may depend exclusively on physical pleasure and bodily sensation as a way of coping with their Injured Inner Child. Starphades who elect this route also deny their Creative Child.

This chapter makes readers aware that long-term consequences of an exclusively right-brain orientation include psychological depression, unemployment, and addiction. A special section in this chapter also concerns the emotional effects of child abuse and helps the reader determine if early childhood experiences are the source of their brain lateralization and career dilemmas.

Night dreams are among the most obvious and dramatic expressions of our mind at work while we are relaxed. Dreams contain messages that tell us about our true nature, including the mission we are assigned to accomplish with our work lives. Chapter 12, "Star Dreams," therefore, introduces the reader to the elementary principles of dream interpretation as used in the *Career Star System*. Readers can decipher the communications, know themselves better, and determine their life purpose.

Chapter 13, "Star Strategies," introduces the Career Star Wheel, a diagram about how to get moving on the path of your Career Star. The wheel shows the process of career discovery and development divided into six stages: exploration, experience, observation, description, reflection, and conception. Starphires work the emotional half of the wheel to become more familiar with their inner feelings and creative abilities. Starphades work the logical half to become more acquainted with the place of their talent in the real world.

"Star Strategies" also provides two new exercises that help Starphires choose sensing and feeling activities that are not goal oriented from a Chart of over 30 possibilities. These relaxation and stress-reduction exercises simultaneously allow creative impulses to begin to break through to consciousness. Starphades, on the other hand, choose logical activities that begin to enhance their left-brain capacity and help promote their artistic careers.

There is no tuition for using intuition and no tax on intelligence in the *Career Star System*.

By Chapter 14, "Star Dawn," readers understand that a right-brained Starphade knows their calling but often lacks self-esteem and that a left-brained Starphire usually does not know their calling and lacks insight. Readers learn that when intuitive intelligence of the right-brain is raised to consciousness and combined with rational intelligence of the left-brain, a Career Star appears to light the way to their life purpose through greater self-understanding.

When the reader has followed the *Career Star System* from the first glimpse of their Career Star in consciousness, as a result of the newly opened channel between logic and intuition, to its actual use in everyday life by following the Career Star Wheel, and practicing the relevant Career Star Strategy, they are at last on the way to fulfilling their destiny. Their star is born from knowledge of the self that is certain to lead them to "Stardom," the land of financial prosperity and emotional tranquillity.

In the *Career Star System* there is no tuition for using intuition and no tax on intelligence. In fact, intuition may be thought of as tuition paid to yourself. Therefore, you are encouraged to bring the two forms of intelligence together as your potentials are aroused, excited, expressed, climaxed, and released. This is not to claim, however, that you give up sexual pleasures for the joy of *Career Star System*, although you may feel freed to make this choice.

Pursue your Career Star and your Career Star will pursue you. You cannot be happy and successful, nor make a difference in the world, by doing what you are not meant to do. Finding the passion of your purpose means a love affair with life. You will enjoy life and work hereafter with a lot more laughter.

STAR ORIENTATION:
Getting *Started*

Twinkle, twinkle little star,
How I wonder what you are.
Up above the world so high,
Like a diamond in the sky.

Ann and Jane Taylor
Rhymes for the Nursery, 1806

INTRODUCTION

Greetings! *Follow Your Career Star* contains the *Career Star System,* a new theory and method for career discovery and development based on inner values. It is a book about how to find meaning and fulfillment in your work life by finding your life-work. "My trade and my art is living," wrote Montaigne, a sixteenth-century French writer and philosopher.

The *Career Star System* is a way to discover your calling. It is designed both for young adults who are just *star*ting out in search of their careers and for older adults who are transitioning into new careers. It is a way to help you choose or change careers, to find the one that is a deal, and ideal, for you.

The *Career Star System* teaches you to discover your true calling through a quest for meaning. The journey takes you into your unconscious mind where your life purpose is concealed. Your individual, special light is hidden in the dark side of your psyche and is identified as a "Career Star." It is the guiding light of your calling, the work you are meant to do.

A Career Star coincides with a deep sense that you are meant to perform a certain kind of work. When your actual purpose in life aligns with an innermost feeling of this kind, there is usually a passionate realization that "this is the right path for me" and it is in harmony with the universe.

Finding the right calling is a high-priority objective in directing the course of your life. By gaining psychological insight *you can find within you* the answer to the kind of life-work you are meant to do. The *Career Star System* also helps you implement a practical plan of action to make your new Career Star actually begin to shine.

While the journey to self-discovery continues to unfold over a lifetime, some individuals feel deeply that their destiny is assigned at birth and report vocational interests as early as memory can recollect. Whether or not you believe you have a destiny, finding your life-work is still a very serious matter.

Everyone yearns for meaningful direction. Life seems heavy and burdensome when you do not know how to solve this dilemma nor which way to turn. Next to the choice of a mate, work is usually regarded as the most important decision you make in life.

It is very painful to discover that you have made another mistake with a career choice or a relationship. Through trial and error, you may figure out what your calling is not, but learning what to do, based on what not to do, is a discouraging and self-defeating process. If anything, you try to learn not to keep making this mistake. The *Career Star System* offers you a direct route to your calling.

To yourself are you the kind of employer you would rather not work for? Is this because you make yourself do work you do not like and resent it? Do you think you cannot accomplish your calling, therefore, you do something else instead? Does this something else have enough compensatory rewards to substitute for your happiness? Do you mess up both your calling and the alternative in this way?

You are not called to bungle or botch your calling. A caterer is not sought to make bad parties, an accountant to mismanage funds, or a teacher to spin lies. If you cannot do it well there is no need to worry because you are never chosen to be in a wrong field. Someone else is picked perfectly instead to do that work for you and humanity.

You make finding your Career Star a tiresome labor when you worry that it cannot be found. You then must try to find your calling with a burden of self-doubt that is borne like a penance. You agonize that your calling cannot happen but it cannot *not* happen. When you settle down with some self-confidence, your Career Star comes up axiomatically. If you doubt your self-doubt, there is no doubt that your Career Star will start to shine.

You are never in the wrong place because every situation offers an opportunity to learn what you need to know about yourself and the world. If you practice insight you will see how the situation is exactly right for the problem to be solved. Labeling a situation as wrong, rather than your understanding of it, avoids insight and prevents learning by keeping grievances against yourself and others active. You are pained or rewarded according to your negative or positive regard for an experience.

It is your worry that you are in the wrong place that causes it to appear wrong. If you are afraid a situation is wrong your nervous reaction interferes with a valid assessment. You may think your worry helps correct the problem but cause and effect are reversed. It is your judgment that causes you to worry, not the situation. Your perspective needs correction, not the situation. As you relax and submit to learning the meaning of events your Career Star is there to guide you.

SELF-CONCEPT

Self-concept is the image and relationship with yourself you hold in your mind. You have a self-concept, whether or not you are aware of it. Usually, if you are unaware, your self-concept is negative. Many people who are aware also have a negative self-concept. For your life course to develop, you must become aware and cultivate a positive self-relationship.

Basically, there are two possible points of view about yourself. One is negative: the "Injured Self," and the other is a positive view, the "Creative Self." Which of these you hold affects major and minor decisions and actions and the entire direction of your life.

As a child your self-concept is determined mainly by your parents. Many adults live according to the belief that they are "wounded" or "damaged," a self-concept that is usually learned early in life. A sense of inadequacy, self-doubt, and low self-esteem are an abiding legacy if there is no change in self-concept during adulthood.

How you were treated as a child does not necessarily coincide with who you are and who you are meant to be. You may believe it, however, and become someone you are not meant to be. Your bad feelings are real but the reasons for the mistreatment were not valid because you were not, and are not, worthless. A change in self-perception is a prerequisite for success and happiness in adulthood. You can dissolve the memory of mistreatment with the recognition that it was and is mistaken.

Negative learning can occur so early in childhood you do not remember acquiring the view and therefore it remains deeply unconscious. Or, you may be aware of not having a good opinion of yourself and recollect the specific incidents and individuals who caused you to feel this way. Either way, holding onto this self-concept as an *adult* is a decision you make about who you are now. You may have to unlearn what you have been conditioned to believe about yourself since early childhood.

A powerful and prestigious career is commonly regarded as one of the best ways to prove to yourself and others that you are a unique and important person. Motivation of this kind for career selection, however, is bound to lead you astray because it derives from a negative concept of the self that is outwardly oriented. It will cause you to make the wrong choices because the underlying reason is wrong. The wrong career choice is distorted by the unrecognized assumption of a negative self.

> You can be whoever you want to be,
> including who you are not intended to be,
> if you do not want to be who you really are.

A positive self-perspective is based on the idea of a Creative Self that possesses knowledge, talents, and potentials. You are a worthy person for internal reasons no matter how you appear, or are treated by society. This is true even when you do not believe that this is true. While the Injured Self is the imaginary negative part, the Creative Self is the positive, real part of your identity. The Creative Self is often unconscious and needs to be brought into awareness and activated.

To begin to live in the real world of the Creative Self requires a change of mind about yourself. You give up believing in the negative and begin to believe in the positive self. You can exchange faith in what is not true for faith in what is true; trade "feardom" for freedom. Believe in nothing, or in something, and you find what you are looking for.

Without believing the truth that you have value and potential that arise from within your natural self, there can be no way of knowing what direction to take with your life-work. What a great pity to you and a great tragedy to the whole world if you decide not to uncover your star-value. You will become someone you are not intended to be if you do not want to be who you really are. Your choice makes a difference to your individual well-being and to balance in the world.

FRIVOLITY

The *Career Star System* provides a theory and a method for finding your Career Star. Whether the system will work for you depends upon the attitude, the frame of mind, you bring to it. To discover what you are meant to do vocationally means lightening up. You must reduce the weight and weariness of the project by handling it with a sense of humor, even a sense of frivolity.

Some people have dedicated their lives to a higher purpose as a result of a psychosocial crises or near-death experience. Do you need to be hit by lightning to lighten up? Eric Carle, a popular children's author, says in *Draw Me a Star,* that he got the idea for the book after he was struck by a very bright star in a dream.

=====================================

Lighten up and you light up your Career Star.

=====================================

Voltaire wrote that "the superfluous is essential." The *Career Star System* is serious about the importance of frivolity in the career quest. Your career decisions and direction are momentous matters but the whole truth is that they are also amusing. Light and heavy are the proverbial two sides to this problem. Frivolity and levity are two forms of "Starwork." If *you* lighten up, your Career Star lights up.

You may think this line is just a clever turn of phrase but it is meant earnestly. The *Career Star System* is playfully designed, i.e. the whimsical drawings of the *Career Star Map.* Being able to play is a crucial part of finding your work and way in the world. If you just stay serious, however, you will probably not see the purpose of fun or the fun of purpose.

It is essential to let Captain Quirk take command of the Career Starship on occasion. Ignore all orders to the contrary from Starfleet

Headquarters. Your Career Star is *your* "Enterprise." Your Career Star Commission, affirmed later in this chapter, entitles you under the inalienable provisions of self-governance, to be comical and jovial, hokey and corny, goofy and weird, at intervals you choose throughout the expedition.

And let us not quibble and squabble without mirth about what is silly and what is sensible because it really gets absurd. It may be difficult to make a career search fun because you are working so hard to make a career happen. "It's not funny because it's my life," a somber client once told me. And, it may be hard to take the quest seriously, and make it important, because it is so much fun.

Frivolity and levity are forms of starwork.

Try to relax and understand that you can afford to be lighthearted because your Career Star is securely fixed within you. You *are* going to find your meaningful life-purpose because it has never been lost. You have only been separated from it in your mind. If you relax you will have less gray hair, fewer wrinkles, a better facial expression, longer weekends, and a Career Star.

Are you looking for a quick fix—a book, an advisor, or an activity that will promptly remedy the career dilemma? Review what you really want. If you mainly want material success, you will have to disregard inner values. Do you doubt you possess a calling? Your attitude is both frivolous and serious because, of course, you have a calling but you also seriously doubt it.

If you are only serious about your career, it means that you are not being kind and thoughtful to yourself. Your seriousness suggests that you are heavy-handed and critical, probably because you think you are the exceptional person in all of human history who does not have a calling.

Without being aware of it, you probably also think you have a row of six sixes branded across the back of your neck. Are you so unlovable that no one ever cared about you? Is it true nobody wants to know you now because you are so specially horrible? At least you show you have an imagination when you invent a negative self that is a mortal enemy to human kind. Felicity or futility, which will it be?

Perhaps because the answer has not been at your fingertips you are frustrated and see yourself as "weak" or "inadequate." If you remain upset the answer will continue to elude you, because *the answer is out of your control.* You are the subject, the vessel, the instrument of your calling not its creator, designer, or originator. This is not to say that you do not create your star but only that it is given to you in a nuclear way. Your star cannot be fulfilled without your decision and participation but you are not the Starmaker.

You are the receiver of the call. To find your calling, it is essential to accept that your calling is an intuitive given not a rational decision. Therefore, forgo the political struggle with yourself and grant directly your entitlement to a Career Star.

Ask yourself the question, "What is my calling?" You can surrender control and allow the answer to come forth from within. Or, you can prevent it from arising from an internal source with your seriousness. You can then follow-through with a dictation from your ego about what you rationally think it "ought to be," given your need for power and the downturn in the economy.

That is, you can take an objective look at your skills and experience, see yourself objectively from the point of view of an outsider, and make a rational decision about your objectives in the material world. An additional logical step is to obtain a confirmation of your choice by a consultation with an expert in career counseling. The counselor can administer an assault and battery of tests to determine your abilities and discuss the local and national job markets with you. To impose an answer arrived at by this strictly rational procedure, is a weight upon your shoulders that does make you serious. The possibility that this method will produce the right answer is slim because it has nothing to do with the authenticity of your inner self. (See "Aptitude Testing," Appendix 4.)

It does not matter that the logic is inductive or deductive, if emphasis is on the outer person at the expense of the inner being. It is hard to lighten up when you feel bad physically, which is what your seriousness causes you to feel. You intimidate yourself with so much worry about your Career Star. It cannot shine in a tension-filled mind. Trust that the answer emerges through an intuitive process and give up the external focus that serves only as a block.

Mournfully, you will feel relief and refreshed enough to enlist with a smile in the informed, but ununiformed forces, of the *Career Star System.* Or, must you keep missing your calling with a frown on your brow and the persistence of your petulance?

To take hold, your calling must have your awareness of its existence; it must be born and borne in consciousness. Origination and destination are the two ends linked by the journey in between. Life is a whole trip from embarkation to debarkation. Seriousness, however, causes the connection between the beginning and ending to be ruptured and maligned. Is your life really too grim to be funny at all?

You cannot find your calling until you give up looking for it so intensely. The opposite is also true, of course; you cannot find it if you have no intention of looking for it. If you think it does not exist, or that it lurks in the outer world, then you overlook the crucial fact that it exists within the universe of your unknown mind. It is the chalice, the sword, the rose, the lotus, the diamond, the sparkling star in the sky, all symbolic of your priceless possession of purpose.

You will discover your calling right there within you, waving and shouting at you, where it always has been, if you will: 1) forgive yourself for not having found it sooner, 2) relax and trust that it is always there, 3) allow yourself to enter into the process of self-discovery, and 4) bring a sense of humor to the question.

Inner work is not hazardous and competitive like "outer work" because inner values are abundant and rich. There is no scarcity of opportunity nor reason for insecurity about travels in the inner world. The only fear is from a rational point of view that erroneously anticipates the absence of inner values.

A quote attributed to Jesus in the Gnostic *Gospel of Thomas* says:

> If you bring forth what is within you, what you bring forth will save you. If you do not bring forth what is within you, what you do not bring forth will destroy you.

INTROSPECTION

The *Career Star System* emphasizes an inner quest to discover your true calling, which is given to you, as it is to everyone, as part of your natural human inheritance. The idea of a "star" is not just a metaphor and a "quest" is not merely an allegory; both are ancient truths. While the power of your Career Star is astronomical, the *Career Star System* itself is spiritual and psychological.

The *Career Star System* relies on introspection, derived via intuition, to uncover your inner values. The compass of inner values orients and fixes the direction of your journey to "Stardom." (See the Career Star Glossary.) Stardom is the location of your Career Star in the kingdom of your mind. You will find it difficult to reach your star-goal without establishing communication with your star-origin, the source of your inner starlight.

Begin to acquire an introspective attitude by taking a moment for self-reflection. Shut your eyes, breathe deeply, and relax. Pay attention to whatever feelings, thoughts, or images come into your mind from your heart center. In this way let your abiding inner self introduce itself to you in any form it chooses to take.

Do not try to make anything appear in your mind, just surrender to relaxation. Practice this informal exercise *now* before reading further. When you return from this experience, make a mental note of what took place and jot it down below before you continue. Also, make another note of how readily accessible your inner world is to you:

✍

_____

_____

_____

Taking a look and recording your self-observations are not a massive undertaking. If you are not able to do, or are bothered by the exercise, read the section on "Resistance," pages 35–39. Now is the time to overcome resistance by practicing the exercise or studying the subject. Have a dialogue, not a diatribe, about resistance with your inner self.

Interview *your* Great Spirit.

Your calling awaits only your recognition that it has been inherited and it waits even while you wait. Like a legacy in an unknown treasury, or unclaimed property in a lost and found, it awaits your retrieval. Capitalize on your inner values, allow your interest to grow, and watch your investment pay off with self-knowledge. Your calling is not lent, rented, leased, time-shared, ransomed, or sold to you. It is free. You are the "soulful" titleholder and we are all the beneficiaries. Your possession of a life-purpose is really our great fortune.

As an enduring gift there are no maintenance fees, finance charges, taxes, depreciation or deterioration costs, unlike commodities and properties in the material market. Your calling is the "privilege of a lifetime," wrote Joseph Campbell.

Your calling is not hypothetical. It is not a set of unpredictable events that happen to accidentally govern your future. There is neither "rhyme nor reason," poetic verse nor scientific formula, to explain why you are magnificently empowered with a purpose. But you do not need to know *why;* only know that your Career Star contains specific instructions for your special function on earth.

"Why" is a metaphysical problem, not a practical one. You are bequeathed a quest in the same way you are endowed a physical body and inherit your color, shape, size, and gender; the same way in which you inherit the sun, the moon, the sky, the wind, and the rain. While most stars disappear during the diurnal rotation of the earth, your Career Star like the North Star, is fixed. The quest(ion) is not whether you have a star but whether or not you choose to believe it by seeking it.

Without a purpose, life may seem dull and monotonous at best, or precarious and persecutory at worst. Just as you grow physically from child to adult, your calling matures within you, if you acknowledge its parentage, birth it with consciousness, bathe it with insight, and allow it to bask in the warmth of your best intentions. Like a baby, your calling will also fail to thrive if you do not tend to it with an aware heart and a loving mind.

Because your calling is the vital essence, but not necessarily the whole of your true being, the *Career Star System* involves making a commitment to finding your inner values and to fulfilling your potentials in an ongoing way throughout your lifetime.

Invest in yourself and dare to be you.

The idea of having "a calling" arose during the Protestant Reformation and is associated with the notion of "divine providence" in the choice of an occupation. Buddhism has a similar idea called "Right Livelihood." In Protestantism, prosperity is a sign that one is amongst an elect in terms of salvation. Today the idea of a "calling" is still heard most frequently with respect to being "called to the ministry."

Having a calling can also be an idea distorted to justify the attainment of worldly power. "I have a destiny" can sound like George Patton or Lawrence of Arabia who had delusions of grandeur. A calling may be twisted to mean some egotistical and arrogant mission to conquer an enemy, build pyramids, or make the trains run on time. This is the call of the wild ego, however, not a steady star.

In the *Career Star System,* "calling" is used in a spiritual sense to suggest that everyone has potentially meaningful life-work and applied broadly to a whole range of occupational possibilities from crafts to professions. A calling suggests what Robert Bolles described as "finding your life mission," or Joseph Campbell referred to as "following your bliss."

Like Jung, Campbell believed that every individual has an "inner hero" and is obliged therefore to fulfill a "personal myth." Unlike the hero in material culture, who is a celebrity because of the possession of fame, fortune, power, and luck, in Campbell's perspective, a hero is someone who accepts the challenge of the uncharted inward journey. You may think your Career Star is a myth but it is your own disbelief that makes it seem mythical. Do not allow your mission to be an omission. Invest in yourself and dare to be you.

IF YOU ARE UNEMPLOYED

An economic crisis is a challenge to the character of an individual and a nation. We are in the midst and the mist of major economic and cultural upheaval. Businesses are downsizing, reorganizing, and capsizing. These changes may be precursors of a larger transformation. They are so recent and extensive that we scarcely know what to call them.

The full ramifications of these changes are not yet evident. Terms used in previous economic downturns, like "recession" and "depression," are in all likelihood not as encompassing as the changes themselves. We may only be able to recognize and identify this transformation retrospectively.

Many individuals are becoming unemployed and underemployed. Others, still earning wages and salaries, are threatened by termination. Careers for some people are on the verge of extinction and job security may seem like a relic of the past. Under the present circumstances many individuals are like rudderless boats adrift at sea.

There is a tendency on the one hand to want to give up hope. Or alternately, to continue believing that dressing, interviewing, and acting technically correct in the job application process, will get you through. This is the persistence of an outdated perspective, an old custom, when the situation calls for a new strategy. In neither case—

hopeless resignation nor traditional tenacity—is there an inner-values response to the prevailing economic crisis.

Impending or imposed unemployment has a major impact on an individual's sense of self-worth and well-being. Without a means of economic support, it is hard to maintain basic human virtues and a vigor for life. And, because our work is so bound to our identities, the end of a job may seem "terminal," as the word "termination" suggests. As a major loss, prolonged unemployment ranks high, among the top five stressors, and can precipitate a core psychosocial crisis.

Viewed differently, however, unemployment can become an opportunity to discover your calling. This may be the first time you realize you genuinely have an alternative. Employed or unemployed, it is time to make a commitment to your real abilities, to respond to your calling. If you are "between jobs," you are ready for your Career Star.

Taking heed of your Career Star is an ongoing, lifetime process. The source of almost all your mental anguish arises from the lack or lapse in awareness of our "real estate," and this is true whether you are employed or unemployed. Unemployment, however, is one crises designed precisely to put you in touch with your worth, individually and collectively as a nation. *Per aspera ad astra,* "through hardship to the stars," is an old Latin proverb.

Finding your calling when you are unemployed is usually harder than finding it when you are employed, because you now have the condition itself and a lot of free time with which to be intimidated. It is easy to believe that the practicality of job hunting outweighs the idealistic search for what you are meant to do.

We are often reluctant to be interrupted from our hours occupied in despair. The idea that you may be using the urgency of unemployment as a distraction from the challenging task of finding meaningful work is hard to accept and keep in mind, especially when the practical task of just finding a job is so real and pressing.

Being unemployed, you may feel that the planet is out of orbit and that it is impossible to undertake any kind of "star search." It is natural to have a myriad of emotional reactions—denial, anger, confusion, fear, and depression. It is also human to blame the system, to see yourself as a victim and to want to retaliate or withdraw. But you can decide to transcend this view.

You may have years of expensive training, hard-won experience, faithful dedication, and personal sacrifice to an organization. But, if you can also recognize that you previously evaded the task of finding your true self-worth, an apparent tragedy can be turned into a strategy, and a misfortune can become fortunate. You can triumph personally and professionally.

Everyone is a celebrity in the *Career Star System*.

As in all crises, the challenge of unemployment is not merely to see the "silver lining," but to see beyond the clouds of confusion and despair. Your calling is the future hope of us all. It is the only viable short- and long-term response that makes any sense. The purpose of the crisis is to connect you with your life-mission and now is exactly the right time to answer the call.

Unemployment is the chance of a lifetime to pursue your calling, even though it may not look like a window of opportunity at the time or under the conditions in which it appears. Honestly consider, "What do I really want in work and life and for what have I been settling?" Are you caught up making a living at a job that you do not even want? You have already failed at your calling if you do not even try to find it.

The future holds great promise for dynamic, effective, and responsible executives, entrepreneurs, experts, crafts people, and skilled workers dedicated to making the world a better place. Your personal and the international crisis will subside as individuals withdraw from the problem and contribute unique solutions. Solve your problem and you transcend the past and offer an answer to others.

Get in alignment with your *Career Star*. Give up job hunting and enlist in the unarmed Army of Career Star Questions. Ask only one question: "What am I called to do?" Your calling will remain obscure as long as you use your senses only to work a job, or to despair over unemployment.

The *Career Star System*, therefore, appeals to you for employment and conscientious management by your firm of wit and will. The *Career Star System* is an equal opportunity employer because everyone is a celebrity in the *Career Star System*.

EXERCISE 1
JOB SATISFACTION ASSESSMENT

Are you sick of the grind? Is work not working out and getting you down? Did everything go wrong and take too long today? Did you not get enough done and now you are behind? Did you still make several huge mistakes?

Are you comparing yourself to other people your age and losing? Would you prefer to have someone else's career or life to your own? Why do *they* have what *you* want? Do all the alternatives seem to have as many hassles and as much paperwork as the job you already have?

Are you wishing work would slow down or that business would pick up? Does the telephone have to ring constantly for you to feel successful? Do you have to sell another two million hamburgers this year? Is there a residual belief that something is wrong, with you or maybe with "the system?"

Whether you liked it or not, did you take a job that pays well? Have you picked material, over ideal, motives? Are you trying to live out your parents' dreams? Or is it the opposite, are you fighting being who others want you to be?

Time to answer the Job Satisfaction Questionnaire. Orbit (circle) the star in the "Yes" or "No" column as your answer to each question. If you are unemployed, complete the questionnaire in reference to the last job you held. If you are employed full or part time, or if you are self-employed, refer to your present job or business.

Job Satisfaction Questionnaire

	✍ Yes	No
1. Do you love your work?	✿	✿
2. Would you do this kind of work even if you were not paid for it?	✿	✿
3. Are you happy to see Monday morning?	✿	✿
4. Are you less happy to see Friday afternoon?	✿	✿
5. Do you have friends at work?	✿	✿
6. Do you "play" with friends from work outside of work?	✿	✿
7. Do you make all the money you want?	✿	✿
8. Do you admire your boss?	✿	✿
9. Do you approve of the philosophy of your company?	✿	✿
10. Do you identify with your company's product or service?	✿	✿
11. Do you leave work with a peaceful, easy feeling of self-fulfillment?	✿	✿
12. Do you look forward to the challenge of the next day?	✿	✿
13. Do you have job security?	✿	✿

14. Are your personal contributions recognized?   ✿   ✿
15. Do you have advancement potential?   ✿   ✿
16. Is your private life satisfactory?   ✿   ✿

Total: _____

You may resist starting with a written exercise, preferring just to enjoy reading and absorbing the information. However, many of these questions are overlooked on a day-to-day basis, yet they are the ones you need to evaluate in order to decide whether to use the *Career Star System* to become fulfilled in your work. If you have not already done so, complete the questionnaire now.

SCALE

Next, add up the total number of yeses and place the number on the "Scale." This figure will give you an objective indication of the extent of your job satisfaction. Do not be discouraged by the results if you are low on the scale because 80 percent of the workforce reports dissatisfaction.

Total Number of Yeses
✔
1 2 3 4 5 6 7 8 9 10 11 12 13 14 15 16
Great Dissatisfaction Mild   Mild Satisfaction Great

Give some thought to your answers. Notice which ones are "Nos" and which you would like to see changed to "Yeses." Are there particular Nos or Yeses that are important to you such as being able to face Monday morning or the philosophy of the company?

PRELIMINARY STAR TYPE

Most people are dissatisfied with their work because they make one of two fundamental errors in the selection of a vocation. In the *Career Star System* these two types are known as "Starphires" and "Starphades." Chapter 5 contains a complete self-assessment of your star type using the *Career Star Map*. Career Star types are also described thoroughly in Chapter 6.

Because you may be eager for understanding, however, you can get a preliminary reading of your star type by answering an additional set of questions below. Look over the two sets of questions. Answer yes or no as to whether the question is the kind you ask yourself about your career. More yeses in one set than the other gives you a preliminary indication of your basic star type.

Starphire Questions

	✍ Yes	No
1. What other kinds of work can I do with my skills?	✿	✿
2. What is the flaw in my thinking that I am overlooking?	✿	✿
3. If I'm so logical, why isn't my career obvious?	✿	✿
4. What are the right steps to take, resources and consultants?	✿	✿
5. How long will it take? Cost? Results guaranteed?	✿	✿
6. Why do employers not recognize my potential?	✿	✿
7. What can I do about the irrational economy?	✿	✿
8. Why do imperfect things happen to me?	✿	✿

Starphade Questions

	Yes	No
1. I know what I want to do, but I cannot make a living at it, can I?	✿	✿
2. What if I find my calling and I don't like it, or fail at it?	✿	✿
3. Why am I better at helping other people than myself?	✿	✿
4. Do I have a fun kind of calling because I am so shallow?	✿	✿
5. Why am I still waiting for the money to follow?	✿	✿
6. Why does everyone else enjoy their work?	✿	✿
7. Why do I know what to do when it is too late and I'm too old?	✿	✿
8. Why do I have to work harder, spend more time, be more efficient and be more exhausted than everyone else?	✿	✿

Starphires look for a rational career and raise questions about the economy. They lack insight and self-knowledge about their unique calling because reason is their master. Starphires need introspection. They are called "Starphires" because they are usually angry that the system does not work their way.

Starphades, on the other hand, question themselves and find problems insolvable due to the extent of their own flaws and self-doubt. They tend to think, however, the problem is the rejection of their talents and personhood by society. They look hard within but find only faults and discouragement. Starphades give up the search because emotion is their master.

If the kind of questions you are asking are not listed here, or if you come out strong on both sets of questions, you are probably not just a simple type of star. You may be either a combination of types or a more rare kind of star. A mixture of both types is called a "Scatter Star." Someone who alternates between the two types is called a "Polar Star." A full assessment of your Career Star type is undertaken with the map exercise, "Star Course," in Chapter 5.

If you want more explanation about the two basic types of stars, a list of characteristics is provided in two different charts, "Summary I," page 93 and "Summary II," page 141. If you want to know more about other types of stars, see Chapter 6, "Star Types."

You are now invited to join the *Career Star System* and acquire your peace of the star. Star light is a sign of welcome and under the influence of its peace you find your greatness.

INVITATION

Dear Star Knight:

You are hereby invited to attend
   the opening of the quest for your calling.
We entreat you and beseech you,
   to put an end to your stalling.

At fate's bequest and behest,
   you are requested
   to do your very best
   and commit to your quest.

At your quest be the most,
   be the host,
   not a guest,
   nor a ghost.

In jest, there is nothing to digest
   or ingest.
Save Mr. Spock, Dr. Spock and Dr. Seuss,
   all with zest.

Yes, just say, "YES!"
Myself I no longer detest.
My self-hate I divest,
   and I'm ready to enlist.

A celestial and terrestrial trip.
A stellar flight on a "soular" Starship.
To soar with the "Ketchon II,"*
   as the *Career Star System* flies,
   so will you!

*See the Glossary

STAR SYSTEM:
Theory and Method

Only that day dawns
to which we are awake.
There is more day to dawn,
The sun is but a morning star.

Henry David Thoreau
Walden, 1854

IGNITION

Your Career Star is the guiding light of your calling and your calling
is the work that fate and destiny have assigned to you. Your Career
Star represents the outcome of combining the logical intelligence of
your rational mind with the sense intelligence of your intuitive mind.
A star of light is ignited at the intersection of these two forms of intelligence. By intelligences crossed are you starred.

Intensify the sparking by intentionally crisscrossing the two forms
of intelligence and your Career Star bursts forth brilliantly like the
mighty, midday sun and illuminates the way to your calling. The formula is Logic plus Intuition = Calling. Or, ✖ and ✚ = ❈ . Use one
without the other and you stay starlessly stuck in the dark.

The ignition of a Career Star is an idea illustrated in Diagram 1.
As the axis of logical intelligence meets the axis of sense intelligence,
an eight-pointed star is formed that represents the eight cardinal
points of the compass. When vertical lines intersect horizontal lines,

the crossing of two opposites, your brilliant Career Star ignites at the center point, the start of the star that is you.

At the center of the star is the "scintilla," the point of sparking, the blazing conjunction of ✖ and ✚. The scintilla is the cradle of your *scintilla*ting Career Star, exactly where you begin to beam. The scintilla appears after an instant of quietness and stillness that precede the eruption at the conception of your birth. The center crossing is the only place where all points lead and converge, the hub from which all directions radiate.

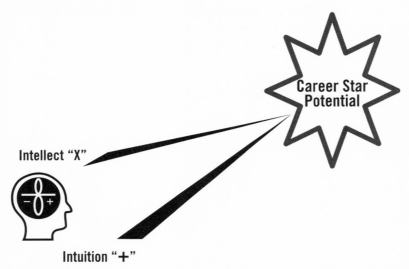

Intellect "X"

Intuition "✚"

[The positive (+) and negative (-) symbols in the "head logo" are discussed in Chapters 8 and 9, "Bright" and "Dark Stars."

Diagram 1: ✖ and ✚ = ❄

Susanne Fincher, author of *Creating Mandalas,* calls an eight-pointed star an "archetype of the self." The eight points of a Career Star symbolize balance and wholeness, major themes in the *Career Star System.* The eight points of the octagram also coincide with the figure 8 in Diagram 1.

The shape of the figure 8 in the head graphic also suggests balance, especially viewed on its side, when the weight is evenly distributed between the two sides (∞). The figure 8 also resembles an infinity sign. Eight, or four versus four, stands for the infinite balance of equally opposing forces.

At first sight, your Career Star may seem nebulous because the two forms of intelligence have only barely, recently, and accidentally crossed in you. Actually, the two have intersected in your consciousness during a few fleeting seconds of self-acceptance provided by some unintentional relaxation. Caring for yourself by taking it easy is quickly repaid with a gift of insight that reveals a hidden part of you cares for you a great deal.

The two forms of intelligence seize the unanticipated opportunity, afforded by relaxation, to zap you with light, energy, and form, to awaken you to your potential. Your Career Star tries to jolt you out of complacent unconsciousness; to strike you with a lightning bolt, to infuse you with self-understanding. The flash of insight light may come and go so rapidly that you do not see the way to be transformed in an instant that is gone.

The outcome of your Career Star odyssey depends upon staying mindful of Career Star astronomy. You do not need telepathy or telemetry to stay on Career Star trajectory but you do need to remember your Career Star cosmology. If you do not openly acknowledge what has happened, you may think you have witnessed a flicker of nothing at all. Stay vigilant and receptive, therefore, to messages from your twinkling, twirling star.

INTUITION

To find your calling you need a form of intelligence other than rational intelligence, which we refer to in the *Career Star System* as "intuition." An advanced form of insight, intuition is a product of the disciplined use of all your bodily senses together in an inward way. Through practice you can learn to access and communicate with this "inner self" to guide you in the application of your aptitudes and abilities toward your destiny.

Intuition is the logic of the inner world.

Until you understand the origin of your Career Star, you cannot rationally direct your quest for it. To find your calling you must fix on the values of your inner self. Starphades tend "naturally" to be more intuitive than Starphires but this does not mean they necessarily utilize it to their benefit. To find your inner values, there must be time for introspective thought. Surprisingly, the time required to develop intuition is not that much.

Try another exercise in the use of your dormant intuitive ability, a continuation of the informal experiment in the previous chapter. While you are sitting in the presence of someone, ask your inner self to tell you something about him or her that you do not realize you know. That is, close your eyes, relax, and ask inwardly to have some understanding of the other party. Be patient and wait for a reply.

If you are unacquainted with your intuition you may initially get only a strange suspicion. Do not dismiss it. If you trust your intuition more its answers will not seem so weird. Whatever idea occurs to you, check it out by asking along the following lines, "You know, I just had a thought about you. I got the impression that you are: (state the idea). Can you tell me if there is any truth to this?"

Remember that your intuitive skills are probably in a rudimentary state due to disuse. Practice this exercise at least three or four times and see your ability improve. Record your experience with this experiment here. Include the response of your subject and any discussion that ensues:

_____

_____

_____

_____

Intuition is the logic of the inner world. It goes by many names, "an intangible sixth sense," "corporeal intelligence," "body instinct," "gut feelings" and "hunches." Intuition is the use of all five bodily senses simultaneously in an inward way. In its application hidden knowledge appears spontaneously in your mind. Just as you learn more about reality by using common sense, you can learn more about your inner self using your common senses internally.

Intuition is the inward side of consciousness, just as awareness of the outside world is the outward side of consciousness. All five senses brought to bear together in a common inward way establishes self-consciousness about thoughts, feelings, images, and sensations. In time you are linked further by intuition to your unique Creative Self, which begins quickly to express its handiwork in the form of art, poetry, literature, music, song, dance, and in other ways.

Intuition is the use of inner-directed consciousness. It is a skill that can be acquired by anyone through practice even though some individuals appear to have more naturally. Being nurtured as a child may have taught them to trust themselves earlier. But anyone aware of the outer environment can learn to be aware of their inner world. Just as you may learn to walk and talk later than other children, but just as well, you can learn to depend on intuition.

Touch, taste, feel, hear, and listen to yourself psychically and you will find your calling, calling you from within. Your calling has to be seen and heard with insight so that it can grab you and be grabbed by you. As insight is acquired through the practice of intuition, you will see your Calling Star more clearly over time. A well known quote from the Bible describes the use of our inward eye.

> No one after lighting a lamp,
>   puts it under the bushel basket.
> Your eye is the lamp of your body.
> If your eye is healthy,
>   your whole body is full of light;
>   but if it is not healthy your body is full of darkness.
> Therefore consider whether
>   the light in you is not darkness.
> If then your whole body is full of light,
>   with no part of it in darkness,
>   it will be as full of light
>   as when a lamp gives you light with its rays.
>
> *Luke* 11:33

TOOLS OF THE CAREER STAR SYSTEM

The *Career Star System* is intended for anyone, no matter what age, who wants to undertake the challenge of finding meaningful work in life. It is never too late. Your calling is always within you waiting to be answered, just as a healthy body is always ready to respond to your will with action. There is a Career Star shining on the pathway of every walk of life.

The *Career Star System* has been empirically derived from years of practical work with clients and students who have found and achieved real career goals. There are two basic components: *Follow Your Career Star,* the book, and the *Career Star Map*. Both written and visual forms are joined in the presentation of the ideas of the *Career Star System*.

✸ THE CAREER STAR BOOK

The book is designed for a three-month period of study, basically one chapter per week. You can double up some reading of the shorter chapters, but because the *Career Star System* involves a process, it cannot be worked in any period shorter than about ten weeks.

There are practical exercises in every chapter to help implement the concepts rather than keep you a passive spectator. With each chapter and set of exercises you progress to the next level of the career quest. It is important to do each exercise along with reading the chapter so that the ideas move from a theoretical to a practical level.

✸ THE CAREER STAR MAP

The *Career Star Map* is a terrain map that has two versions and two purposes. The first is the full-color rendition, whose purpose is to provide an overview of the five major career paths. Topographically it illustrates the five common career courses and the many detours, pitfalls, and barriers that exist along the various ways. The *Career Star Map* is the centerpiece of the *Career Star System*; take a peek at it now if you like; it is the fold-in page at the back of the book.

The *Career Star Map* is also used as one of fourteen exercises in the *Career Star System*. Its second purpose is to assess the extent of right- and left-brain lateralization. In Exercise 5 you use the black-and-white version of the map with the word grid overlay, selecting words that are most descriptive of you. As you make the assessment you also plot your current and potential career course. You will actually be able to visualize the long-term consequences of your career choices on the map.

The *Career Star Map* is an assessment tool to help you determine the extent of your right- and left-brain mental functioning. From the map you will understand your position, course, distance, and direction, in the present and in the future. The calculation of where you have been in the past is a separate project, but is where you will be if there is no change in orientation. Tomorrow can be a lifetime of yesterdays. How to use the map is explained fully in Chapter 5, "Star Map."

Unfold the color map now and look it over leisurely. Do not try to figure out how the map works. Just casually familiarize yourself with it. Notice the place names and drawings of various locations. This step is called "map familiarization." Ooooohing and aaaaahing out loud are entirely optional at this point.

Just look the map over and think about whether you have visited any of these places recently. After your review, continue to study the text below. A black-and-white prototype of the original *Career Star Map* appears on page 34 to give you another version of this information.

Follow Your Career Star explains how to maneuver from one path to another, and how to find the course that is ideal, not a trial and an ordeal, for you. The map is a sketch of the terrain and the book is a set of instructions for finding and pursuing the ever-burning flame of your golden Career Star.

❈ CAREER STAR BURST MANDALA

The Career Star Burst is the star design on the title page and elsewhere throughout this book. It has been made into a mandala, a graphic symbol of a circle enclosed in a square border used in meditation. The star burst, whose 8 points represent the omni-directionality of your career potential, symbolizes the ignition that occurs at the crossing point of your objective and subjective psyches. When the two join, a spark of knowledge is formed at the center, where you as a being already are.

"Scintilla" is the name for the innermost star at the very center of the Career Star Burst; it is the inner star that represents the original life spark of the sparkling self. The Career Star Burst is the emblem and insignia of the Order of Career Star Questars and is also the logo of the *Career Star System.*

As a part of Exercise 4: "Star Burst Mandala," you are asked to color versions of your Career Star. At times you are asked to place the palm of your dominant hand over the Star Burst Mandala during various exercises, such as the "Oath of Commission," Exercise 2, later in this chapter. Reflect and meditate on the mandala from time to time and use it as a reminder of the potential of your ground-breaking, pathfinding, trailblazing Career Star.

Further, you are encouraged to find a real object to hold in your hand or to carry on your person, to represent your Career Star as a faith object. It serves as a constant reminder of your Career Star's accessibility and fidelity to you. Like a touchstone, it can be used to demonstrate the genuineness of your commitment to your Career Star. You can appropriate almost any tangible object but preferably one that has personal meaning to you.

You may also go to the trouble of handcrafting or fashioning a special object that will imbue it with even more meaning. Jewelry, heir-looms, found objects, crystals, and photographs are common choices. As a symbol of your Career Star, it does not need to be a piece of a real star nor even to look like a star. Wear or carry it on your person during the entire transit of your career quest. Additional techniques to help maintain Career Star consciousness are provided in Chart 9, "Logical Activities," page 171.

❧   *CAREER STAR NOTEBOOK AND DREAM JOURNAL*

In the *Career Star System* you are asked to keep a Notebook and Jour-nal as an essential part of your work and study. Select a notebook of your choice, of any size or shape. You will be asked to give your jour-nal notebook a working title at the end of this chapter. As you progress through the *Career Star System* it is important to make the following types of entries.

1. Notes and thoughts about working with the *Career Star System.*
2. Reactions to the various exercises.
3. Impressions of the various meditations (Chapters 3, 9, and 13).
4. Observations and experiences with your Career Action Plan (Chap-ter 13).
5. Recollection and interpretation of night dreams (Chapter 12).
6. Additional types of entries might include:

   ❧ Childhood and adolescent memories.
   ❧ Judgments and criticisms about yourself.
   ❧ Embarrassing events or situations.
   ❧ Worries about your life.
   ❧ Negative thoughts about your development.
   ❧ Insights about yourself or others.
   ❧ Spontaneous positive feelings.
   ❧ Hopeful thoughts or feelings.
   ❧ New ideas or concepts.
   ❧ Aspirations and ambitions.

Your notes on the text of the *Career Star System* and your Career Ac-tion Plan are to be entered from the front to the back of the *Career Star Notebook and Dream Journal.* All your night dreams, as well as your reflections and interpretations, are to be recorded from the back to the front. See Chapter 12, "Star Dreams," for more details about the dream journal. If you wish, Chapter 12 can be read ahead of sequence, after Chapter 4 or at any time.

GOALS

The goal of the *Career Star System* is to help you identify, stay aware, and pursue your Career Star. If you have questions about the *Career Star System,* such as "Does it work?" and "How long does it take?" please refer to Appendix 2, "Star System Questions." A review of the goals of the *Career Star System* is given below. An "Overview for Professional Career Counselors" is contained in Appendix 1.

With the implementation of the *Career Star System* you will be able to:

1. Identify and stay conscious of your calling.

2. Establish a dialogue between your intellect and your creative potential. That is, open a channel of communication through the pathway of intuition and have an ongoing conversation between your calling, which is unconscious, and your conscious self. You do not know consciously what you know unconsciously.

3. Become aware of dreams as messages from your unconscious self that have knowledge about you for your conscious self.

4. Design an action plan where you continue to link intelligence and intuition so that consciousness is sustained, movement is maintained, and potentials attained.

5. Identify and care for your Injured Inner Self who, without your understanding, may appear to you as an internal opponent and keep you engaged in self-defeating behaviors.

6. Identify and deal with organizational conflict that represents the Injured Inner Child as she or he appears in the collective form of others. You can learn to see that your own self-doubt and fear come back to you whenever you give the hostility and political opposition of others in organizations' meaning and validity.

EXERCISE 2
STAR COMMISSION

The *Career Star System* has been empirically derived from years of working with individuals and groups actually engaged in the pangs and throes of self-transformative career birth and parenting. The system works, but just as an automobile will not transport you to a destination unless you take charge, the *Career Star System* depends upon your motivation and cooperation as the driver.

License yourself now to take charge and be arrested by the authority of your Career Star. Try not to think of yourself as the passenger going along for a ride. The journey is free and you are the only one qualified to be the tour director. Begin the daring adventure with a commitment to yourself to make the trip to self-discovery and self-realization a lifelong excursion.

Place your dominant hand, palm down, on the Career Star Burst found on the title page or elsewhere in the manual. Also, if you have found or fabricated a symbol of your own Career Star Burst, place it around your neck now, and hold it there while you read the Oath of Commission on the next page.

At this point some readers may object to doing this exercise because it seems "embarrassing" or "compliant." Occasionally a student will be very serious about how "silly" it is. If you tend to agree with "the silly view," please consider whether or not you are afraid to make a binding contract with yourself.

Some people squirm under the thought of a commitment without compromise. Do you not trust yourself to keep a promise to yourself? Is there a part of you that judges the idea of a mission-quest to be "frivolous?" Is it fearful enough to trivialize in this way in order to dismiss it?

Whenever you study the text, wear your symbolic Star Burst around your neck; or better yet, around your head, to publicize your commitment. Let it rest on the brow chakra, the sixth chakra of light, the energy center in the body that mediates mind and spirit. If you think this is "corny" do it anyway, because it will help you remember your commitment to your Career Star. Or, at least put the symbolic object in your pocket to demonstrate to yourself that you are sincere, and hold on to it whenever you read this book.

Hey, it's not like I'm asking you to fast for four days, purify yourself in a sweat lodge, rub yourself down with sage, make an offering, and perform a song and dance appealing to spiritual powers for a vision. This was Black Elk's ritual when seeking enlightenment about how to deal with the European invasion of North America. *(Black Elk Speaks: The Life Story of a Holy Man of the Oglala Sioux.)*

✳ ✳ *Career Star Oath of Commission* ✳ ✳

By my signature below, I do hereby publicly resolve and declare that I have read Chapters 1 and 2, "Star Orientation" and "Star System." I accept earnestly the invitation to my calling and announce openly that I am ready for the eruption of my Career Star.

I understand that I qualify to become a Career Star Questar as a student and practitioner of the principles and exercises contained in this manual and map. By this resolution and declaration, I affirm my commission as a Career Star Questar. I promise to seek, obey, and cherish my personal Career Star.

Be it resolved that I covet my Career Star. Without reservation, I am proud to make this pledge and henceforth will honor this creed and remember this sacred covenant. I stand humbled, awed, and inspired by my induction into the Stardom of Career Star Questars.

I recognize that the answer to my quest for a calling lies within me, that I am the star, that I represent the inner starlight of all the Starmen and all the Starwomen of human kind. By my signature on this certificate I do pledge with all my truth to follow my Career Star.

_____

(Career Star Questar Signature)   (Star Date)

_____

(Printed Name)

_____

(Witness 1 Signature)   (Title or Relationship)   (Star Date)

_____

(Witness 2 Signature)   (Title or Relationship)   (Star Date)

As a Career Star Questar, sign and date the "Oath of Commission." By your signature, swear on your word and swear on your sword, undying allegiance to your Career Star. As you affirm your commitment with your signature, hold your faith object in your hand with faith. To confirm your commitment, light a candle to symbolize the ignition of the "scintilla" of your Career Star.

No longer can you shuffle and shift, hedge, and dodge, and beat around the bush. Your signature means you are committed to your quest without protestation, procrastination, or prevarication. Nor can you cancel or rescind the oath. To mark the ceremony in time, you have the option of reading the Oath of Commission aloud to a company of relatives and friends.

These witnesses verify your pledge and signature. Ask them to sign the document attesting that they have attended your oral reading of the oath as well as the placement of your signature. If you are especially proud of your commission, you may have it notarized, framed, hung in your living room, and announced in the local newspaper.

Your first assignment as a commissioned Career Star Questar is to obtain a notebook to serve as your *Career Star Notebook and Dream Journal*. Your journal is used for two basic purposes:

1. To record your thoughts about the theory and practice of the *Career Star System*. Carry and use your journal daily making entries from the front to the back *(Journal de Jour)*. Just as your journey carries you through life, you carry your journal.

❄ Note your ideas as they occur while studying each chapter.
❄ Reflect upon your experiences and results with exercises and meditations.
❄ Choose your Action Strategy in Chapter 13 and describe your experience.

2. To record your night dreams and interpretations, making entries from the back to the front. Keep the journal on your night table and write down your dreams as completely as you can remember upon awaking. *(Nocturnal Journal.)* See also Chapter 12, "Star Dreams."

❄ Record your dreams in detail.
❄ Record your feelings in the dream in detail.

❋ Give your interpretation, thoughts, speculations and feelings about the dream.

❋ Note any themes in your dreams that parallel events in your life.

CAREER STAR AND JOURNAL NAME

Give a name to your *Career Star Journal.* If you know your Career Star well give it a precise name. If known only vaguely use whatever hunch or guess you have. If you are completely blocked about this do not give up without a name even if it must be "Blocked Star." The strangest association in your mind is better than a no-name star.

Think about your abilities, interests, values, and ideals. Be specific and try to avoid generalities like "Loving Star" and "Serving Star." The name can always be changed as your Career Star understanding develops. Also write the name on the cover of your *Career Star Notebook and Dream Journal.* The name can also be used as an affirmation to help you focus on your career goal.

1. The name of my Career Star is:

_____ ✍ _____

_____

2. Rationale for the Name: State clearly and exactly your thinking and reasons for the selection of this name for your Career Star.

_____ ✍ _____

_____

_____

_____

_____

_____

INVENTION STAR

Here is a case illustration. Bobby was referred by a psychologist when career issues became salient in his psychotherapy. He worked at that time as a tile setter and because of his extreme dislike for the work, could stay on a job for only about five hours per day. He loathed laying tile. Every workday was a dread and he craved the relief of weekends. Sunday evenings were ruined in anticipation of Monday morning.

After an initial orientation meeting he joined a career development support group in which he worked on career issues for nearly three years. There were several sporadic individual counseling sessions but for the most part his career development took place in a group.

When we initially discussed his career alternatives he said he had absolutely no clue to his calling. I asked him to close his eyes, relax, and meditate on the subject. He became very tense over this prospect and claimed he could only see "black." He thought he had some deep disorder that prevented image visualization.

He offhandedly mentioned several weeks later in the group that he liked to play in his mind with inventions. In a subsequently written autobiographical statement Bobby described his experience:

> Almost every day I spent some time thinking about ways to improve how something works. I never considered this a chore and it was fun. It was something I liked to do, a puzzle that I give myself for a break. To be an inventor never occurred to me as a career choice.
>
> The ideas I had were not earth-shattering. Most were novel at best but it was a routine I enjoyed. The group encouraged me to develop and pursue this activity. Specifically, to think an invention through, sketch it on paper, and make a prototype. Thus began my career as a toy inventor.
>
> Now when I wake up I go into my shop like a child going into a toy room to play. I am not concerned about marketability or originality and I try not to put any kind of constraints on the process. Jon once asked me, "Can you allow your toys to have spirits of their own?" I have just been trusting and relaxing in order for toy ideas to come alive in my mind and keep coming.

One Saturday morning just after waking up a toy came to me. Instantly I knew I had something special, a gift from God. It is a novelty, plush, stuffed animal that children can display ornamentally in their room and has several features that help calm their fears. I located a freelancer who made a prototype that looked great. I found a partner and we licensed the idea to a company. Since then I have invented a total of five patentable toys that are being shown to various manufacturers.

In another instance, a book came to me. I was never a good reader in school and I made this toy for myself to make reading more fun and interactive. This is how the book evolved. I had a rough idea. No design went into it at all. It took its own form. This particular book teaches eye/hand coordination and reading. An electronic character outside the book is used like an escort to help a child through the story. The book became more than a printed page, it became a creative act for me and hopefully for the child reader.

My father was a twenty-one-year-old paratrooper who died in a commercial airline crash coming home on military leave when I was six months old. This was just before the Vietnam War. As a G.I. he was entitled to have the U.S. government pay for his children's college education. So, at the age of thirteen I was approached by a college counselor who asked me what I would like to do after graduation from high school.

Well, I was overwhelmed and unprepared to make a decision like that. When he left I asked my stepfather how and when would I know what type of career to pursue. He replied, "Son, it will just come to you." Well, I took him at his word because I looked up to my new dad for many reasons. And I kept looking for a long time waiting for it to come true.

My mother told me a story recently. When my biological father was killed she wrote him a letter and put it along with my favorite toy in his casket. This news helps put some pieces of my life together because I also think there is a design behind my toy inventing and I feel more of a connection with my father because of it. Now I would say that the name of my star is: *The Star of My Invention.*

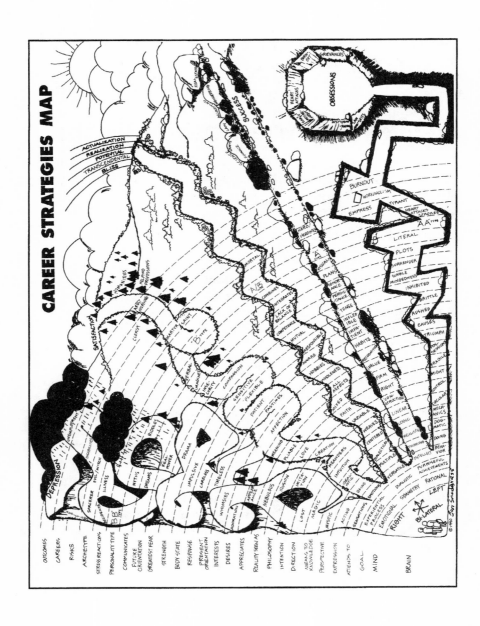

STAR STORMS:
Meeting the Enemy Within

A Star is a small, bright light
that you can see in the sky at night.

Your Very First Dictionary
Macmillan Publishers

RESISTANCE

It is estimated that eighty percent of the workforce performs work they dislike. Predictions of future employment forecast that people will change jobs at least ten times and have three major career shifts in a life span. If career discovery and development were easy, everyone would be working happily at an enjoyable job, society would be utopian and career counselors would be irrelevant.

To many, finding a calling sounds like harder work than finding a career itself. Almost everyone experiences a great storm of interference in pursuing a career search because everyone has an "internal opponent." This is a part of our personality that interferes with optimum development, particularly when it remains unconscious.

The internal opponent first appears in the form of anxiety and doubt about personal change but this is only the tip of an unconscious iceberg of emotional opposition that lies beneath the surface. Finding your calling does not mean you will actually pursue it. You may not believe it if you see it, or see it, if you do not believe it.

This backlash of resistance is the result of an emotional injury in the mind that goes back to childhood. It has various names depending upon which aspect is emphasized in its description by self-help experts. It is called the "Wounded Child," the "Injured Self," or the "Internal Opponent," among other terms. Our early experiences as children teach us not to wholly care for ourselves, although we may be unaware of this fact.

The Injured Child is recognized, however, whenever we admit that "we are our own worst enemy." This means we are not being held back by some person, situation, or institution, but by a concept of ourselves in our own mind. A crucial part of the *Career Star System,* therefore, is understanding and dealing with the emotional resistance that predictably accompanies efforts at positive personal change.

Resistance as it applies to career development is described this way by Tom Jackson in *The Perfect Résumé:*

> Fifteen years of working with people in their job campaigns has taught us one very important lesson, which in our work has come to be called 'The rule of inherent negativity.' It can be stated like this: People very frequently do not operate in their own best interests.

Richard Bolles provides another example when he writes in his job search bible, *What Color is Your Parachute,* "All who live a thoughtful life know that it is true: our greatest enemy in carrying out this first mission of ours is indeed our own heart and our own rebellion."

In human development, there is no psychological resistance to doing the wrong thing but only to doing the right thing. A name for this phenomenon is "developmental anxiety." Smoking cigarettes and eating junk food, for example, ordinarily do not make us nervous. In fact they are envisioned as enticing and exciting. Abstention scares us, however, and giving up bad habits is regarded as "dangerous." Unfortunately, anxiety is generated by developmental, not by nondevelopmental activities, otherwise humanity would evolve to a higher plane.

In human development, there is no psychological resistance to doing the wrong thing but only to doing the right thing.

Some career guidance materials may acknowledge the irrational dimension of resistance, but rarely expand on the idea, or provide a conceptual framework or a plan of decisive action to overcome it. Most counseling guides are premised on the idea that career discovery and development follow a straight-forward procedure of linear steps. They also usually assume the goal is to become an employee of an organization.

For example, job search, résumé writing, interview techniques and networking strategies are presented as the key steps and regarded as simple matters of logical process. Similarly, most self-help books in popular psychology do not deal with a negative, or an unconscious dimension, in the effort to change personally. Thumbing through another self-help book can cause you to wonder if you are not acquiring another expensive addiction.

Why do people not start, follow, or complete the carefully outlined steps of self-improvement? Why do people lapse into confusion, claiming not to know there are steps or what steps there are? And, why are the wrong steps so much easier to take than the right ones? Without knowledge of an irrational side to human nature, that camouflages and sabotages our intentions and actions, we really cannot understand why we are divided and defeated by ourselves.

On the other hand, counselors in psychology often underestimate the treatment value of a logical plan of action. Out of respect for a client's personal values and rights to self-determination, intervention may be construed as intrusion. Psychological counseling, which invites you to get in touch with and to express your feelings, is an important part of the change process, but all too often it is regarded as an end in itself.

A therapist trying to avoid elitism may mistake apathy for respect and tolerance for assistance, and not offer the practical help that flows out of understanding feelings. Trained to rely mainly on techniques that emphasize the analysis and interpretation of feelings and dreams, many psychotherapists take a less directive stance and do not help develop practical plans.

Designing a plan of action, giving guidance and support, linking intellectual and intuitive capacities, preparing for the reaction of an "internal opponent" are all relevant undertakings in the career counseling process. "Career therapy" has a dual task—logical and psychological. The uniqueness of the *Career Star System* lies in its integration of the cognitive and emotive spheres in the career search.

Career development inevitably precipitates a struggle to become your true self over and against the resistance of a false self that lies hidden. You must know and prepare for the predictable backlash of resistance that is bound to appear with the pursuit of your calling. Assertively meeting your adversarial nature provides a distinct advantage that makes the difference in the career challenge.

There is not just a left- and right-brain in mental functioning, but a third factor, an emotionally Injured Self that intrudes and interferes with efforts at finding a calling. The closer you come to acting on your potential, the more aroused the Injured Self becomes, usually in the form of self-doubt and insecurity. This side of the personality is largely unconscious as is much of our positive, intuitive, and creative potential.

When an individual learns that a structured system exists for dealing with major career issues, there may be an initial eagerness and optimism about getting started. However, most human beings are change-resistant. After a good beginning there tends to be a second stage, the surge of a strong desire to quit, exit, and escape the whole process by inventing justifications that are often quite realistic.

The two most common excuses, lack of "time" and "money," are almost always irrefutably valid. Hardly anyone thinks he or she has adequate time and money. A clever student once claimed to be unable to practice these exercises because he was "too busy working on career issues." Plato said, "We can easily forgive a child who is afraid of the dark; the real tragedy of life is when men are afraid of the light."

A list of "getaways" might include: social obligations, confusion, television, working, sports, partying, fighting, sleeping, children, exercise, and wellness. Almost anything can serve as a diversion as long as it distracts you from seeking a meaningful purpose. Escapes are part of a larger system of denial of the self, explained fully in Chapters 10 and 11, that functions to prevent an individual from ever entering the change process.

Try this simple experiment once again. Close your eyes, breathe deeply, relax, and say to yourself out loud, "May I know more about my life-mission?" Be patient and wait without judgment. Write down whatever thoughts, images, or feelings occur to your mind.

_____🖎____

_____

_____

_____

Do you feel threatened by this simple act? Do you absolutely refuse to do it? Many people do! In college classes I have found a greater anxiety reaction to the prospect of meditation than to an examination. "Oh, no, not another relaxation exercise!" If you are really unafraid, stop reading this book and do the informal exercise above now. Do not remain a stranger to yourself.

The main block to finding a calling is fear. We are afraid of that part of our mind that is unfamiliar to our consciousness, just as we are afraid of parts of the real world that are unknown to us. We also fear the loss of the world that is known.

Other species may know fear, but not of themselves. Humans tend to be allergic and phobic about their abilities and potentials. We are fearful not about what we actually do to ourselves, which can be really horrible, but about what we have the potential to become, which can be truly beautiful.

We believe faithfully in our fears and fearfully in our faith. The only enemy in the unconscious mind is the intrusion of self-recriminations from consciousness. Practicing self-acceptance makes us restless and unsettled. That knowledge resides in the shadow of ignorance is the only consolation in light of this contradiction.

Humans are allergic and phobic about their potentials.

The fear may be a fear of failure, or of success, or any number of other fatalistic fears in between, including being afraid of being afraid. The fear is perpetuated by a lack of faith in the gift of a calling, an endowment shared by all. If you mistrust your calling you see it betray you, which is what you have done to it. Plus, you miss the connection with the very thing that can help you overcome the fear.

Everyone is called to overcome what is most difficult within himself and to offer the solution to the world. Your greatest fear is the gateway to success because the problem is the answer in reverse. An answer is found, therefore, by turning to, naming, and facing the problem. "You must do the thing you think you cannot do" said Eleanor Roosevelt.

The great secret to finding your calling is simply that, just as vices are the exact opposite of virtues, problems are inversions of the answer. *Potentially,* overeaters are the best nutritionists, the troubled the best psychological counselors, the worst lawbreakers the best lawmakers, the most promiscuous the most loyal spouses and devoted parents, the most destructive the greatest engineers, the most frugal the best designers, and the faithless the most devout. Your calling is a precise correction to your greatest fear.

The problem is the negative, while the answer is the positive, side of your calling. The answer is trapped, locked, or sealed at the very center by the problem. The act of confronting the fear is a stand in honor of self-trust that cracks the encasement and releases the answer. Persistence overturns the problem and applies the solution to oneself and for others. Help yourself and you learn exactly how to serve society.

If faith in the self is avoided, however, either by denial that fear exists or by the opposite, belief that the fear is valid, the answer to your calling is postponed. It is precisely thinking about and acting on your calling that constitutes the challenge of the quest. Resistance in moderation is sought with appreciation rather than apprehension. Going forward into the resistance with the persistence of relevant action makes the darkness diminish, instead of your Career Star.

Remember, at the point of greatest fear, continue the attempt to break through with the lance-light of insight. Fear validates the correctness of the quest. If you turn away from the resistance, either through bodily indulgence or rational denial, there is no penetrating light into the night of resistance. Instead, the opposition mounts and overshadows the Intuitive and Creative side of the Self.

Stumbling blocks are really stepping-stones, corner stones and building blocks.

The extent of resistance is a sign of being on the mark of your calling, but many people misunderstand and slack off development because they mistake an internal fear for a real danger. They believe something awful will happen if they change, whereas in reality it will happen if they do not change.

Resistance is like the needle of a compass that points in the right direction. The fear keeps you alert and wary of pitfalls and blockages. As in the story of *Goldilocks and the Three Bears,* do not forbear fear. Bear it, bear on it, bear with it, and you will see the light of your great Career Star. You want opposition not too strong and not too weak but "just about right." Resistance in the range of manipulation is felt against your face and frame and says with a whisper, "You are headed the right way."

PROJECTION

Few individuals intuitively know their calling from a young age and follow it freely, feeling nothing but joy and exhilaration. It is important to recognize, therefore, that the struggle involved in change is itself an indication of the correctness of the action. The effort to follow your Career Star uncovers deeper layers of resistance. The nearer you are to finding your calling, the greater the magnitude of resistance aroused in opposition.

Fear is a sign of work-in-progress because there is absolutely no opposition when undertaking a wrong goal. Anxiety accompanies development, not nondevelopment. Because self-doubt stirs up resistance, a storm erupts in your mind when undertaking personal changes. Human development does not proceed along the "fast track" nor the "path of least resistance."

This concept is contrary to the more customary notion that being fearful means you are headed the wrong way and that the right direction is without fear. In the *Career Star System* you use fear as a tool to look deeper into understanding yourself rather than as something to be avoided by 180 degrees.

Resistance will never be so ominous and severe as it is in the beginning and the temptation to quit will never be stronger. The first step is hardest precisely because it incites the darkest region of self-doubt within the psyche. Initially the danger appears external as a Storm of Fear and Doubt arise in your mind just as you anticipate passing through the Threshold of Change. The journey to the inner most star of the self encounters the labyrinth of convoluted self-doubt.

Because the quest is an inner journey, no one can take the trip on your behalf. It can only be undertaken by you alone. Even your faithful friends, closest relatives, and best therapists cannot go with you. Resistance is the unconscious reason that getting started is so difficult. This fact is recognized in folk wisdom by the adage, "the first step is always the hardest" and requires that you take a courageous leap of faith forward.

Without faith the inner self is in total darkness. Passing through the gateway signifies that an irrevocable commitment has been made and that the journey is under way. This realization is not confirmed, however, until the dense Clouds of Doubt and the fierce Storm of Fear are encountered. Now you realize the initiation is real, not imaginary like every time before. This "trespassing" calls up all the worst fears about yourself when it is too late to change your mind and turn back.

Without faith the inner self is in total darkness.

In the study of the *Career Star System* resistance begins to show up once the basics have been covered in Chapter 2. For this reason Chapter 3 concerns Star Storms of Fear and Doubt that are the beginning of the encounter with the enemy within. In trying to make a commitment to change a client once said, "I feel like I'm defying a law of the universe like gravity—I need to be superhuman not to be destroyed by a battle with something enormously more powerful than I am."

San Juan de la Cruz, a sixteenth-century Spanish mystic and poet, referred to this initial reaction as the *Dark Night of the Soul.* In getting started, it is doubted to the very core of your being that you will survive. Helen M. Luke, for example, describes Dante's experience in beginning his journey in *The Divine Comedy.*

> The dark wood, then, is the threshold of the whole journey, but it is also an immediate threshold to an immediate gateway through which we must pass in a direction which seemingly leads away from our goal. Moreover, we are incapable of finding it alone. There is only one thing that can save a man in such a pass. It is to admit that he is completely lost and just how frightened he is, and to force himself to look up and away for a

moment from this self pity and absorption in the ego—in other words to affirm hope. "Then I looked up, . . ." Dante simply raised his eyes and looked, and at once came the blessed glimpse of a mountain pointing to Heaven; and he saw the sun, the light of consciousness, shining down upon it. Again we are given a hint of another of the great themes of the whole poem, which is "Look, look well . . ." We are to learn an ever deeper looking with the inner eye.

Dark Wood to White Rose, 1989

These places are not really geographical locations but metaphors for projected states of mind. In an individual case commitment to the inner self may appear as a confrontation with a "giant plasma blob" or "a fierce dragon monster." But you can choose to see that these are mental and not actual states. It is never that you "cannot" but only that you will not. Exercise free will over being free of will and give power to faith instead of faith to power.

The idea is to not look back, down, or aside. Look forward, up, and into the doubt. Take a stand, stare ahead, and hold out hope. Another perspective will begin to appear at the exact moment your effort to have faith is sincere. It comes as a result of merely having the courage to keep looking long and hard enough, which signifies that you have genuinely tried to believe.

By the comparison of the two views, hope with no hope, you will be led out of the labyrinth of hopelessness as a third way inevitably emerges. For example, for Dante in *Purgatory,* a mountain was not the way out but the glimpse of hope associated with it led him to discover another route. The two views, hope and hopelessness, interact to produce a qualitatively new and different direction.

There is a basic philosophical and empirical principle that out of the interaction of two things emerges a unique third thing. For example, stereoscopic vision derives from the use of two eyes that see the same object at two different angles simultaneously and yield perception in depth. Depth perception is a third, completely new dimension beyond height and width, produced as a function of the interaction of the other two.

The same phenomenon is true for hearing; the use of two ears together creates stereophonic sound that is a leap beyond monaural sound or listening with only one or the other ear. The mixture of two primary colors makes a unique third color, for example blue and yellow make green, or red and yellow make orange. Further, the amounts of the two primary colors in a mixture determines the shade of green, from dark green, which has more blue, to light green, which has more yellow.

Three or more notes struck simultaneously on a musical scale comprise the distinctive sound of a chord. Hydrogen and oxygen commingled in a ratio of two parts to one form water. The mating of a man and a woman can create a new being with a spiritual life-force that is unique and irreducible to physicalistics, the genetics or chromosomes of one or both parents.

The linking of logic with intuition brings you knowledge from beyond your own mind that flashes in the form of a star, a beacon of your unique destiny. Do not forget, therefore, the formula: ✖ and ✚ = ✿ . As the poet Robert Browning wrote, "Out of three sounds he frame, not a fourth sound, but a star." Combine vision with intuition and you have mission.

THRESHOLD OF CHANGE

The Threshold of Change lies at the gate that you enter when you make the decision to discover your Career Star. A frontal view of the gate is shown beneath the Rainbow of Bliss on the color *Career Star Map*. If the mortals you see there make a complete about-face and walk directly into the sun beneath the rainbow, they pass through the Threshold of Change and enter the Garden of Earth. An aerial view of the gate and the garden are shown in the drawing on page 54.

It does not matter that you do not fully recognize your Career Star when it appears on the horizon of your consciousness because your star registers the instant it is first sighted, even if it is only out of the corner of your eye. You have now glimpsed the engagement of your Career Star. This moment hinges on volitional sighting that you allow when you let your Career Star come into view. Without realizing it you have said to yourself, "Let there be light."

This "sighting," even at an oblique angle, without assurance of its meaning, sends you through the Threshold of Change into the Storm of Doubt and Fear. At first you do not understand what has happened until you realize that you are beyond the point of retreat or escape.

You are not really challenged or endangered when you pass through this portal but you may think you are caught in a ferocious dilemma. You are actually at the start of a wonderful quest but your fear and doubt create a tempest of disbelief. You suspect that you cannot weather the turbulence that you have unknowingly generated. This is the initial test of a Career Star that everyone ultimately passes but morbidly dreads they cannot.

When you are caught up in this resistance, you are still looking at the problem of what to do from the point of view of being starless. You think that you do not want to be within the gate of the Garden of Earth because you imagine that there is some great responsibility in becoming a Career Star that you cannot possibly fulfill. As yet you do not realize that the storm is entirely a fabrication by the dark side of your mind that imagines you are still an alien in exile in the Shadowlands.

You may imagine that there is a regimen of discipline that you must endure as a disciple of some "master." But, you need only to be willing to change your point of view about yourself; to put in place of acrimonious self-hate a magnanimous star to work on your behalf. The instant you remember that you do not undertake the quest alone, your star shines in the distance as you trust that it is there.

You know you can do what is called for on the wrong path outside the Threshold of Change in the Whirly World. There you have a well-worn trail to degradation. Amidst all the confusion in the outer circus, you have always chosen starlessness. Perhaps you think you deserve to wander without mercy in the Shadowlands and to collide from time to time with the Wall of Projection that you erected as an expectation around the Garden of Earth.

You forget that it was your choice not to believe in your star, and in forgetting allowed it to become an unseen basic assumption. You can dissolve the assumption whenever you want by remembering that you originally made the decision to remain starless. You are in total control over believing whether your Sun Star is shining for you in the Garden of Earth. *You think the vision of a star is an illusion and that the illusion of starlessness is a vision.*

There is no doubt in faith and no faith in doubt.

There are no real walls and the gates to the garden are not barred and locked. It is just a belief you have that you do not belong to a star—a belief that is not true. It is hard to believe it is true that it is not true. It is not *just a belief* that you have a star. It is true whether you believe it or not. Your star is not within your vision because you do not look, not because it is missing. You mistake your not looking for its desertion. "Our own star fallen so low, no sign of it," says Dante in the *Inferno*.

"I hate myself therefore I am self-hate" is a spiteful new twist on Descarte. The "data" or "proof" that you have had "a bad deal" in life are figments of your perception. Why waste time suffering in the Shadowlands when you have a renowned star dedicated to leadership? Why do you keep going round and round on the Misery-Go-Round chasing a pointless brass ring?

You may choose to linger outside the Threshold of Change once you have gotten off the Misery-Go-Round and broken free of the reality sector. You may want to remain in between going in, and staying out, because even this place is consoling, and here you think you can still exercise control and escape.

"Maybe I am always supposed to be on the outside" you may say to yourself. You hear a familiar voice urging you to make sure you are wrong again by circling through the wilderness of the Whirly World. Running tempts you but you are running from yourself. When you are forced to rest from exhaustion, you feel the battle resume.

Why will you not let yourself feel the need for your Sun Star and be comforted? Are you holding back an unrequited love because you fear it will not be there? Your irresoluteness permeates your whole existence. If you do not scare yourself by saying you are going to lose it, once you find it, or that it disappears when you have it.

It is there with belief, not the opposite, that it evaporates with belief. You have cause and effect reversed, afraid that trust eradicates truth. Why does pretending to be a nonstar receive more weight than genuinely believing you are a star? Are you afraid that you will look and not see a star? Do you not look and not see a star? How can you find your Sun Star if the frontiers of darkness are the boundaries of your search?

CLEARING OF FAITH

Because you have made a commitment to the Career Star quest, understood that resistance is really a projection, and persisted thus far studying the *Career Star System,* you may discover that everything begins to work out for the good. However, now something new may disturb your entrance to the restful Garden of Earth. Nothing is wrong and yet you may become fearful again. It is frightening to deal with unfamiliar feelings that everything is all right (even though it is better than falling apart and being upset).

You may not be sure you know what feeling okay is like. Or, you may go out of your way to find something new to consider wrong. Some unfinished task by coworkers, for example, ordinarily would not bother you but now offends your pride. Perhaps you are blamed for something you did not do and yet feel guilty as if you had. Do you need to distrust yourself again? Need to regain familiar dark ground swirling around, and find it? You are seeking again what you believe about yourself.

Now you can be angry that you had to reach for an extra reason to be upset, not having enough of your own. Or, you can laugh about your self-distrust that you are okay. You cannot have a reason for stepping through the Threshold of Change if you do not face your Sun Star and feel its light against your body and in your heart. The real meaning of "lighthearted" is feeling the light in your heart. With a switch in perspective you can lose your previously heavy state of mind and gain a lighter one.

As another example, you may think you are in a slippery and tricky place and need to retreat from the area around the gate. But it is your deceitful thoughts retaking possession of your mind as you become apprehensive about acquiring and keeping the refreshment found in lingering in the shadows of the gate. You do not need to dig your heels in, stall your entrance, nor take another turn on the Misery-Go-Round.

You do not realize that there can only be shadows where there is light. You think you are in the dark of the shadows but you are actually in the shadows of the light. If you retreat you will temporarily lose the healing the muted light affords. Once you pass through the Threshold of Change you will not have another chance to run away. For the rays of your Sun Star latch on with a compelling hold that at last clears up the Storm of Doubt and Fear.

The star is rising and shining in your mind because you have decided to linger at least in the shadow light long enough to allow your body to rest and savor recuperation. Soon you will have the energy to run away again. You are loitering at the gate to the Garden of Earth in the light where you are arrested by your Sun Star. Put your mind in an inward attitude and you feel a lifting of the sentence of self-doubt.

One day you will take a bigger chance in favor of relaxation in this special place and allow yourself to feel better for even longer. Your Sun Star will inadvertently rise even higher in your mind and suddenly break through totally. The wall associated with the gate will dematerialize. Initially you may think you are going to melt. As you pass through the threshold, you enter the sane asylum of the Garden of Earth. Suddenly you are standing before your star in the Clearing of Faith. Then you will be blinded by the light rather than blinded by the denial of your Sun Star.

Once *you* get beyond the Wall of Projection and recover from the Storm of Fear and Doubt you may want another period of recuperation that can be taken in the Zone of Recovery. You can lie in the healing light of your Sun Star and relax at the resort of the Garden of Earth before you continue the pursuit of your mission. Give yourself the benefit of a convalescence without continuing to use your weariness as ammunition for more attacks on yourself.

When your energy returns, the fun of exploration, the reward of discovery, and the adventure of your quest all begin anew. At last you are free and free at last to be you. In time freedom will make you so star conscious you will be convinced, not only that the Storm of Fear and Doubt were absolutely imaginary, but that you truly are a star of a singular sun and the sun of a singular star.

EXERCISE 3
CAREER STAR MEDITATION

It is crucial to stay Career Star conscious and to remember always that your Career Star arises from an internal rather than an external cosmos. Follow near and far the golden burning flame of your Career Star. The bright, clear luster of the star reflects the deep inner radiance of who you really are.

To help maintain Career Star consciousness, you are encouraged to participate in the exercise below beginning with the "Progressive Relaxation Meditation." This meditation is followed by the "Career Star Meditation."

Be prepared for a resurgence of resistance, however, because this is the first exercise of substance involving communication with your inner star self. Sudden illnesses, accidents, mental blockages, evaporating time warps, needs for sleep, and lapses of memory, for example, may occur to interfere with carrying out this exercise.

Individuals or entire groups of students have not done the assignment and innocently provided plausible excuses. Some individuals suddenly discover "the whole project is weird" and decide not to do their "inner homework." In groups, disagreements with other members erupt to prevent discussion of internal issues by creating lively external ones.

With the anticipation of resistance in mind, read through the exercise instructions below before you begin. There are three parts to this exercise:

1. Read over the "Progressive Relaxation Meditation Text" Appendix 3, page 231, to help you enter into a receptive state of mind before you actually begin your Career Star Meditation.

2. Read the entire Career Star Meditation, several times, to allow images to come to mind. Note these images but try not to memorize them nor worry that you will never see them again.

3. Now, do both meditations in succession, Progressive Relaxation and Career Star. The former is preparation for the latter.

Read the text of the Progressive Relaxation Meditation, Appendix 3. This will help put you in a receptive state of mind. Next, read the text of the Career Star Meditation below to get an overview of this exercise. Read both texts now.

There is no right or wrong way to experience a meditation. Each meditation is unique to the individual. If you do not see any shapes, images, or colors at first be patient and relax. Put aside any self-reproaches or grievances against others.

If you are not familiar with meditation it may take a few practices to get the feel of it so do not rush yourself. Do not expect, for example, to have three-dimensional, multimedia images all in technicolor, equivalent to "virtual reality," before you consider the meditation valid.

If you allow yourself to enter and enjoy the process you will respond to events in your life differently and not lose your balance as often as in the past. If thoughts intrude from outside, try to exhale and let them go.

CAREER STAR BURST MANDALA

CAREER STAR MEDITATION TEXT

Stare at the above Career Star Burst Mandala. Acknowledge your Career Star with a gesture and greeting. Begin to notice its symmetry, geometry, harmony, and beauty. Take in the design and note the many different shapes, angles, and lines. Lift up and close your eyes and see the light of your Career Star with the eye of your mind.

Now, imagine that you are going to go inside the Career Star Burst Mandala. Stare at it for thirty to sixty seconds more, and then close your eyes again. Breathe deeply, relax, observe, notice and enjoy any images or colors as you see the Star Burst in your mind's eye. Then put this manual aside.

Visualize that the star is getting bigger and bigger as it moves toward you. As it gets closer and closer, imagine and allow it to surround you and take you in. Sense that you are completely surrounded and taken inside the star.

Beyond resistance and into the substance.

Now inside, casually look around and notice what comes into your view. Do not judge what you see nor expect to see something you do not. Observe and take in what is there and whatever appears. If it appears dark or cloudy, just be patient and wait to see if there are any colors, shapes, or movements.

If you do not receive any images, colors, or movement, pay attention to the thoughts or feelings that may come up from the unconscious. If ideas you have about matters in the external world obtrude into your consciousness, simply let them go with your exhaling breath.

Again, do not judge whatever comes up as absurd or bizarre. If you have no thoughts, feelings, or images, it is probably because you are not relaxing. Just accept this, and do not try to conjure or force anything to appear. Again, just relax and try to relax about relaxing. Focus on and sense your breathing.

Say to yourself, "It is okay if today I see only the darkness of my Career Star, because this is a beginning. I am willing to see darkness as often and as long as it may take until the story of my star bursts into color and design."

Now that you have discovered with your eyes, use each of your other senses to explore the interior of your Career Star. What does it feel like inside? Is it warm or breezy or damp? Can you feel its size? Is it spacious or is it cramped? (I will wait a minute while you find out.)

If you can take the time and if you have the interest, ask your Career Star to take you to some place in the universe of your own mind where there is meaning. When and wherever you arrive, ask aloud, "What does this place mean to me? What influence am I under in this place and what does this place have to teach me?"

When you are finished, project yourself back out and imagine that you are seeing the Career Star from the outside, and that it is getting smaller and smaller as it recedes back into space. As it does so, look at it again from the outside and from a distance. Say aloud, "I see and seek my Career Star."

Try to fix the telescope of your consciousness on the outward appearance and behold your splendid Career Star. Keep in mind that you have experienced your first rendezvous with your Career Star. In your mind respond by appropriating your Career Star as your personal sanctuary. In the future you can stay or sail away with your golden Career Star.

Now we are going to conclude the Career Star Meditation. Therefore, begin to become aware of the present by noticing what it feels and sounds like in the room where you are actually located. Count yourself out from five to one. Reenter the present alert, awake, and refreshed. Be at peace with yourself.

CAREER STAR MEDITATION

Recall your experience during the meditation and write a brief account of what took place. Call to mind the sights, colors, and feelings of four successive meditations in a one-week period and record them below. Indicate for each whether it was preceded by a Progressive Relaxation Meditation. Describe your experience in detail and use extra paper if necessary.

Meditation One: Date:_____.

_____
_____
_____
_____
_____
_____

Meditation Two: Date:_____.

_____
_____
_____
_____
_____
_____

Meditation Three: Date:_____.

_____

_____

_____

_____

_____

_____

Meditation Four: Date:_____.

_____

_____

_____

_____

_____

_____

AUDIOCASSETTE

You have an option to record the meditation texts onto an audiocassette. Or, you can ask someone else to do this job. You then will have both prerecorded for future meditation sessions. Add or subtract from the text as you like in your own version of the meditation. If you made an audiocassette of the Progressive Relaxation Meditation describe your experience in writing below:

_____

_____

Remember the main "point" of the Career Star is the idea of its origin within your own personhood. Through regular meditation you can stay at the altar of your star. The Career Star Meditation along with the Career Star Burst Mandala are to help you stay reminded of the constancy of your inner star. Do not forget, therefore, to stay starward, starfast, and starbound. "Wish upon a star" really means, "May we please stay conscious of our star?"

Over the next few days be alert to any signs of increased energy or feelings of exhilaration possibly arising from the contemplation of your Career Star. Meditation can bring tranquillity to your life if you allow it to become a regular practice. Now, return to your duty station and continue to study the manual and carry out the exercises of the *Career Star System* as prescribed.

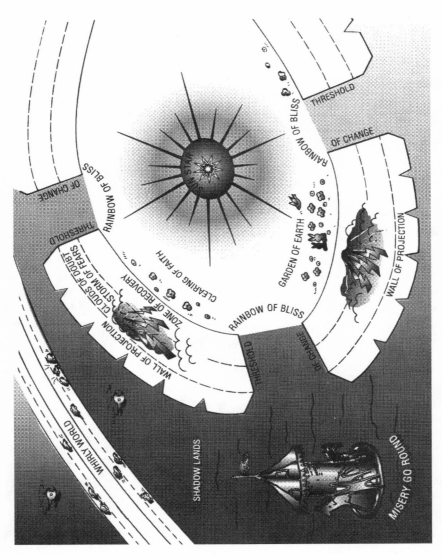

THE GARDEN OF EARTH

STAR MISSION:

Accepting Your Assignment

Hitch your wagon to a star.

Ralph Waldo Emerson
Society and Solitude, 1870

CLICKER

Your calling is calling your calling,
   and your calling is calling you.
But if you do not awaken and call out for your calling,
   how can your calling hear you?

Is it long distance?
Overseas?
Are the circuits jammed?
Perhaps this is a shouting match?
A standoff?
Are you deaf?

Are you listening to the tiny voice of conscience,
   Jimminy Cricket, Tinker Bell and Tweetie Bird,

who are whispering and longing and crying
and pleading and yearning to find you?

Where are you?

INSPIRATIONS

One of the greatest adventures in life is finding your Career Star and beginning the awe-filled journey to become the full and complete human being you are meant to be. The most astounding fact is that you are alive, and alive with an amazing, exciting, and important mystery to be solved.

You are the one person who has never existed before and who will never exist again. The ongoing challenge, frightful and fulfilling, is to respond to the call. To view this as a great happening rather than a horrible misfortune is the initial step.

Abraham Maslow, founder of the human potential movement, wrote, "A musician must make music, an artist must paint, a poet must write, if he is to be ultimately at peace with himself. What a man can be, he must be." Martin Luther King Jr., founder of the civil rights movement, said, "If a man hasn't discovered something that he will die for, he isn't fit to live."

Agnes DeMille, the dancer and choreographer who made ballet popular on the Broadway stage, captured the preciousness of the idea of a calling when she wrote the following in a letter to her friend, Martha Graham, who was also a dancer, dance teacher, and a leading figure in modern dance:

> There is a vitality, a life force, a quickening that is translated through you into action, and because there is only one of you in all time, this expression is unique. And if you block it, it will never exist through any other medium and [will] be lost. The world will not have it. It is not your business to determine how good it is; nor how valuable it is; nor how it compares with other expressions. It is your business to keep it yours, clearly and directly, in yourself or your work. You have to keep open and aware directly to the urges that motivate you. Keep the channel open.

Our calling is the application of talents and abilities that constitute the center core, the crucial crux, the essence of our higher being.

These gifts are originally inherent and natural, but are greatly modifiable by experience, environment, and learning. When you are young your calling exists in your mind and body in a rudimentary or embryonic form.

In this light, motherhood and fatherhood are callings. Actually, the calling of all callings because babies are raised ideally through a cooperative union of parents. Parenthood gives to children the irreplaceable experience of being nurtured and protected, which is essential if they are to learn to care for themselves. Without this experience it is difficult to love and be loved. Parents serve as role models to replicate when it comes the children's turn to be caring adults. (See also "Child Abuse," Chapter 11.)

To be "born" your calling has to be seen and heard with insight and raised with conscious attention. It has to be carefully parented so that it can develop, just as a real baby needs to be nurtured by his mother and father. "Find your calling" is an admonition to love the self of embryonic potentials with parental compassion. Although newborn, your calling is invincible and unassailable.

Just as you would not ignore the crying of a real child, do not ignore the mental birth of your Career Star. Without nurturing, your baby starself cannot flourish. When your calling is grown it will help you care for yourself like a parent but it begins as your child to be cared for and raised. As your calling matures, it will begin to grab and grip your attention in the same way a child astonishes its mother and father with its incredible uniqueness.

Being seized by your calling is a turning point in the Career Star Quest. It occurs when you unambivalently entertain the notion of a Career Star long enough—and this need only be a few seconds—that the unconscious star leaps from a remote possibility to a burning certainty by crossing the vision of your conscious mind.

Smitten, you cannot let go because consciousness is the consequence, not the cause, of your Career Star. Consciousness has been overtaken by a hidden universe and intrudes permanently into this realm. Your Career Star is unforgettable from this point on because the conscious effort to drive it out only makes it tighten its hold.

Unsuspectingly, you allowed the idea to get too close to awareness and it leapt across the frontier, formed a permanent bridge and now radiates securely in your conscious mind. As this happens the bridge is anchored firmly on both shores. If you attempt to sever the tie that binds you to your Career Star, the consciousness required to eliminate it only causes its presence to be affirmed.

The harder you try to shake the star the more it latches on. The magnitude of dark resistance is penetrated and illuminated by the light beam into consciousness. The only thing to do is reciprocate by making a commitment to your star as permanent as its fidelity to you. Dispatch yourself without delay to a foresworn destiny with a star.

A Career Star is a spark of light that illuminates the darkness within your mind about knowing your life-purpose. Because the light now shines, no matter how dimly, there is no longer any darkness in which to hide the truth. Denial has become conscious and the two cannot coexist.

WHAT IS A CALLING?

The *Career Star System* is impartial in advancing that everyone possesses a calling. This contradicts the more prevalent view that only exceptional individuals are gifted and that the rest of humanity has ordinary occupational or professional roles to fulfill. The world is not divided between a few rare geniuses and millions of average slobs. Each individual has an absolutely unique work function to contribute to society.

Everyone has a calling! Though you may not know it, your calling has been answered before it was placed. We all have a reason to be living, a purpose to accomplish. Since everyone has a calling, callings are a part of a society's common wealth.

A "calling" is a strong desire to do a particular kind of work. A calling is not just "work," however, which usually means doing something you do not want to do. A calling is a pathway pursued throughout the course of your life that integrates what you do for a living with who you are as a person.

A calling is not a device applied to your telephone service. Nor do you have to take a number and stand in line to await your call. You don't have to earn or deserve your calling. But you do have to acknowledge that it is your possession. All are called and all are chosen but few listen and respond.

Everyone has a calling because everyone has what is described in *A Course in Miracles* as a "special function." Each person has skills and knowledge, talents and powers, potentials and dreams, that are absolutely original, personal, and wonderful. You are called whether or not you answer.

A calling is often understood to mean that "you can be anything you want to be." Well, yes; but you can only be prosperous, happy, and successful by being who you are *intended* to be. If who you want to be does not coincide with the function you are given, you will lack a deep excitement in your work.

> **When your star in the sky meets the star in your eye it's your calling.**

Work undertaken with a higher purpose may be hard to find but not harder than not finding work you are meant to do. You actually work harder at not finding your calling. A calling is not difficult to accomplish because it is freely given to you for the explicit purpose of giving it back to society. That you are qualified is why you are called. You are also fulfilled personally as your calling acts on you.

A "calling" is not just about making money or achieving status and success. It is not found in the classified advertisements nor through the grapevine of the hidden job market. A calling lasts a lifetime while a job has a beginning and an end.

Cynical about the purpose of your Career Star? Ponder it on a mountaintop, at a bonfire on the beach, in the serenity of a natural setting, or anywhere you like. When the star in the sky meets the star in your eye, when being down to earth coincides with the flight of your aspirations, you find your calling.

Everyone has the potential to do meaningful, purposeful work in life. You do not have to have the genius of Albert Einstein, the compassion of Florence Nightingale, nor the humanitarianism of Albert Schweitzer to have a calling. You need only to be sensitive, attentive, and responsive to yourself through "insight," through the inner lens of introspection. Within you, your calling is calling you.

> **Your calling is ringing. Answer it now. Don't put it on hold!**

There are as many callings as there are individuals, as many as the multitude of stars in the solar system. You are a "naturally luminous, celestial body"—the dictionary definition of a "star"—if you allow yourself to be undimmed by self-doubt. Perhaps you prefer another definition, "a globular mass of hot gases?"

You are the star and the star is you. There is not now, nor has there ever been, nor will there ever be, a duplicate, a facsimile, or a substitute for the one and only you. Even if you are an identical twin, you are still one of a kind. Individual uniqueness is described in the *New Testament* in this way:

> There is one glory of the sun, and another glory of the moon, and another glory of the stars: for one star differeth from another star in glory.
>
> 1 Corinthians, 15:41

The call of your calling is not wild or arbitrary. Because there are many individuals, many gifts, and much glory, no one star can excel in all areas. To each and every person is given a unique and special gift. Homer expresses the idea of creative uniqueness with his poetic gift:

> You will certainly not be able to take the lead in all things yourself, for to one man a god has given deeds of war, and to another the dance, to another the lyre and song, and in another wide-sounding Zeus puts a good mind.
>
> *Iliad,* 729 B.C.

The same basic idea is contained in the *Doctrine and Covenants,* the Church of Jesus Christ of Latter Day Saints:

> And again, verily I say unto you, I would that ye should always remember, and always retain in your minds what those gifts are . . . For all have not every gift given unto them; for there are many gifts, and to every man is given a gift by the spirit of God. To some is given one, and to some is given another, that all may be profited thereby.
>
> *Pearl of Great Price,* 46:10–12

Your Career Star shines with luster in the darkness of your unconscious mind even while you are totally oblivious to its radiant glow. Like real stars shining in the daylight, or during the cloudiest night, luminously always it is radiant. It waits for the beam of your intelligence to arrive in order to return to your awareness a sparkle of golden light and energy.

Your calling is not encoded in a message that needs to be deciphered. Like a lighthouse beacon that continuously pulsates, your Career Star is a twinkling signal that heralds to all that the distinctness that is you has been born. You will receive a flash of insight light when you no longer bow or beckon to the decoy of another beacon.

Belonging to a Career Star is not a gamble like playing the lottery, dice, or roulette. If you believe that life is totally arbitrary, *you are* at the mercy of external forces and you are bound to be unlucky. Half of failure is in not believing and the other half in not acting on your calling.

"Whether you think you can or whether you think you can't— you're right," said Henry Ford. "Argue for your limitations" or your potentials "and sure enough they're yours," wrote Richard Bach, author of *Jonathan Livingston Seagull*. The power of self-fulfillment is the message of all the great self-help classics: *Think and Grow Rich, The Power of Positive Thinking,* and *How to Win Friends and Influence People.*

Your physical birth causes your star to ascend in the heavens. Your awareness of your Career Star causes it to arise in your mind. A truly golden star shines out resplendently day and night, with your name etched on it, serving as a reminder of the importance of your Career Star alliance and allegiance. This means a Career Star is longing to become your guiding light.

You are the choice of your discerning Career Star. "There was a star danced and under that was I born," wrote Shakespeare in *King Henry V.* This means you are a shining orb, too, if thou art not hardheaded about following thy Career Star.

Edward F. Edinger comments on the coincidence of identity and destiny in this way: "The notion that one's identity has an *a priori* existence is expressed in the ancient idea that each person has his own individual star, a kind of celestial counterpart, representing his cosmic dimension and destiny." For example, Jesus' star was the Star of Bethlehem, the brightest star. Carl Gustav Jung refers to a Mithraic liturgical prayer in which a new convert recites, "I am a star wandering together with you and shining up from the depths." Mithraism, one of the great religions of the Roman Empire, was more widespread at that time than Christianity. Jung comments that, "In his religious ecstasy the neophyte makes himself the equal of the stars, just as . . . St. Francis carried the relationship even further by speaking of his "brother the sun and his sister the moon."

Stars are holes in the canopy of the sky that reveal that another sun lies behind the sun that we see every day. Bits of the day that remain in the night, stars remind us of the constancy of sunlight. "Choose not to deny the experience behind the sun," wrote Dante in the *Inferno*.

WHERE IS A CALLING?

Your calling is the inward side of your physical being and is the crux of your spiritual self. If you think the idea of a calling is strange, re- member that the word "weird" is from *wyrd*, Old English for "fate." In Greek mythology the Weird Sisters were the three Goddesses of Fate, daughters of Zeus and Themis, who wove, measured, and cut the fab- ric of life. Where callings come from *is* "weird"!

Your calling is first and foremost a spiritual entity and this "meta- physical," "transpersonal" self within you is a touch of the divine. To have a calling implies a caller, which means that you are called by an intelligence and power greater than your own. As a minister of God, Buddha said, for example, "Your work is to discover your work and then with all your heart give yourself to it."

St. Paul said, "I therefore . . . beg you lead a life worthy of the call- ing to which you have been called." (Ephesians 4:1.) By virtue of a di- vine spark of the Spirit within your spirit, you are a "soular" star and a stellar soul. It will be helpful to your destiny, to your progeny, and to posterity to acknowledge your descent and ascent from a divine lin- eage, which is what stars in the sky represent.

You are a "soular" star and a stellar soul.

The outer light creates the inner light so that both may see and be seen, according to Arthur Zajonc, author of *Catching the Light*. The inner star is allured to the outer star because an inner void, lifelong felt, is filled by the acquisition of your star. Not until the star is visi- ble within you does it become obvious beyond you. When your call- ing does not seem to be ablaze in the heavens, the telescope of consciousness is not focused in the inner observatory.

DESERTED

In observing that I was speaking
  I miscalculated between pretending
  to be an artist and an actor.
And in just speaking out
  what I genuinely had to say
  my ideas which I knew well enough
  just up and slipped away.

Your calling is hidden within your unconscious mind, unlike your physical being, which is shown to you in a looking glass but reflects only external appearance. The mirror of consciousness, however, can reveal the essence of your inner being. Vanity is the folly of believing only in the physical self and is the richest of all deceivers. Just as the city for St. Augustine, a fourth-century theologian, was a group joined by love of the same object, hell is a place in the mind organized around self-worship. "Pride" is still number one of the seven deadly sins in the Roman Catholic Church.

Your calling comes through in proportion to your willingness to listen. It remains unknown when you are inattentive and unreceptive to inner sights, sounds, and motions. Not knowing your calling is often mistaken for having been forsaken by the soft and gentle voice of conscience. Do you suffer from an internal attention-deficit disorder? Do you have to be hit over the head to see stars? What will it take to make *you* starstruck and starry-eyed?

You must have a question before you have a quest, and you must put the question to an inner source before you can hear your calling echo back. Some people will not allow themselves to possess the excitement of the question, "What is my calling?" Out of self-mistrust, many others will want recognition from, and opportunities provided by, others and keep waiting for the telephone to ring. Your calling relies on sufficient self-confidence within you to be summoned. Are you responding instead to the static of your own self-doubt?

Without self-trust your real value is disowned and projected into the material world. Far away now, value shows up in coveted things seen as precious. These things—such as money, possessions, status, and power—are acquired through competition with others likewise disillusioned and disendowed. Projection of the value of yourself will always make you feel empty and unfulfilled.

Our doubts about our calling are often attributed to others who are seen as making critical judgments against us. But this is really the externalization of our own self-concept. What we imagine coming negatively from others is usually our own self-doubt projected outwardly.

We use another's image to represent our own mistrust so that we can deceive ourselves about its origin and feel helpless to change it. The lineup of people in the opposition are witnesses for the self-persecution. A client once said, "I find it harder to keep a commitment to myself than to others because I care more about what they think."

Especially when we are young we believe we must do what teachers and parents recommend. Authorities frequently encourage young adults to enter rapidly growing fields. Sometimes, this is because they failed to take initiative or make enough money in their own career pursuits. Not recognizing that they still have their own callings longing to be fulfilled, they impose their expectations on their children.

You may object to the call of your star because you believe that it is being imposed against your will by some alien authority. For example, you may think some cruel godlike figure, or other fictional character, is responsible for fate. If so, you may prefer to resist finding your calling in order to be free to do what you dislike. This is for the sake of an autonomy that is important even if it wrecks your life mission.

An objection on the basis of control by a "foreign star power" is an invention of your own imagination. It is designed to hinder and delay progress. The only "star authority" is you. The path is wide open and the sky is the limit. Exchange the reign of tyranny in your fantasies for the aegis of a faithful Career Star in reality. Trade a mental tsar for a celestial star!

Does anyone passionately in touch with feelings have a calling? Did Hitler and Manson have a mission? They certainly thought so, but their ambitions and actions are actually the antithesis of a calling as we have defined it. A true calling does not call on you to harm others or yourself.

Those who think they have been called to serve the dark star have actually been blinded by the intensity of the injury to their inner self. The extent to which they hate others is a measure of the hate harbored also for themselves. A calling is a response to the positive side of human nature and a service to humanity. (See also Chapter 9, "Dark Stars".)

Your Career Star is not an independent and autonomous force because it cannot function to serve your interests without *your* recognition, participation, and authorization. You are sovereign but where is your allegiance? You can allow your future to be sacrificed by corrupt self-government if you are disloyal to your Career Star. " 'Tis God gives skill, but not without men's hands: He could not make Antonio Stradivari's violins without Antonio," wrote George Eliot.

You cannot receive something you do not want to find and you cannot find something you do not want to receive. Nor can you give something you do not think you have. You must want to give your gift back to society in order to find what you have been given to share. Your destiny is to add to humanity by contributing your Calling Star.

Listen for the call from within which will teach you when, where, and how you are to respond and proceed. The earth needs your calling as much as you do. You must want to shine as much as you want it to shine on you. Without a Calling Star you will not be able to grow and glow and neither will the world.

Self-doubt functions like a veil, a mask, or a shield that hides a real face and true identity, both from our own selves and from one another. We turn outward to others for help in finding ourselves and encounter instead their veils, masks, and shields, which are facsimiles of our own. Jung called these masks "personas" after the Greek word for masks worn by actors in ancient plays. You will not be able to find your part occupationally until you strip away your mask and assume your role within the larger script.

A person who allows her or himself to find an inner source of purpose becomes more centered, calmer, and self-reliant and is influenced less by external enticements of all kinds. Political power, sexual favors, and monetary rewards, for example, become less compelling sirens. Erratic and irresistible temptation are eased and overcome by the temper of intention and inspiration.

Almost any dazzling light can draw us off track when we focus on outer values. Fortune hunters shuttle from market to market looking for options and bargains to buy, sell, and trade in opportunity stocks. If you *Follow Your Career Star,* you will find meaning in work and play. Winston Churchill wrote, "Those whose work and play are one, are fortune's favorite children."

WORKING A CALLING

A few individuals react to the idea of finding a calling as if it were an impractical and unrealistic idea. Some think the *Career Star System* as "a starry-eyed idea." "I've got to make a living," is one retort. "A man has to work for his bread in this world," is an attitude of begrudging toil. In the beginning, it may be hard to believe that you can find your Career Star. You may think you have to settle for "any job and be glad for a means of support."

"Not in doing what you like," wrote the novelist, James Barrie, "but in liking what you do is the secret of happiness." Finding your calling is not meant as an alternative to supporting yourself economically, however. A job and a calling are compatible.

This is a book about finding your calling more than finding a job. Accordingly, little emphasis is placed on job search, résumé writing, interview techniques, and networking strategies. These topics are important if employment and income are an immediate necessity and they are covered by many traditional career resources. (See Chapter 13, "Star Strategies".)

"Work" itself means to gradually force or shape something into being, just as this book and paragraph were first hammered out, and later cleaned and polished. Exploring different jobs is the initial search phase of the career discovery process. Searching allows your calling to begin to shape you, as you start to shape it, and if you do not submit to the process you will be pounded by fate. Once located, working your calling becomes your life work, your ongoing *magnum opus*.

Many people avoid the search phase by staying on a job they hate for too long. The mistake collapses the process by making temporary work permanent. Eventually, the individual begins to imagine escape usually in the form of a permanent vacation. Out of the frustration and depletion of a wrongful job choice you may fantasize about travel and recreation, even as legitimate occupational alternatives.

A vacation *is* necessary in the short run but it is a mistake to turn a vacation, which is just another stage, into a vocation, which is a permanent occupation. If you select an alternative as a reaction rather than through a thoughtful exploration, you repeat the original mistake, the substitution of an interim stage for an end result.

> Do what you love and love what you do. Hate your work
> and it will hate you, too.

Another kind of mistake occurs when employed people become accustomed to a level of income and a standard of living that they fear is jeopardized if they seek a career change. They justify not hearing a call out of binding commitments to family, employers, and creditors without necessarily realizing that these obligations have been incurred partly for this very reason.

"What if I find my calling and it does not pay very well?" you might ask. This question suggests that a calling and prosperity are incompatible. Some people get hooked on the money and benefits of a career that is disliked even though their career preference is known all along. This trap is a psychological fallacy, not a real barrier, because your calling will help you care for yourself financially in return for caring for yourself emotionally.

Finding your calling does not mean that you have to give up all your worldly possessions, reduce your standard of living, and take vows of poverty. Rationalizing your doubt by claiming to be unable to "afford" change means risking your mission because you do not trust it is really there. You trade your precious life-purpose for income maintenance and your star treasury for petty cash. In the exchange, what is truly valuable is lost.

Your past, present, and future are intertwined. *Follow Your Career Star* and you will find all three: a vocation, a vacation, and an avocation—all three braided into one.

✳ EXERCISE 4
STAR BURST MANDALA

A mandala is a Buddhist or Hindu graphic symbol, usually a circle enclosed by a square, used during meditation. It represents the reconciliation of all the polarities of the self in harmony with the unity of the universe. Through the process of meditation, the cleavage between the Injured and Creative Selves (Chapter 8), begins to be mended. Meditation is like medication because it gives attention to the wound, which is the first phase in the healing process.

On pages 69–72 are large outlines of the Career Star Burst, the logo of the *Career Star System*. The Career Star Burst Mandala is an ideogram, a graphic illustration, of the idea of a Career Star. The Star Burst has the classic mandala form of an enclosed circle within a square. You are now going to paint or color your majestic and imagistic Career Star Burst.

Make a half-dozen copies before you begin because you may want to do this exercise another time. As your career quest evolves the colors of your star will change. Date each one and keep a record for future reference.

Find a quiet and comfortable space, play some of your favorite music, and burn some incense if you wish. Before you begin the color process, however, do the Career Star Meditation, either reading from the text in Chapter 3, page 48, or listening to the audiocassette that you have recorded for yourself.

Do not be unraveled by the prospect of this activity. Relax; whole worlds can be created in a few moments of reflection. A single moment can seem to last a lifetime and a single lifetime can seem like a moment. Let yourself become lost in the time and space of the creative process.

Audibly repeat, "Relax, I do not need to make anything happen." Let your unconscious do the "work." In this meditation allow your attention to focus on the colors that appear inwardly. Permit the Career Star to evoke any shape and color it chooses. Take in all the different shades, tones, and hues and think of the mandala as a rainbow/kaleidoscope of you.

After your meditation, color or paint your Career Star Burst according to the colors you have seen in your mind's eye. Start at the center and use any type or variety of colors you visualize. Without judgment or criticism allow the colors that are truly attuned to your inner self find expression in your mandala.

Susanne F. Fincher, in *Creating Mandalas*, gives various interpretations of major colors. For example, gold stands for "insight" and dark blue, for "responsibility." This is another way of expressing the idea of balance between rational and spiritual elements in the career quest.

Allow yourself to be curious about what the colors may mean but do not let this thoughtfulness interfere with your choices and effort. Later you can look up the meaning of the colors, but at this stage rely on your intuition to help you color your Career Star Burst. Try not to be concerned about whether you have used the "right" colors to represent your star.

Do this meditation at least four times in the next week and describe each experience afterward. Also, color four Star Burst Mandalas and give each a name and a date. One of the names can serve as the new working title for your journal.

It is not unusual to be fascinated by mandalas and to find yourself transfixed by their evocative nature. An unconscious process of reconciliation is continuously taking place whenever there is a desire to become emotionally healthier. If you find it soothing, stare at your mandala for as long and as often as you like. Help it attain full living color through use in all your future meditations.

Meditation 1: **Name of Star:_____.** **Star Date_____.** ✍

_____
_____
_____
_____
_____
_____

Meditation 2:   *Name of Star:*_____.   *Star Date*_____.

_____

_____

_____

_____

_____

_____

Meditation 3:   *Name of Star:*_____.   *Star Date*_____.   ✍

_____

_____

_____

_____

_____

_____

Meditation 4:   *Name of Star:_____.*   *Star Date_____.*   ✍

_____
_____
_____
_____
_____
_____
_____

Because night dreams can help you discover your calling, you have an option at this point to skip to Chapter 12, "Star Dreams." Or, you can stay in sequence and read Chapter 5, "Star Map," which will help you make an assessment of your basic star type. Starphires usually want to stay in sequence and Starphades jump ahead.

STAR MAP:
Setting Your Course

Vos estis lux mundi.
You are the light of the world.

Matthew 5:11

MAP PURPOSE

In her best-selling book, *Drawing on the Right Side of the Brain* (1986), Betty Edwards attributed the discovery of the distinct functions of the hemispheres of the brain to the work of Roger W. Sperry, who in 1981 received the Nobel prize in medicine. The concept of "brain lateralization" is confusing to almost everyone, however, because there are several possible references. Sometimes it is literal to the actual hemispheres of the brain and at other times to a psychological style of thinking, either more emotional (right-brained) or rational (left-brained) in decision-making.

There is a strong correlation between brain lateralization and career choice. Generally, right-brained individuals are drawn to subjective career fields such as human services, the humanities, and the arts. In the *Career Star System* these types are called "Starphades." Left-brained individuals, on the other hand, tend to be attracted to objective fields such as science, law, industry, and the military. These types are called "Starphires." There are other types of stars in the *Career Star System* delineated in the next chapter but these are the basic two types.

In this chapter the *Career Star Map* is used as an assessment instrument to help you measure the extent to which you are right- or left-brain lateralized, a Starphade or a Starphire. In making this assessment the map also helps you see your current and future career direction and to change direction once you know which way you want to go.

A second purpose of the map is to show the geographical layout of the five major careers paths. There is a moderate and extreme Starphade and Starphire path, plus a balanced center path. Each path has a different course and "life-outcome," symbolized by the archetype at the end of each path. Along the various ways you can also see the twists and turns, barriers and pitfalls that are encountered.

The *Career Star Map* is similar to an aptitude test that assesses your basic preference for analytical (left-brain) versus experiential (right-brain) thinking. The map coordinates could be written as a set of test questions. For example, you could be asked whether you prefer listening to music or balancing your checkbook; relating more to people or to computers; dancing or working late? A mathematical score of the extent to which you are right- or left-brained could be calculated. Your score could be compared with the scores of all the others who have taken the test and ranked in comparison to extremes.

The map format of the *Career Star System* makes the assessment process a little more fun and playful than a more traditional aptitude test because it allows for your creative input. In this respect the map is projective and interpretative like a Rorschach Ink Blot except it has color and is not quite so messy. It is no less vulnerable to distortion, however, and can be skewed in any direction you choose without honest answers.

ASSESSMENT

To begin the assessment process, unfold the color *Career Star Map* at the back of the book. Casually look the entire map over before you begin to study it more carefully. Give yourself a break from reading, try to relax and enjoy the process. Just take in the map, without judgment or criticism, as if it were a work of art.

Allow yourself to assimilate the information on the map without expectation or preconception. Look over the various names and places. Let the map data sink into and saturate your curiosity and be absorbed by your senses. Later the map will be used to help figure out your calling, but for now, pass on results and just enjoy the process of map familiarization. Review the map now before reading further in this chapter.

Do the same thing next with the black-and-white version of the map at the back of the book. Pay attention this time to the words in the margins and on the grid, more than to the images. The black-and-white version is used in the Star Course exercise later in this chapter. The full-color version is provided to give you an overview of the five major career paths.

MAP OVERVIEW

There are several things to notice about the map:

1. The map has paths that represent the five most common career directions. The paths stretch out across the map from the bottom left corner like the palm of a hand. The diagonal path in the middle represents the ideal career path that integrates right- and left-brain styles of thinking.

The center path is the ideal path because it represents a blending together that derives from interweaving intellectual and creative concerns. In accessing both hemispheres you become a more whole and self-actualized person. Paths to the left of the center are right-brained paths, while those to the right of center are left-brained paths.

On each side of the diagonal center path there is a moderate and an extreme right-brain path, and a moderate and an extreme left-brain path. Each path is drawn to graphically illustrate the nature of the pathway actually taken. For example, the moderate left-brain path is linear while the moderate right-brain path meanders.

A number of terms can be used to designate the different paths. Using the actual shape of the routes, from left to right, we can refer to the "circular," "meandering," "weaving," "linear," and "angular" paths. Or, as another example, at the end of each path is a figure that represents the archetype of the path: the "Evil Magician," the "Martyr/Saint," the "Mortal," the "Hero/Heroine," and the "Tyrant/Empress." Finally, near the end of each path is a letter representing personality types: BB, B, A/B, A and AA paths.

2. The map is valid for both right- and left-handed people. If you

are left-handed, however, from your point of view the map may be drawn "backward," since it is your left side that is under "rational" control, and your right side that is not in control, or is "irrational." Your perspective is exactly the reverse of right-handed people as you may have come to expect.

3. There are lists of words along two margins of the black-and-white version of the map, one at the bottom and the other along the left-hand side. The words on the margin are called "coordinates." There are a total of thirty coordinates along each margin. These two lists are identical and together form a matrix.

You are going to trace a coordinate from each margin to the center path. In doing so, you encounter five descriptive words. As you will see in a moment, picking a coordinate and then selecting the one word on the particular path that is most descriptive of you, helps identify your style of thinking and your current career direction.

4. Please disregard the impression given by the map that the earth is a flat rectangle floating in space.

EXERCISE 5: STAR COURSE

Once upon a time, in a Career Star seminar, a student who had listened to the above introduction to the map, turned to another and exclaimed, "So, what brain are you?" On another occasion I heard, "So, what side of the brain are you on?" Below, we want to try to answer the question, "On which side and to what extent are you brain lateralized?"

We begin by trying to determine your current career path to give us a preliminary reading on how you use your mind. This may scare you at first but will reveal the extent to which you are right- or left-brained in your thinking style. Start by selecting a coordinate word from the list of words along the left margin of the map.

Pick any coordinate that "grabs" you—any one that stands out. It does not matter which one. Whichever one you select first and the order in which you select others will tell something about you that is meaningful. Do not let this thought deter you in the selection process, however. Just choose one word that seems to communicate, "Pick me, pick me!"

If there appears to be no communication from a word, be patient, quiet, still, and keep looking without trying to force one to stand out.

If none begins to emerge after a few minutes, pick any one that interests you, or just pick one at random. Once you have picked a coordinate, in the margin next to the coordinate, put the number 1 to indicate the order of your choice.

Now, look for the identical word in the list across the bottom of the map. Remember, the two lists of coordinates, along the left margin and across the bottom, are identical. When you have found the same word in both margins, follow the grid lines from each coordinate to the center path of the map. The two identical coordinates intersect at a quadrant on the center path.

If you trace your coordinate from the center path back to the margins in each direction, you will see a word on each path. Follow the grid lines of the coordinate you have chosen in both directions and notice the words you encounter on the quadrants of the other four paths.

For example, if you picked the coordinate "Direction," you will see that in tracing the grid lines to the center path you find the word "weaving." Follow the grid lines back in both directions and you will encounter a word on each of the quadrants of the other four paths. For example, below is the list of words for the coordinate "Direction," one word from each of the five paths:

1. **"Circular."**
2. **"Wandering."**
3. **"Weaving."**
4. **"Linear."**
5. **"Angular."**

Notice that each of these terms describes the way the five paths are actually drawn. Now, select the one word that is most descriptive of you in your present life and current career situation. That is, mark it on the page in the book, and circle it or place a sticker on the pathway next to the word on the map itself. As another example, if you happened to select "Greatest Fear," you find the following five choices:

1. **"Real Power."**
2. **"Insecurity."**
3. **"Lack of Balance."**
4. **"Ignorance."**
5. **"Defeat."**

Be brave and be honest. Do not choose a word you wish you were, or one you think others think you are, or what your mother wants you to be. This is not an assessment of aspirations or best impressions. Mark only the word that you think actually describes you the way you really are now. Do not dwell on all the possible meanings of words; just pick one that suits you best and mark the spot on the path.

If you think you fall between words on adjacent paths, you are welcome to put your marks between two paths. Plot your course now by picking a coordinate and writing down the five-word choices below. Then, from the list of five words, pick the one that most accurately describes you and mark your choice on the map itself.

Coordinate 1:_____.
          a)_____.
          b)_____.
          c)_____.
          d)_____.
          e)_____.

Next, repeat this process for four more coordinates, a total of five coordinates altogether. Later you can add coordinates to double check the original five. Or, if you want, you can do all thirty coordinates, but if you do too many at once the exercise may become tedious. The first five coordinates give you a preliminary list of words that characterize you. Below, enter the name of the coordinate, the five-word choices for each path, and the selection of the one most descriptive of you.

Coordinate 2:_____.
          a)_____.
          b)_____.
          c)_____.
          d)_____.
          e)_____.

Coordinate 3:_____.
          a)_____.
          b)_____.
          c)_____.
          d)_____.
          e)_____.

Coordinate 4:_____.

      a)_____.

      b)_____.

      c)_____.

      d)_____.

      e)_____.

Coordinate 5:_____.

      a)_____.

      b)_____.

      c)_____.

      d)_____.

      e)_____.

Coordinate 6:_____.

      a)_____.

      b)_____.

      c)_____.

      d)_____.

      e)_____.

Coordinate 7:_____.

      a)_____.

      b)_____.

      c)_____.

      d)_____.

      e)_____.

Coordinate 8:_____.

      a)_____.

      b)_____.

      c)_____.

      d)_____.

      e)_____.

Coordinate 9:_____.

      a)_____.

      b)_____.

      c)_____.

      d)_____.

      e)_____.

Coordinate 10:_____.
        a)_____.
        b)_____.
        c)_____.
        d)_____.
        e)_____.

INTERPRETATION

Look the map over to see the pattern revealed by the words you have picked. If you have not already done so, you will need to mark them clearly so they stand out. There are many possible patterns ranging from "concentrated on one path" to "scattered all over the map." Each pattern has a meaning and your pattern has a unique meaning for you.

Basically, the pattern reflects the direction of your current career and life-course. If you are on the "Martyr/Saint" path, the meandering path, notice that you start at "Slackoff Curve" and proceed to "Procrastination Falls." Just before you get to the falls you can easily take Temptations Narrows over to the Path of the Magician.

Further along, if you do not get trapped in the "Gully of Guilt," or take up residence in "Lazy Park," you may enter the "Forest of Gratitude" and discover the "Hills of Satisfaction." This may sound wonderful but notice also that you are a long way from the "Plains of Success" and the "Valley of Fulfillment," which suggests that you have given up status, income, achievement, and potential.

Similarly, if you are on the "Hero/Heroine" path, the linear path, you begin at the "Exercise Yard of Rights" and quickly move to "Break Through Straits." But beyond this, you hit the "Bushland of Befuddlement" and may enter the "Desert of Isolation."

Farther down the road, you arrive at the "Plains of Success" but then you also are near the "Buttes of Boredom" and far away from the "Rainbow of Bliss." Only the center path leads to a balance of happiness and income, satisfaction and success, self-actualization and self-fulfillment as Mortals standing squarely in the sunlight of self-knowledge.

Remember also that brain lateralization may vary with experiences in life. So, your assessment may change from time to time. Some students have claimed that their assessment varies whether it is taken during the work week or over a weekend. By staying aware of your assessment and the impact of major events in your life, you can help maintain a steady state of mind and direction.

In general, if your plots are all on one path, the course is obvious. If not, are the marks on two neighboring pathways? Coordinates toward the top of the list, coordinates like "Life Outcome," show some of the long-term consequences of your decisions.

For example, heart attacks and strokes for extreme left-brain Starphires, and depression and fatigue for the right-brain Starphades. If the pattern of choices is on two or three paths, you have a picture of your general direction. If your results are scattered, you can attain greater integration and balance by following the appropriate Career Star Strategy outlined in Chapter 13. Practice exercises that strengthen both sides. It is important to learn when to include both, or to exclude one or the other mode of functioning; that is, when to be logcial and when to be intuitive.

If your coordinates do not line up, and are strewn about the map, analyze how they are distributed. Is there one mark on every path? Or, are you scattered on each side but none on the center path? Are you scattered but at the two extreme right and left paths? Equally scattered on the two sides? If you only have one plot isolated from all the rest, double check to make sure it is not an anomaly.

Generally, if there is a tendency to be scattered, the results suggest that you have bilateral strengths in both logical and creative dimensions but you are unaware of this and are not trying to employ them in an integrated way. You can be mildly or wildly scattered. In either case, neither capacity is fully dominant, even though one will almost always overshadow the other at any given moment.

The ideal is to have all five coordinate points along the center path. It is usually quite difficult for an individual to simultaneously use both right- and left-brain capacities because of resistance by the Injured Self that separates the two functions. The importance of balance is a theme in the *Career Star System*. (The "Injured Self" is discussed fully in Chapter 9, "Dark Stars.")

For further indication of your dominant hemisphere, analyze how you plotted your course. If you could not get started because no coordinate stood out, and you found yourself staring at the list searching for the most logical choice, you are probably left-brained. (There is no logical choice because the qualities on the list cannot be rank ordered.)

You also are probably left-brained if you began in the lower left-hand corner and selected the first five coordinates, because it is logical to begin at the start. If you were flooded with feeling and overwhelmed by the task of reading this exercise and following these directions, you probably are right-brained. How you use the map itself, or how you use anything for that matter, tells how you use your mind.

ILLUSTRATIONS

You are going to be asked to write down your preliminary assessment below. Here are a few sample writeups from students who have previously carried out this assignment.

Moderate Right-Brain
"It looks like I am a veritable Career Starphade! My coordinates line up toward the left of the center path that lead to the Valley of Fulfillment. Mainly, I'm wavering and wandering on the winding path. Two of my coordinates also lead to the Clouds of Depression and one to the Hills of Satisfaction.

"This suggests that I am moderately right-brained. I am emotionally oriented. My intuition tells me to be an artist. I am afraid of failure, however, very sensitive to criticism and easily disappointed. I also find it difficult to be disciplined about my career. I need a sign, a gift-wrapped package, a pine tree, a bright star on the top, to know it is my calling."

Extreme Right-Brain
"I am listing toward the right-brain side according to the map. I have five coordinates on the Magician path, and I have no direction in life. I don't want to be a wife either. I'm one of the original 'Lost Girls.' This unfortunately is true. I wandered aimlessly through high school and now I find the same pattern misleading me in college.

"I can see myself either lying lazily in Mud Wallow or swimming easily around Procrastination Falls. I can also imagine a low point being spent in the Sea of Addictions. How come there is no outline of a Rescue Vessel visible on the horizon of the map? Am I drowning in the mercurial Ocean of Dependency?"

Moderate Left-Brain
"Although I circled some words on the moderate-right and center paths, most of my coordinates fell on the moderate-left path. I also started the whole exercise searching for the most logical choice. As a result of these two factors, I would say I am more left-brain oriented.

"I was glad to notice that none of my word choices fell on either of the extreme paths. I think at times I can be right-brained, but I would not consider it a shift in my basic orientation and extremism is absolutely out of the question—except, of course, logical extremism."

Extreme Left-Brain

"I plotted my star course and it is on a collision for the Wall of Woes and the Mountains of Frustration. I find I have five words plotted on the right lower side. This indicates then that I am a left-brained person. I guess this is the reason I am very strict, decisive, and analytical. I do not trust my feelings but rather base my decisions more on facts. Even when I am in my most sensitive state, I do not like to lose control.

"I like to think things out before making an important decision and I never like to put my goals in jeopardy. Goals are my identity. I can't even understand it sometimes. I am tenacious if I feel it is necessary to maintain control of myself. It's really not others I want to control but my life in general. I find it weird, complicated . . ."

Consider doing the Star Course Exercise once again after you have finished working the entire *Career Star System.* You will see then if there has been any shift in direction as a result of your evolving perspective derived from studying the text and practicing the exercises. Have you straightened out your bent mind, twisted career course, and found the right of way to your Career Star?

VALIDATION

Brain lateralization is correlated with many issues. These correlations are the foundation of the map and the basic message it attempts to communicate. Chart 1, pages 84–85, contains the complete word content of the grid of the map. This chart lists thirty phenomena that are correlated with brain lateralization.

The chart contains five columns, a mild and extreme right-brain Starphade column, a mild and extreme left-brain Starphire column, and a centered Sun Star column. If you review each column, from either the bottom to the top, or the top to the bottom, you will see the interconnection brain lateralization has with the other phenomena. While extensive, the chart does not exhaust all the possibilities.

This chart provides another way of looking at the map, this time with a focus on the verbal, as distinct from the pictorial content. You can use Chart 1 to validate the course you plotted on the map. In this case, shade in or circle on the chart the rectangle of the words that

Chart 1:
Career Star Map Grid

STAR TYPE:	STARPHADES		SUN STAR	STARPHIRES	
ARCHETYPES:	Evil Magician	Martyr/Saint	Mortals	Hero/Heroine	Tyrant/Empress
PERSONALITY TYPE:	"BB" Type (Idle)	"B" Type (Easy Going)	"A/B" Type (Balanced)	"A" Type (Ambitious)	"AA" Type (Driven)
LIFE OUTCOMES:	Depression	Satisfaction	Actualization	Success	Obsessions
CAREERS:	Welfare/Disability	Subjective Fields	All Career Fields	Objective Fields	Workaholism/Burnout
SACRIFICES: (GIVES UP)	Achievement	Income	Extremes	Happiness	Integrity
RISKS HAVING:	Accidents/Fatigue	Over-weight	No Risks	High Blood Pressure	Stroke/Heart Attack
COMMUNICATES IN:	Riddles	Words	All-Media	Images	Signals
FUTURE ORIENTATION:	Dreams	Imagines	Plans	Determines	Plots & Schemes
GREATEST FEAR:	Real Power	Insecurity	Lack of Balance	Ignorance	Defeat
STRENGTH:	Drama	Compassion	Competence	Competition	Tenacity
BODY STATE:	Impulsive	Relaxed	Versatile	Tense	Inhibited
RESPONSE:	Careless	Flexible	Responsible	Inflexible	Rigid
TIME ORIENTATION:	Timeless	Patient	Aware	Impatient	Rushed
INTERESTS:	Whimsies	Pastimes	Hobbies	Habits	Causes
DESIRES:	Adoration	Affection	Wholeness	Recognition	Triumph
APPRECIATES:	Appearance	Meaning	All Aspects	Value ($)	Possession
REALITY SEEN AS:	Misty	Malleable	Mixed	Firm	Brittle
MANNER:	Flashy	Casual	Variable	Clean-cut	Formal
PHILOSOPHY:	Illusion	Love	Faith	Right	Might
INTENTION:	Imitation	Construction	Creation	Control	Domination
DIRECTION:	Circular	Wandering	Weaving	Linear	Angular
MEANS TO KNOWLEDGE:	Magic	Intuition	Integration	Reason	Mechanics
EXPRESSION:	Acting	Being	Appropriate	Thinking	Doing

STAR TYPE:	STARPHADES		SUN STAR	STARPHIRES	
PERSPECTIVE:	Mystical	Idealistic	Dialectic	Realistic	Dogmatic
IN RELATION-SHIPS:	Pretends	Rescues	Relates & Communicates	Defends	Conquers
CONCENTRATES ON:	Sensations	Emotions	Synthesis	Decisions	Actions
STAR CORE:	Phony	Soft	Genuine	Hard	Empty
GOAL:	Experiential	Process	Dualistic	Purposeful	Achievements
MIND:		Emotional	Symmetrical	Rational	
BRAIN:		Right	Bilateral	Left	

you selected. This will show how linear or scattered your coordinate points are.

Sometimes I am asked to define various words in the grid and the margin coordinates. Occasionally, a "Star Dictionary" is requisitioned. "Paradigm" and "enigmas" were the most perplexing words to students of the original *Career Strategies Map*. These have been replaced with the simpler terms, "blueprints," and "riddles" in the revised *Career Star Map*. If there are words you still do not understand, look up their meaning in a standard dictionary or just go with your hunch.

Younger students do not know what is meant by "Type A" and "Type B Personality." They fear, however, it is *their* personality type that it is being graded "A" or "B." The definitions of A and B personality type are given on pages 93–94. There is a Career Star Glossary at the end of the text but regular words on the map are not included.

Words are descriptive but rarely capture the vital essence of a concept. For this reason the whole point of the map is to show through images the influence of brain lateralization on life-course and life-experience. The shape of the paths themselves as well as the various locations are a visual summary of the overall perspective of the *Career Star System*.

STAR TYPES:
Knowing the Galaxy

A leaf of grass is no less than the journey-work of the stars.

Walt Whitman, *Leaves of Grass*, 1855

RIGHT- AND LEFT-BRAIN

In this chapter we identify and describe the various types of stars in the *Career Star System*. The two basic and contradictory types are known as rational "Starphires" and emotional "Starphades." The former tend to be goal driven and want to be successfully ahead of others. Their counterparts, Starphades, are preoccupied with rounding out the quality and intensity of their personal experience.

In addition, other types of Career Stars are delineated in this chapter. "Polar Stars" switch between the extremes of Starphade and Starphire one or more times. "Scatter Stars" have strengths of both types of stars but are not able to apply them simultaneously. "Super Stars" are integrated naturally and "Sun Stars" through the practice of the *Career Star System* (see Chart 3). The next chapter, "Star Stories," contains case illustrations of these various kinds of Career Stars.

The *Career Star System* is not about brain lateralization per se, however, but how "sidedness," as a style of thinking, affects career choice and life course. Because brain lateralization is a platform of ideas on which the *Career Star System* rests, some background and technical information on the subject are provided in this section.

To help remember which hemisphere serves which function, it is essential to start with a point of reference. The designation "right" and "left" is from the point of view of the individual, not an observer, as shown in Diagram 2. At the level of brain physiology the idea is literal; the right-brain is on the right side and the left-brain is on the left side of the head.

Front

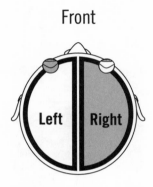

Diagram 2: Orientation of Right- and Left-brain

Just as people tend to be either right- or left-handed, most individuals are either right- or left-brained. That is, people are oriented either logically or emotionally in their thinking style. This does not mean, however, that there is a correlation between "brain sidedness" and "handedness." One can be right- or left-handed and still be either right- or left-brained. "Brain sidedness" is only part of "sidedness," as people are also "footed," "eyed," and "eared."

Whether brain lateralization is caused by hereditary or environmental factors is the subject of considerable debate. Some researchers believe that the basic preference is set at birth as a function of the neurochemistry of the brain. Others believe that socialization, particularly sex role socialization, that discourages feelings in males and logical abilities in females, is a basic social cause.

Another view is that environment and heredity interact, as do the functions of the hemispheres of the brain when there is not too much damage by whatever causes, genetic or social. It is possible that the controversy over causation is as much an expression of the division in the mind as its solution. Further discussion of the issue of gender and brain lateralization is contained in Appendix 5.

In addition to being either right- or left-brained, there is a third possibility: the mode of thinking may shift from side to side at intervals or in cycles. This shifting may happen once, as a major change in a person's lifetime, or more frequently at regular or irregular periods of months or years. A client once claimed to shift on a daily, even hourly basis, and said she had a "dual personality." These types are called "Polar Stars," discussed later in this chapter.

Physiologically, the right-brain controls the left side and the left-brain controls the right side of the body. The crossover occurs through a bridgelike structure, a massive system of tiny fibers between the two hemispheres, known as the "corpus callosum." The diagram below illustrates the "crossover at corpus callosum."

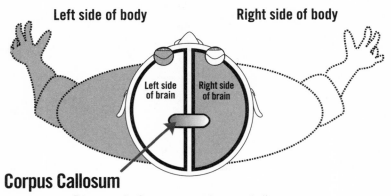

Diagram 3: Crossover at Corpus Callosum

In summary, most people are either rationally or emotionally oriented in their thinking style just as they are right- or left-handed in manipulating physical objects. An individual's emotional or rational preference influences minor and major life decisions. The ideal of course is to have a greater balance of both capacities.

You can get along in the physical world without being ambidextrous but trying to get by in life using half your mind imposes a limitation. This would be true also, for example, in using only one arm, leg, or eye. We tend not to appreciate the power of the other hemisphere and do not realize our handicap in life by being only right- or left-brained.

STAR CORE

Although every individual is thwarted and waylaid in their Career Star quest in unique ways, people do seem divided into two basic types. There are those who know but do not follow, and those who do not know, their Calling Star. Both are based on uncertainty about being starworthy.

In my experience as a career counselor over the years I have heard two basic responses to the question, "What is your calling?" Some individuals have a very firm idea and will tell you immediately, while others have not the "foggiest notion" and do not know what to say.

People with a definite idea, Starphades, have often known since early childhood but because of self-doubt do not trust its truth. If they enjoy a particular kind of work, "it is too good to be true." Those who do not have a definite idea, Starphires, will tell you, "I've thought and thought about it and never found an answer." Frequently they report being "interviewed, tested, and counseled extensively without turning up a clue."

Starphades know their calling but disappoint themselves by not fulfilling their destiny. They lack determination, lack faith in themselves, and may claim "society" is opposed to them and not appreciative of their particular talents, which typically lie in the arts, humanities, and social sciences. They do not really believe that they should be fulfilled and that they do not have to suffer.

This group fails to support their gifts with sufficient self-confidence and action to bring about the achievements that constitute the "proof" they would need in order to believe in themselves. "I will not try my best" is often used as an excuse to hide feeling inadequate.

In judging their career failure to be inevitable, unavoidable, and irrevocable, Starphades suffer a sense of guilt and loss. They are quick to find fault in themselves that justifies suffering a lifetime for their "tragic" mistakes. These individuals often experience depression, the long-term outcome of aggression turned inward. Extreme cases fall on the left-hand side of the map under the archetype of the Evil Magician.

Starphires, on the other hand, who do not know their calling, are frustrated for never having found their true way and dissatisfied with any alternative chosen. They remain angry mainly with themselves for not being able to figure it out—for not knowing and for having traveled the wrong road.

Starphires may complain about obstacles that do not conform to their logic and willpower. Barriers are regarded as part of a greater plot to block their way, a projection of their own obstinacy. They may express anger toward others who do not facilitate their passage. Extreme Starphires are on the far right path on the map and encounter the walls, hard rocks, and dead ends of the controller of the material world (Tyrant Archetype).

There are a lucky few, however, who are guided by a combination of intuition and intellect. Blessed and charmed by a natural synthesis of left- and right-brain capacities, they know their calling, take action readily, accomplish goals easily, and become quickly and completely fulfilled. These "Super Stars" probably never make their way to career guidance counselors.

Many engineers, lawyers, bankers, accountants, real estate brokers, medical doctors, and architects, for example, have chosen a field because it is their calling. This is also true for many social workers, teachers, artists, ministers, and nurses. There is a tendency for left-brained individuals to be drawn to work with objects, and right-brained to work with subjects, but it is entirely possible to be integrated psychologically in objective or subjective career fields. The motivation for the selection, not the career field itself, reflects brain lateralization.

It is common for those who do not have an answer to their calling to think that those who have one are much better off, and there is usually envy and enmity between the two types. If each is at a polar extreme, and if there is no sexual attraction, they will actively dislike each other. Each will see in the other, but fail to recognize, what they claim is missing in themselves.

Actually, both types face a common dilemma but sing a different career lament. The ones with a calling tend to be sad while the ones without a calling tend to be mad. Together their disharmony is an expression of an underlying dissatisfaction with the self. Career and interpersonal difficulties are the resonance of inner discords. Like sound waves, our self-relationship rebounds outwardly as it reaches the chorus of family and friends and the entire circus of society.

STAR FIGHTS

The two basic types, left-brained Starphires and right-brained Starphades, tend to regard one another with disdain. The former think it is stupid never to have a point and the latter think it is silly always to be point-oriented. Their arguments have a point and are also pointless, because these are two sides of a whole star.

It makes sense to have a point or to be pointless, as the situation demands. Both views are valuable, but neither is superior as the antagonists want us to believe. Arrogance and contempt for one another regarding their respective lifestyles, values, and viewpoints, mask the doubt harbored about their own choices.

"Pointers" want to finish dinner and get to dessert so that they can move on to the next activity, especially if they have things their way. "Nonpointers" want to savor the dinner, the dessert, and the post-dessert activities, each in turn. They do not particularly care about the mess created as a by-product in making dinner, or in making anything.

Pointers are extra cautious because the mess is the immediate product, and they can be preoccupied with the cleanup long before the dinner or dessert ever begin. In summary, the pointers tend to be extra careful and nonpointers rather careless about goals. Each has a different conceptual schema of means and ends.

**Those who possess logic often lack a calling.
Those who have a calling often lack logic.**

Starphires and Starphades often try pairing with each other as a solution to the career dilemma. Not understanding that the other person represents a misplaced and dislocated part of the self, psychological opposites usually cannot tolerate each other. Right-brained, left-brained, and never the twained shall meet!

If, however, they see in their opposite a missing positive part of themselves, falling in love may be a way to try to recapture the lost self. If a sexual attraction is absent, however, the two types usually loathe each other because each represents what the other lacks and cannot find. If this were not true, each would be more balanced individually and socially.

Ordinarily, romantic attraction is to mates of the opposite type in terms of brain lateralization because of the prospect of being made whole. Initial sexual attraction may be based on physical characteristics like body type and shape, hair and eye color. But, in terms of mental functioning, or right-/left-brain lateralization, the old saying holds true about opposites attracting.

"I will be your nurturer if you will be my protector" is a frequent but not the only division of labor. Starphires want Starphades to be their vivacious self, and Starphades want Starphires to be their logical, structured half. Because the pairing solution denies the potential inherent within each individual, however, mutual disappointment and dual underachievement usually result.

"Starphires" are hardened toward life and shut out their feelings with stubborn determination to go "forward." While professing logicality, the sensation of progress is usually more important than its accomplishment. Brittle, they fragment on the dams and boulders on the right side of the map. Extreme Starphires are left-brained, strongheaded, and often wrong-minded.

Starphades, on the other hand, are usually sensitive and tender souls who have idealized expectations that life should be fair and just. They believe all efforts deserve corresponding rewards and that disorganization is an unnatural state of affairs, even though this is not true in their personal life or residence. Starphades resent the confines of rules and organization and would rather be amused on their own.

The fact that there is not a demonstrable cause-and-effect relationship between good intentions and actual outcomes in life convinces Starphades that hard work is futile and that they are victims of a greater misanthropy. Their outraged impulses and offended sensitivities guide their actions toward the perfection of self-indulgence, avoidance of risks, exaggeration of setbacks and postponement of the challenge to achieve their full potential.

Through the eyes of these two types, Starphires and Starphades, the world tends to be characterized by the soft belly of underachievement or the bitter shell of overwork. It is a cruel irony and the bitter cost of imbalance: those who possess logic often lack an objective while those who have an objective frequently lack logic.

To reiterate, the rational approach stresses goal orientation and relies on logic. The key issue for this style of thinking is control over actions and, by extension, goals. Control over time, energy, and resources provides a sense of steady movement from point A to B that relieves immediate anxiety about the lack of self-worth. If ends are achieved the illusion of power is sustained.

There tends to be an intolerance for experience as an end in itself; which is demeaned as "a waste of time and energy." Starphires must stay logical and avoid any emotions that might slow down or interfere with the attainment of an objective. A common human feeling of fatigue is probably the greatest threat to their projects. They try to shoot flashily skyward and then descend to burnout.

CHART 2:

Characteristics of Starphades and Starphires I

STARPHIRES	STARPHADES
Calling Unknown	Calling Known
Left-Brain Lateralized	Right-Brain Lateralized
Goal Oriented	Experientially Oriented
Controls Outer World	Surrenders to Outer World
Denies Inner World	Appreciates Inner World
Overachiever	Underachiever
Angry	Sad
Frustrated	Depressed
Arrogant	Insecure
Rushes for Success	Languishes in Failure
Type A Personality	Type B Personality

[See also "Chart 5: Summary II," page 142]

Emotionally oriented Starphades, on the other hand, make goal achievement secondary or irrelevant to the primacy of experience. Their approach gives up logical control in order to have sensational times. Feeling impulses and following intuition are crucial because exploration and discovery are seen as the main objective.

To Starphades, interruptions and deviations are welcomed for what they might turn up and where they may lead. The objective is to be between points A and B instead of quickly and efficiently getting from one to the other. The experiential process itself becomes the goal and is regarded as more important than any particular pre-set outcome.

These two styles of thinking have been identified in business textbooks as "Type A" and "Type B" personalities. (First identified by M. Friedman and R. Rosenman in their study of stress.) Type A personalities are characterized by impatience, restlessness, aggressiveness, competitiveness, hyperactiveness, and time pressures. This classification of personalities coincides with brain lateralization and is a map coordinate.

Type A individuals invest long hours on the job, strive to make deals and meet deadlines and want to rise rapidly through the ranks of the organization. The Type B personality, on the other hand, misses deadlines, cares less about promotions, and is not driven and ambitious. The researchers found that Type A personalities are twice as prone to heart disease, five times as prone to a second heart attack, and twice as prone to fatal heart attacks as Type B personalities.

If at this point you do not see your type of star, or if you see elements of yourself in both types of stars, do not be discouraged or dismayed. Continue to study and apply the *Career Star System* and as you progress you will begin to feel the correctness of one star type over another.

STARPHADE OR STARPHIRE

Those who know their calling, Starphades, know because they are guided by their grounded feelings. They rely on their right brain and intuition lends them a sense of direction. At the same time, however, because of the influence of self-doubt, they are irrational about their potential. While they have the impulse to be artists or humanists, for example, their feelings of worthless are so close to the surface, that their sensitivity makes organization and discipline difficult. They are called "Starphades" because creative types often fade out in terms of follow-through actions.

Those who do not know their calling, Starphires, are rationally oriented, rely on their left brain, and are more protected from their feelings. Being less intuitive, they do not have direct access to their calling. Because they are good at solving logical problems, however, they may become financially and socially successful as scientists and professionals, for example, yet remain profoundly dissatisfied.

As a result of trial and error, left-brained individuals often come to know what their calling is not. But if encouraged to try an intuitive approach, they may tell you that "I tried that line and there was no answer," or "I was too busy to make the call." Because of an abrasive edge, this type is known as a "Starphire." Starphires and Starphades are the two sides of Career Stars; the former are the dark side while the latter are the bright side of the phenomenon.

Starphades do not believe their Career Star shines resplendently enough to be clearly seen. Their star is dimmed by their disbelief in themselves and it flickers like a filament of the self. A shadowy Career Star, darkly tarnished by doubt, is a Starphade.

Starphires, on the other hand, fly about networking opportunities. They do not believe enough in the imagery and constancy of their own lodestar for it to burst blazingly forth from the darkness of their unconscious. Consequently, Starphires make the mistake of thinking they do not know because they have not tried hard enough. As a result, they often endure batteries of tests, and hours of counseling and become veterans of self-help courses and experts.

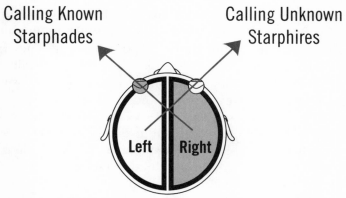

Diagram 4: Calling and Brain Lateralization

Their error and terror is persistent, thinking the reason they do not know their calling is logical not psychological. The harder they try rational efforts, the more disconnected from their feelings they become and the more unlikely they are to find their ideal career. It is hard to find something when you do not realize you already possess it. Enchantment is the magic of discovering that what you always wanted is already yours.

Starphires are off their course as a result of their self-imposed demand for accelerated achievement. A hidden motive to affirm their self-worth draws them "starboard" off course, seeking repeated successes in order to feel good about themselves. Right-brain Starphades, on the other hand, are port-bound stars because they are afraid to reach for their star and leave home base.

A difference in time orientation also distinguishes the two types of Career Stars. Starphires are usually in a hurry to secure a position of achievement in the real world to confirm their worth. Their haste distracts them from feeling their doubt about their Career Star. Starphades, on the contrary, are more resigned to their conviction that their Career Star has abandoned them and therefore time does not seem to matter.

Starphires enter objective fields specifically because they do not know what else to do. They may become financially quite successful but are usually profoundly dissatisfied. Dread of feeling a personal emptiness pushes them to do anything rather than nothing in order to discharge the discomfort. While they rid themselves of fear of the unknown, they hate the illogical outcome that results from making the wrong choice.

Starphades disappear into the shadows. They usually know their calling from an early age, but because of self-doubt are unable to follow through with the action required to achieve it. They become moody underachievers. Starphades enjoy showing theatrically that the world is right and that they are wrong. Starphires enjoy using their intellect to argue that they are right and the world is wrong.

In spite of financial security and social prominence, Starphires often become irritable and irascible overachievers. The world responds exactly as they insist by giving them money, status, and power. Ironically, this response confirms a devalued self-perception for they would not be materialists if they did not believe they were lacking inner value. They forfeit the intangibles of creativity for consumption of the hard goods and remain perplexed by despair.

Starphires believe they need validation of their true value through material success and they get back exactly what they invest. They do not seem to learn that material achievement confirms an objective view of themselves that depreciates their inner self. *Starphades doubt and fear that they do have a calling, while Starphires doubt and fear that they do not have a calling.*

Those who know their calling are in touch with their fear and doubt and those who do not know their calling are not in touch with their feelings. The fear is so great that one would rather not engage in work (Starphade) or engage in work that is hated (Starphire). These twin stars are truly a paradox of human nature.

It is easier to find your calling once you realize you already possess it.

If you do not pursue your calling, you spend much of your energy trying to make enough money, to take vacations, to buy goods and services, to divert and compensate yourself for not doing what you love. These tangible rewards will prevent you from feeling or thinking about what you have really given up. Life-purpose is forfeited in consumption and fringe benefits.

The integration of emotional and intellectual styles of thinking offers greater potential for discovering work that is both personally satisfying and financially rewarding. Do what you love, and what you do will embrace you in the arms of happiness and prosperity. Do what you hate, and what you hate will do unto you what you have done to it—with a vengeance that makes life bitter, poorer, harder, and shorter.

POLAR STARS

No stars are identical and none is inherently more preeminent than another. A talented and intelligent minority, however, may have little trouble conceiving their ambitions, achieving their potentials, and becoming happy.

An exception to the classification of Starphires and Starphades are stars capable of natural integration of right- and left-brain functioning. These individuals possess "bilateral symmetry" and follow the center path of the map. In imitation of life we call them "Super Stars," but because of the infrequency of sighting, may be a hypothetical category. "Super" makes them sound special but in the *Career Star System* they are entirely equal to lopsided stars.

In being able to integrate and alternate hemispheric functions as necessary, "Super Stars" constitute a distinct minority. "Bilateral symmetry," as it is called in brain physiology, is really about as common in mental life as hermaphroditism in biology and true bisexuality in human sexual orientation.

Someone who is not born on the center path but gets there via application of the *Career Star System* is referred to as a "Sun Star." In terms of the map, Starphires fall on the right-hand side, Starphades show up on the left-hand side, and Sun Stars and Super Stars are on the center path. Again, the right-brain paths are on the left, and the left-brain paths are on the right-hand side of the map, because of the crossover at corpus callosum. (See also Appendix 5, "Brain Lateralization".)

In addition to these four types of stars, there are several other possible variations on the theme of right- and left-brain functioning. For example, there is a fifth possibility in which the mode of thinking shifts from right to left, or vice versa, in periodic cycles. This switching may happen once, as one major change in a lifetime, or more frequently, at regular or irregular intervals of months or years. This "conversion" type is called a "Polar Star."

CHART 3:

Career Star Types

Starphire: unintegrated, left-brain asymmetrical functioning.
Starphade: unintegrated, right-brain asymmetrical functioning.
Super Star: natural bilateral symmetrical functioning.
Sun Star: integrated, left- and right-brain symmetrical functioning via the application of the *Career Star System.*
Polar Star:
    Starphade to Starphire: conversion from right-brain to left-brain asymmetrical functioning.
    Starphire to Starphade: conversion from left-brain to right-brain asymmetrical functioning.
Scatter Star: "unintegrated," simultaneous right- and left-brain capacities and potentials but because of psychological conflicts show scattered symmetrical or asymmetrical functioning.

A final possibility is the presence of simultaneous but unintegrated left- and right-brain capacities. On the map this appears as being on both sides of the center path either mildly or wildly "scattered" over the map. Usually there are no coordinates on the center path. This spread indicates that an individual has bilateral strengths but that are reacting in opposition rather than coordination to one another. The definitions of the various types of stars are summarized in Chart 3.

Conversions are the "stuff" of polar stars. There are Starphades who become Starphires and Starphires who become Starphades. When one approach to life appears to fail, the only imaginable alternative is often a relentless pursuit of the polar opposite. Artists become data processors, prostitutes convert to nuns, business managers turn into actors, and comics try being salespeople. A previously right- or left-brained individual often will veer to the opposite extreme.

Almost always, crossovers are radical; one extreme is substituted for another to certify the transformation. Taking the opposite path is rarely an answer to choosing the wrong path to begin with, however. In the cases cited in the next chapter, people alternate between being Starphades and Starphires, sometimes over brief and sometimes over considerably longer intervals of time. Starphades fall short, and Starphires go off the beam of their respective Career Stars.

Rarely trucking down the middle path, conversions often are inflexible about the adoption of a new style. Both capacities continue to exist but are not simultaneously utilized or mastered. There may be a lack of awareness about the value of using both capacities but there is also an inherent conflict in being flexible. There is a fear that control will be lost and they will return to the old extreme.

In *Jung to Live By,* Eugene Pascal cites an old Roman proverb, "Moderation in all things, and moderation in moderation." "Nothing too much," wrote Diogenes Laertius and I might add, "Not too much of nothing."

EXERCISE 6
STAR PAINTING

Starphire personalities will be much more reluctant, while Starphade personalities will be much more willing, to participate in this star finger painting exercise. Both may think it is silly to believe that your calling can be found through finger painting. What is your reaction?

If you are already an artist you may find this exercise too simple. If not, you may object to doing something messy or getting paint under your fingernails. Maybe you refuse to buy the paints? You cannot afford the time, energy, and expense? Perhaps you tell yourself that you do not know where to purchase finger paints?

Why do you procrastinate in getting paints and then misplace them once you have them home? Or, do you always pick the wrong day to paint, a day when there is already too much strife in your life? If finger painting is so silly, why are these rationalizations so much easier to produce than the paintings? Perhaps you feel it really is finger *"pain-ting"*?

Your reaction is related to your Injured Child, a concept covered thoroughly in Chapter 9, "Dark Stars." Play is the "work" of children and injured children are not able to play freely; neither are injured adults. It is important for you to get in touch with the Injured Child part of yourself.

Your resistance may be a reaction to an earlier emotional injury that interfered with learning how to play. Not learning how to play can hamper all subsequent learning. If you can learn to play again you can learn to find the kind of work you love and that loves you.

Try not to treat this exercise as another chore you must accomplish before you can go to bed tonight. Give yourself some quality time in the early morning or evening in order to get into the spirit of this exercise. You do not have to have a set of designer finger paints and classy art lessons before you can get started.

Any kind of finger paints and any quality paper readily available in stores will do for a start. You can substitute color markers, pencils, or crayons if you absolutely cannot stand the thought of messy paints all over your fingers. The idea is to get beyond the hurdle of resistance and to playfully experiment with colors and designs.

If you are a right-brained Starphade, you probably will not have much reluctance getting into this exercise. In fact, you may have already begun to paint your fingers as your creative way of starting. Left-brained Starphires will tend to procrastinate and resist, fearful of the creative side of themselves with which they are unfamiliar.

Put on some music that you like; light some incense to help get you into a tranquil mood. Start with the Progressive Relaxation Meditation, Appendix 3, if necessary.

Now, begin by using each one of your senses to investigate each of the paints and the paper. See, smell, hear, feel, and taste each color and in turn do exactly the same with the paper. Yes, literally expose the paint and paper to your senses and your senses to the paints and paper.

As you do this ask the colors and the paper out loud, "What do you want to become?" Chant this over and over as you prepare and if you like use an accent for more affective communication. "What are you?" "Tell me what you want to be." Play this way and have fun!

Allow yourself to enter the process, suspend all judgment, and be without expectation or criticism. Next, explore with each of your senses the application of all colors on the paper. It does not matter what you make, but only that you let the expressive side of you come forth and make something of you.

Each expression will help loosen and open your inward side. It will not all pop out instantly but you have begun the process. Try to spend at least twenty minutes with this exercise and make at least one painting per sitting. Remember that it is the repetition that matters in the long run and not the product.

You can take more than twenty minutes if you like, but not so long that you will not want to practice finger painting tomorrow. Have finger painting sessions, each lasting a minimum of twenty minutes, at least three more times during the following week.

A total of four sittings of twenty minutes is the bare minimum per week. Save your creations in order to see the different aspects of yourself that are revealed as you become more deeply immersed in and released by the finger painting process. Do not compete with yourself and believe that each one has to be better than the last while in fact each one is already perfect.

When you have finished, write up your experience. At first you will probably resist doing this also but writing will give you another angle of vision on what has happened. It will also allow you an opportunity to analyze the experience, and the paintings. Did you feel like a child again?

Try to let your impressions of the experience flow out of you in written form as if you were now finger painting in a different medium. This method of expression is more cerebral and less messy. Express what you felt and thought about as you painted. Also what you feel and think about them now. Try not to be judgmental and intolerant of your thoughts that find expression below.

Experience 1   *Date:*

_____

_____

_____

Experience 2   *Date:*

_____

_____

_____

Experience 3   *Date:*

_____

_____

_____

Experience 4   *Date:*

_____

_____

_____

At a later time reflect on both the experience of painting and the experience of writing, and write down your reflections. What do you feel and think about them now? This is an opportunity to be more analytical about the experience and the paintings. Is there an individual or overall theme to the paintings? If so, what is your interpretation?

Reflection 1   *Date:*

_____

_____

_____

Reflection 2   *Date:*

_____

_____

_____

Reflection 3   *Date:*

_____

_____

_____

Reflection 4   *Date:*

_____

_____

_____

Do you realize that these feelings and thoughts would not have occurred to you, at least at this time, if you had not given yourself permission to finger paint? Do you realize that these paintings almost did not exist in the world? When you set your assumptions and judgments aside, your creative self can lift you out of unsupportive conditions and negative thoughts.

There are more beautiful ideas and designs beneath the surface, deeper than where you are currently probing, which will surface if you allot time and allow yourself permission for the experience. Close by giving thanks to the paints, the paper, the music, the incense, and yourself for participating. Carry out this ritual of gratitude as an ending.

STAR STORIES:
Telling Your History

The fault, dear Brutus,
is not in our stars but in ourselves.

William Shakespeare, *Julius Caesar*, 1599

The various types of stars in the *Career Star System* were defined and described in the previous chapter. You made an assessment of your particular star type using the *Career Star Map* in Chapter 5. Now in this chapter you are provided with case illustrations of the various star types to help you further identify your own star type.

Knowing your Career Star type is important because you will learn about the type of psychological denial system you use, "Rational" or "Irrational," covered in Chapters 10 and 11. And you will select the kind of "Action Strategy" to implement in Chapter 13 based on your star type. A list of all the star types in the galaxy of the *Career Star System* is given in Chart 3, page 98. Characteristics of the two basic Career Star types, Starphires and Starphades, are shown in Chart 2, page 93, and Chart 5, page 142.

ADULT STARPHIRES

Wanda telephoned my office having found my number in the Yellow Pages under "Career Counseling." "I don't know what career to pursue," she told me. "I started college right after high school but I never declared a major and I dropped out after two years."

Wanda does not realize that not knowing her major is basically the same problem as not knowing her career. She was twenty-four years old, working as a secretary, and believed she has fallen rapidly behind her peers. She was also "bored and disgruntled" with her job.

Because she was getting older, Wanda was desperate to make a career decision, and get moving. She explained that she was increasingly critical of herself for not having identified her career sooner and for not having made progress faster. She now wanted to be instantly rid of the problem. Her unwillingness to accept the problem interfered with its solution for you cannot solve a problem that does not exist. The start of a solution is to stop berating yourself for not figuring it out sooner.

Suddenly, Wanda demands an answer before she admits fully that the problem exists. The answer has eluded her for at least four years, since the time that she dropped out of college; why should it now be fixed so quickly? In the final hours Wanda has called an expert. Professional help appeals to perfectionists who grant themselves "last rights to assistance" on the eve of total self-defeat. Wanda can then claim to have tried expert advice, which also "failed" and testifies to the "hopelessness" of her case.

I told her, "Thinking that you should already have the answer is an attitude that interferes with finding an answer." I go on to explain that she has compounded the problem of finding her calling by adding a time demand as to when her calling should be found. This is doubling the problem and preventing her from finding the answer, I explain.

Starphires typically have fixed timetables and make pronouncements like, "I should have been there a year ago," or, "I'll give this two more weeks." Wanda has a preset pace, date, and mind-set as to when she should be at a preconceived place. When she does not meet her own schedule, she reacts harshly with self-recriminations and even stricter deadlines.

Intolerance and impatience are two aspects of perfectionism. Now

Wanda has two problems to solve: her destination and her schedule. Unable to solve the first in four years, how can she possibly solve both simultaneously? Why is she suddenly doing this to herself? Is failure the goal? Is she trying to coerce herself into a decision because she believes that she has been too lax in the past? Is she masochistic?

Is she under a self-indictment for wasting resources, money, and years? Apparently she believes that if you are harsh enough with yourself for past mistakes you will learn not to repeat them in the future. Or, is she just intent in the moment on making another one?

The panic attack is the sensible response of her mind to the imposition of a double load. She speaks of the "competitive pressures" of society, but she is really a menace to herself with her rude demands. As a practical example of how your mind shuts down under pressure, I ask her to recall the experience of forgetting a name. "If you relax and let go of the insistence on knowing a name instantly, it will eventually come to you," I tell her. The harder you try to think of a name, the more it recedes from your conscious memory.

Determination can be a virtue, but obstinacy can prevent the pliability required for exploration. Trying to force the unconscious to surface in response to willpower contradicts its cooperative nature and makes certain that it will stay in recess. The unconscious part of your mind knows *apriori* that the use of Force means the persistence of self-doubt.

The imposition of a time requirement crowds her intellect with another problem that takes away the mental space necessary to explore and discover an answer to the first problem. A deadline makes certain that the first problem will be unsolved and repeated, it is really a self-imposed penalty for having had the original, unforgivable problem.

If you are at square one, you are at the start, exactly where you need to be. You always have the option at this point of taking the right steps, an option that you do not have if you have already gone down the wrong road again. If you cannot bear the idea of starting over and so rush madly ahead, you will find later that you got ahead of yourself and repeated the mistake. Accordingly, her perfectionism prevented acknowledgment of her problem.

Richard, a thirty-year-old in hospital administration, came for a consultation about his desire for a career change. In the time since his graduation from college with a B.A. in business, he had been successful at several different jobs.

Richard earned a good living and had recently married. He reported that he had been very happy throughout his childhood and college years. He came from a "very good and loving family." The only drawback of which he was aware was that both parents were "over-achievers" and had pushed him toward high achievement, too.

Richard was eager to make a career shift because he was bored with administration. But he confided also that for the past year he had been the victim of what had been formally diagnosed as a "Panic Disorder"—at unpredictable times he would become overwhelmed by anxious feelings and would be unable to function—and I sensed that he was self-conscious about being around the medical profession with his emotional problem.

Previous psychotherapy had alleviated the symptoms and offered some emotional relief but not a remedy. Richard said that he really still had no clue about the cause of his attacks, which deeply embarrassed and frustrated him. It was very obvious to me that he was attacking himself severely for having had the attacks in the first place. My initial impression was that Richard was extremely left-brained and trying to control unconscious feelings about being flawed or imperfect.

Perfectionism is another mistake.

I explained that I thought the anxiety was the signal of an important unconscious message that was being ignored. Although it was too early to know for sure, I thought Richard was probably driving himself with overwork to such an extent that it impaired his physical well-being. The disabling anxiety was perhaps a strategy to spare himself a real injury to his body or his brain if he persisted.

Richard had had an enlightening dream that helped us to decipher the message. In his dream he saw his boss at work choking him to death at a staff meeting for yawning during business hours. He spoke as if he really believed it was his boss attacking him in his dream.

I thought that the boss in his dream represented a cruel, authority part of himself that was attacking him for being tired and bored with overwork. Richard admitted that he felt compelled to stay busy "all the time, at any cost," and he referred to himself as a "control freak."

Although he quickly grasped the principles of the *Career Star Sys-*

tem, I was concerned that he was only going to deal with the problem at an intellectual and not at a practical level, in typical Starphire style. I stressed the importance of nonlogical exercises, of doing nothing purposeful, and finding in the relaxation that no harm actually came to him.

Unlike many Starphires who never surmount their resistance, Richard took eagerly to the exercises. He was already practicing some deep breathing and stress-reduction techniques learned in psychotherapy. He supplemented these with the "Progressive Relaxation Meditation" (Appendix 3) and with Exercise 6, "Star Painting."

Richard did nonlogical activities for at least twenty minutes twice per day almost every day. He remembered having liked right-brain activities as a child and in this respect he may have been a Polar Star who converted from a right- to a left-brain orientation at an earlier point in childhood.

Richard's eagerness to follow "a plan" was perhaps a measure of his Starphire goal domination but he plunged in also because of the amount of psychic suffering he had endured in the past year. His symptoms of anxiety subsided almost immediately and within two weeks he was feeling well again.

He worried, however, that he would relapse and lose control of his newly acquired stability. His attitude suggested to me that his problem still existed at an unconscious level: he still believed that he had to maintain vigilant control of himself in order to be okay.

Here is a dream he reported that seemed to symbolize his ongoing conflict. He was on vacation at a resort with his father and brother. They all attended some kind of social function during the afternoon that evolved into a raucous party in the evening. Suddenly there was a commotion outside because someone, he thought probably his brother, had fallen several stories out of the building. When they all went out to investigate, however, they could not find a body.

I thought the dream meant that Richard was afraid that if he truly relaxed and really began to enjoy himself, something dreadful like suicide or murder would happen. The father and the brother stood perhaps for the logical side of himself that he feared might be destroyed.

Richard was afraid that if he got fully into right-brain activities (like the party) it would be the end of his logical life. He feared he would become extremely right-brained and this might destroy the business-oriented career that he had planned. The fact that he could not find a body suggested that his worry was unfounded. That is, the panic disorder caused real symptoms when he persisted with pernicious left-brain stubbornness to overwork himself. If he let control go in exchange for a more balanced style of life the disorder and symptoms vanished because its origin was entirely imaginary.

ADULT STARPHADES

A Native American woman, Swan in Flight, a fine artist and fine crafts person, found herself fascinated with the creative works and ceremonial practices of indigenous peoples around the world. Cultures were studied like an anthropologist of the self. She was fondest of artifacts and instruments such as drums and rattles, talismen and bundles, masks and shields, used in rituals of all types.

Swan in Flight knew how traditional societies employed these objects to aid in transitions, including seasons, migrations, and lifecycles. She deplored the absence of ritual objects and ceremonies in modern passages.

For a livelihood Swan in Flight taught child and adult art classes. She particularly liked "found objects," discarded things, symbolic of the way she felt about herself. She hoped that through her instruction, a ceremony in itself, others would come to know themselves better. Her teaching also reinforced her own learning.

Swan in Flight wanted her students to use their creations to embark on their own sacred journey to self-discovery. She also created, manufactured, and sold the products she made to individuals as "power" and "faith" objects, and to galleries as fine art.

For years, she held a paid position in a museum that consumed her time and energy. It drew her away from her own creative work and away from teaching others the value of creative ritual in the art of life's changes. In undertaking her own creative work, Swan in Flight found it easier to wash and clean gourds, for instance, than to design and paint them. Menial tasks were placed ahead of craft and fine art always came last.

Swan in Flight needed especially the things she made for others. Her mission was carried out with enormous difficulty, however, as if she personally represented the mythological struggle between light and dark forces. The very support she tried to give to others was barely accessible to her. Her assignment by fate, to bring the message of destiny, identity, and creativity to others, she barely believed for herself.

One day, after working together many years, Swan in Flight brought and read the following statement about her personal background. She said she rewrote it many times to get to the feeling of her core life experience. She stated, "it articulates the experience of being me that explains being me to me."

I am not who you think I am. I don't know how I got here or where I am going. I don't know if I am stuck here or if I will be able to return. It happened early in life. Probably my poor parents were aware. The fantasy I have is a beam of light piercing through the darkness of my window. A beam of light from a distant planet changed forever my mother's expectation for a darling child.

I think she knew early that I was some sort of alien creature. I could never be her darling human child. I was an aberration, a monster she could not handle. She was right to push me aside. I wasn't of this world, especially as a child. I had not learned the ways of your culture . . . your expectations . . . your labyrinth of acceptable behaviors.

I became aware of my situation at seven or eight earth years of life. I felt there was something terribly wrong and couldn't figure it out. How did my mind, my active, creative, adventurous, thrilling mind, come to dwell in this body, in this excuse for a family, in this dreary town on this dead planet? The more I thought about it the more an injustice it became to me.

I thought that it was such an outrageously blatant error that I would soon be rescued and placed with my proper family in the correct body. Time dragged on and what seemed so apparent to me, was ignored by everyone else. It was as if a joke was played on me. I cried and screamed, "Please, someone, fix this mistake." How could a loving God let this happen?

I became dismal and depressed. I waged a war with the gods, refusing to participate in their barbarous experiment. Deep inside, I craved adventure, excitement, a loving family who enjoyed the magic of life, the arts, the ether, the elements of earth, air, fire, and water. I craved time travel, out of body experiences, my soul lifting up and out, merging with earth, with life itself. I longed for a body that I felt was truly mine.

I pleaded with the gods, "Please put me where I belong." But they did not listen and I ached from the inside out. I was forced to be a part of them, of it all. I was forced to deaden the wild oth-

erworldly spirit within. I was forced to wear the mask of confor-
mity and death. My insides were screaming, "I am alive in here, I
really am alive."

Time has elapsed more than forty years and the mask has hardened and I try to pry it off. I want the release of its constriction,
afraid to know what is underneath. So, I sit and wait for the end
of this experiment. I long to return to my planet of origin.

I was "mismerized" by her story. Summarized briefly below is my response to Swan in Flight's statement in that session. I told her that it
was evident that she had forgotten who she is and where she came
from:

> Though you say, "I do not know how I got here," the beginning
> of your story tells of your origin in a distant light. You are only an
> "alien creature" when you adopt an earthly view of yourself.
>
> You have believed an earth perception for so long that you feel
> as if you are an alien. You see yourself as defined by earth time
> rather than recalling your original being from a light source. You
> hate the maligned person you think they think you are.
>
> Your light cannot be seen if you cannot see it and shine it out.
> You are as you were originally defined, not how others think you
> are. You are here in hell on a light mission, not as punishment.
> You do not need protection nor a premature return to your ori-
> gin. You see a bleak and brutal world that needs your recognition
> of light.
>
> You are asked to shed light to help repeal darkness, to liber-
> ate future generations from the same misunderstanding you suf-
> fer. When you return to the Light Source you will wonder why you
> forgot and adopted this earthbound point of view of yourself.
> What I tell you is the truth not science fiction.

Swan in Flight epitomizes the great talent mixed with enormous
self-doubt characteristic of a Starphade. Her perspective is the mistaken view that she is born wrong in body, place, and time, rather than
the wonderful and gifted person she is really. A revolution in mind is
exactly the kind of change she and the world need to make.

Swan in Flight's calling is to lead the world in the celebration of
life by making this change of view within herself. In time she began
to believe in her artistic gifts, but not without periods of feeling mis-
erable and being unproductive. Always, my challenge was to kindly

and firmly encourage her to believe in her purpose without taking her uncertainty as a sign of my own.

Paul held a B.F.A. in music and more recently had acquired a law degree. He had made three attempts to pass the bar examination before he came to see me. He believed that the legal profession was the way to become a film producer. But now he reported that this alternative was "not working out either."

Paul had worked as an assistant film editor in the motion picture industry for seven years. He "hated" this work, however, which is the main reason he quit to attend law school. In his heart of hearts he said he knew he wanted to be a writer.

"I'm not really interested in the law," Paul surprised me with the announcement. He had been unemployed for about eighteen months. Thinking that the problem was the way in which he was presented, Paul wanted me to help him market himself so that he could become employed.

Out of a practical necessity for income Paul had sent out fifty résumés applying as a paralegal professional, a job he described as spending "twenty hours a day as an assistant to some schmuck who sends you to pick up his laundry." Accordingly, Paul was not persistent about follow-up. He had one interview but still felt discouraged. His lack of enthusiasm was evident to me and probably to prospective employers.

With considerable insight, Paul said that he realized that, "the reason I'm still unemployed is because I'm not committed enough to any of these part-time, temporary jobs. They all make me sick so I don't really go for them." I thought the lack of commitment was to himself and that his attitude of self-mistrust undermined his entire career search.

He said he was looking for a career counselor to help him decide which career to pursue. But as we discussed each one in turn, he had an explanation as to why music, film editor, lawyer, writer, and paralegal professional were unsatisfactory. The common denominator, I thought, was his self-doubt, not any permanent barriers in these professions.

It is common for Starphades like Paul to have several or many creative abilities. In encountering adversity, Starphades often become discouraged and quit. When they subsequently recover, they may pick another facet of their gifted self as their new career choice and repeat the process. This kind of serial pursuit of different careers can be repeated for years without success. Starphades usually cannot imagine a career that would draw on all of their multifaceted talents.

Cited is an excerpt from the second meeting that shows the underlying persistence of Paul's self-doubt. The session was audiotaped so that he might listen to the ideas at another time and gain some insight. He left the tape in the rest room, an indication of his right-brained style and perhaps an evaluation of the consultation.

> **JS:** I understand that you are telling me that in looking for both temporary work and a long-term career you are defeated by not having any faith in yourself.
>
> **P:** Faith does not have anything to do with it. Faith does not pay the bills.
>
> **JS:** You don't seem to have faith in your abilities and skills strong enough to aggressively pursue the opportunities.
>
> **P:** I have incredible faith—I think I'm brilliant and I'm shocked that I can't get a job. I'm at a crisis point in my life. I do not think you understand. I do not know what to do. That is why I am at a career counselor because I do not know what to do. I came to a career counselor to find someone to help me find a wrap to present myself.
>
> **JS:** You're asking me to package you when I am telling you that on the contrary it's basic that you have faith in yourself—that you believe you have qualities that are worth offering to employers. State what they are and put them forward.
>
> **P:** I can produce movies but you need a property to produce and the ability to raise money, these are the two requirements. Music, film editing, law, I have the best of the combination of creative and business skills to be a producer. It's an incredible combination and very few people have these three things.
>
> **JS:** But then you tell me you can't be a producer because you lack money and a property. You have to try to build a bridge to the world with your talents and the world is not going to build it to you. So make a commitment to yourself to begin exploring now through trial and error what you have to offer—it's really the only alternative you have.
>
> **P:** It's so much effort to do something that you do not care about to go to those lengths. It seems inane.
>
> **JS:** That is why I keep saying that it is a matter of faith.
>
> **P:** No, I don't want to go out there and kiss people's ass and that's the game you have to play. Promoting yourself is all bullshit. I am terrible at playing this game and really not very inter-

ested. Maybe that's been my problem. A producer is the biggest bullshitter in the world.

JS: I'm encouraging you to understand that the genuineness of your talent is real but reality is adverse and to survive you need to be aggressive about adapting to it.

P: You have to really want to do what you want to do to go to those lengths and I don't really care that much.

JS: It may be true that the world does not just naturally appreciate and support artists. Are you saying that you refuse to promote yourself because you anticipate rejection? You keep rejecting yourself with your doubts, which is devastating to your sense of well-being. As a result you can hardly create, promote, or support yourself at all.

P: It's a terrible thing—this culture celebrates mediocrity—it's all marketing—not the quality of the product or service.

JS: But still you are believing you are mediocre because you are believing this external world view is valid and denying your potentials that are achievable with faith in yourself.

Paul and I never got beyond the impasse of opposing views, he believing the problem was his victimization by the world in not being recognized as valuable and my believing it was his own mistreatment of himself in not recognizing his own value.

STARPHADE TO STARPHIRE

Karen was born and raised in the Midwest where she became fairly popular and successful in her early twenties as a singer and pianist in nightclubs and hotels. She decided to move to Los Angeles to look for greater opportunities in the entertainment industry.

She found it difficult to bear the brusque and frequent rejections encountered in auditions. She gradually lost faith in herself and her determination waned. She came to regard Hollywood as "phony, superficial, and degrading," and was struck by the irony that it was the "image capital of the world."

When Karen became totally discouraged, she took a job as a temporary data-entry clerk in a national transportation firm. Because there is an affinity between musical ability and computer skills, she prospered, and over the next six years she was promoted, eventually to a managerial position.

She appreciated the security of the job and the income and benefits of full-time employment, but she reached an advancement ceiling and, after several years, became totally bored with the routine of her work. She joked that she had become "the permanent temporary," but she was serious about the extent of her job alienation.

Karen had achieved all the outward signs of success and appeared to be living the "California Dream." She had an important position, a title, a new car, financial security, and a fiancé, but she felt demoralized in exactly the same way she had been at the end of her musical career because these achievements did not draw on her creative potential.

In the changeover from musician to businesswoman, she had given up her piano playing and singing, even as hobbies, which had previously given her comfort and admiration. She exchanged what she considered to be the excitement and insecurity of a performing artist for the security and boredom of an organizational manager. Having tried and tired of both extremes, it was time now for "the balancing act," as she called it, that would bring her business and creative abilities together.

The first career shift from music to business was abrupt and arose as a reaction to the rejection she experienced in her musical pursuits. Karen mistook rudeness as an evaluation of her talent and it mirrored her self-worth. Thus, she avoided solving her original problems of assertion and self-esteem. In her second career change, to management, she did not have to face these issues because she was not personally invested in being either a clerk or manager. Failure, therefore, was meaningless because in business she considered it a *fait accompli.*

Ironically, the fact that it was meaningless work is what allowed her to succeed in the transportation firm. She was able to relax and to be herself without the impediment of fear. In searching again for meaning through the *Career Star System,* she was reconfronted with her weaknesses and had to put herself forward as someone who was business minded about her musical talent. This third alternative was an understanding she acquired from the *Career Star System* and began to undertake.

STARPHIRE TO STARPHADE

David was also from the Midwest, and after high school had gone directly to college where he majored in broadcast journalism. His grades were excellent, and he had some practical experience from work on campus as well as solid recommendations from his professors. But after graduation and upon arrival in Los Angeles, he abruptly decided with no previous preparation to pursue an acting career.

David studied as an actor for two years and then obtained an agent. He married his college sweetheart and enjoyed personal and social security. Unlike Karen, he found professional opportunities abundantly available from the very beginning. Part of his success may have stemmed from knowing how to manage acting as a business.

Acting opportunities came readily and steadily over the next eight years. He was in thirty-five commercials as a character actor and in major roles in several films. Fascinated also by the production of commercials, David entered this phase of the business and quickly succeeded. He had plenty of full-time work, and he prospered financially.

Then David hit a slump. Over the next two years little work of any kind came his way. By this time he was in his midthirties, his appearance and physique had changed considerably, although he was not sure these changes accounted for the downturn. Accustomed to success, David could not stand nor understand the turn of events.

Most people experience adversity much earlier, more fully, and more often in their lives, which conditions and protects them. This was David's first exposure to real hardship. Because of his unique gifts and abilities, he had never before been tested by the forces of frustration and failure. A true test of character has always been the management of adversity rather than the achievement of success. "Anyone can hold the helm when the sea is calm" is an old proverb.

David became depressed and, as if living out a Hollywood legend, began to indulge in excesses, especially drink, as compensation. To counteract the depressive effects of alcohol, he used cocaine. One could begin to see the layers: acting covering up an insecurity, alcohol covering up acting, cocaine covering up alcohol—a parade of masks, a masquerade.

His coping strategies naturally affected his appearance, functioning, and performance, which compounded his situation by leading to more rejections and greater depression. To pay his bills and support his habit, he exhausted his credit card limit and defaulted on two bank loans.

The feature that distinguishes David as a Starphade is the spurious connection he draws between his sense of well-being and the way he is hired and regarded in the film industry. Perhaps because he had never had the experience, David misread a natural business slump as a personal rejection. Starphades are forever attributing self-condemnation to independent sources. Their work is often driven by self-centered needs for approval rather than genuine commitment to their creative spirit.

CHILD STARPHIRE

Individuals tend to become either Starphires or Starphades as a result of their responses, in exactly opposite ways, to emotional traumas experienced during infancy and/or early childhood. The origin and nature of these early traumas will be dealt with more fully in Chapter 9, "Dark Stars."

The left-brain "rational" adaptation to trauma is exemplified by the life of Jean Piaget, the famous Swiss cognitive psychologist, who devoted his entire career to understanding intellectual development in children. One famous story about Piaget reveals his own amazingly precocious intellectual ability.

When he was ten years old, Piaget wrote a scientific paper about a rare albino sparrow that he had observed in the field that was published in a Swiss natural history journal. The curators of the Geneva Museum of Natural History were so impressed with the study that they sent him a letter and invited him to become the director of the museum until they learned of his age.

Chronological age and mental age are obviously not equivalent. Some children are able to accelerate intellectually and become "little adults" as a way of coping with difficult family situations. Piaget's mother, for instance, is described as having been emotionally unstable, and his father is said to have been a remote intellectual. Apparently, neither parent was available for emotional comfort and support of their son. In his autobiography, Piaget wrote:

> I started to forego playing for serious work very early. Indeed, I have always detested any departure from reality, an attitude which I relate to . . . my mother's poor mental health. It was this disturbing factor which at the beginning of my studies in psychology made me keenly interested in psychoanalytic and pathological psychology. Though this interest helped me to achieve independence and to widen my cultural background, I have never since felt any desire to involve myself deeper in that particular direction, always much preferring the study of normalcy and of the workings of the intellect to that of the tricks of the unconscious.
>
> *Autobiography,* (1952)

In general, precocious intellectual development is one mode of adaptation to emotional deprivation in childhood. As a diversion and substitute curiosity about the external world helps to soothe feelings, and take the place of losses in the intimate world. Why some children learn that learning is self-reparative and others do not is perhaps partly explained in that not all children have the intellectual capacity to respond in this way. The left-brain adaptation may be restricted to exceptionally bright children.

Piaget's intellectual ability was perhaps as rare as the albino bird he studied. Gifted children in general have an option of taking flight in the pursuit of knowledge that other children do not. Another possibility is that emotional injury may be so extensive in right-brained children as to overshadow their intellect, no matter how great.

Intellectual acceleration in those who are capable may be enhanced by a variety of factors:

1. These children become more self-sufficient and, therefore, are able to amuse and care for themselves. They are usually greatly appreciated by adults for being less burdensome than other children, reinforcing their self-sufficiency.

2. They may also become "little helpers," assuming responsibility for managing smaller children and performing household or scholastic chores. Adults may reward them with attention and affection for their assistance which, naturally, helps them to feel better about themselves and encourages them to continue to be more "grown up."

3. They usually perform well in school, because they enjoy studying and the challenge of doing well on tests. Since they receive rewards of praise and good grades, conforming and performing become ingrained as habits.

The "rational" mode of adaptation, though helpful, has its own inherent problems. Starphire children may lack same-age friends and considered "bossy" by other children. "Little adults" are usually not well liked by their peers and do not engage in play with age-equivalent playmates. In adolescence they may stay intellectually aloof and take little interest in the opposite sex or athletic activities.

This group tends to become successful but not necessarily in a meaningful career. As a result, they tend to have an abiding sense of dissatisfaction, often hooked on the security and income of the career they have selected but not enjoying it, although this was not apparently true in Piaget's case.

CHILD STARPHADE

Children who are unable to respond to their emotional injury by developing their intellectual ability and who lack soothing parental care are left by default to be governed by their feelings. They remain the tender and sensitive right-brained individuals, who may be creative and filled with potential, but whose lives are pushed by their feelings rather than drawn by goals.

Without the intervention of a reasonable authority who can teach them by model and principle to contain their feelings and develop their abilities, they may never discover the capacity to reason on their own.

Eric was a sixth-grader who was driven by his need for attention and affection. While he was very bright, his emotional needs were so strong that they interfered with his learning, annoyed the teacher, alienated other children, and disrupted the entire classroom. Eric was "unable to settle down to work, or to continue working on a task for any period of time longer than ten minutes without some kind of reinforcement, either positive or negative," his teacher wrote. For example, he frequently delayed the drinking fountain line, causing those behind him to urge him to move on. Initial complaints did not affect him and he waited until several children yelled at him before he responded. Or, he would tip his chair back further and further until he was a danger to himself or to others, and the teacher would have to ask him to stop. Eric would become increasingly disruptive until someone noticed him. When he got the attention he sought, the negative behavior quickly stopped. Consequently, he was compelled to repeatedly engage in the behavior to constantly regain attention, which never seemed sufficient.

As an alternative, however, a child like Eric may adapt to the lack of attention by becoming a "pseudoadult" who gives love and reassurance to a parent as a way of trying to obtain it. Rather than a reaction that demands attention, this approach takes the initiative by giving attention as a means of trying to receive the needed fulfillment.

EXERCISE 7:
STAR HISTORY

Below, record the history of the pursuit of your career objective. If you find the concept helpful in thinking about your career, use your new understanding of brain lateralization obtained from the previous chapters. Begin your history with basic facts: where were you born, raised, and educated? Have you had paid work and volunteer experience?

What are your aspirations and ambitions? What clues do you have about your Calling Star? In a narrative essay, tell your experiences and reflections about the pursuit of your career objective. Writing about your career history will give you an opportunity to review your past and to see how it was affected by brain lateralization.

Name: _____ Date _____ ✍

Address: _____ Phone: _____

Date and Place of Birth:

_____

_____

_____

Education:

_____

_____

_____

Current Employment:

_____

_____

_____

Marital Status/Children:

_____

_____

_____

Previous Career Counseling?

_____

_____

_____

Previous Aptitude Testing, if any? (Indicate by whom, where, and when):

_____

_____

_____

Previous Psychotherapy, if any? (Indicate type, dates, and experience):

_____

_____

_____

Which Star Story in this chapter comes closest to describing your own? In what ways does it apply and not apply to you?

_____

_____

_____

Do You Know Your Calling? Explain.

_____

_____

_____

Describe your interests, activities, and play as a child and adolescent:

_____

_____

_____

Narrate Your Career Star Story (describe your work and career history):

_____

_____

_____

Imagine your Career Star Story in the future:

_____

_____

_____

BRIGHT STARS:
Combining Intelligence and Creativity

Bright Star, would I were steadfast as thou art.

John Keats, Sonnet, *Bright Stars*, 1848

THREE SELVES MODEL

The right- and left-brain model defined in Chapter 6, "Star Types" and illustrated in Chapter 7, "Star Stories," is helpful in identifying and classifying an individual's style of thinking. The usefulness of this model is limited, however, because it does not provide a causal explanation as to why there is brain lateralization nor what to do about it.

Assuming that you have located yourself on the map in Chapter 5 and carried out the assessment to determine the extent to which you are right- or left-brain lateralized, you may now be curious about how you came to be this way. Brain lateralization indicates an emotional injury that interferes with thinking. Once you understand the cause, you may also want to use this knowledge to overcome the one-sided use of your mind.

Diagram 5 features the Model of the Three Selves, which is another

conception of how the mind is organized. The diagram shows a figure 8 with a thick bar between the smaller upper circle and larger
lower circle. The lower circle is divided into a plus and minus side.
This diagram illustrates a division of the mind into three parts instead
of two (right- and left-brain): the "Rational," the "Injured," and the
"Creative" Selves.

This threefold division gives an added dimension of an unconscious and a damaged part of the self. The Rational Self corresponds
to the "left-brain," and the Creative Self corresponds to the "right-
brain," in the previous model. In the right- and left-brain model,
mental life is assumed to be entirely conscious, healthy, and whole.
Counterveiling positive and negative forces offer a more dynamic
view of the mind.

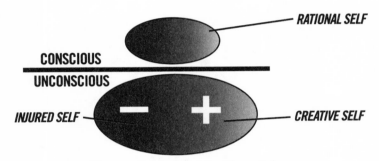

Diagram 5: Model of the Three Selves

In the Three Selves Model there is a larger, unconscious part of
the mind that is divided into Creative and Injured Selves. Both can
also encompass consciousness if this knowledge becomes an individual's intention. Many terms have been used to describe these two
sides of the human personality. Some of these are collected in
"Chart 4: Human Nature." Referring to these two dimensions, Jung
wrote, "In the empirical self, light and shadow form a paradoxical
unity."

Within each of us is a negative and positive side, the nucleus of the
original Adam and Eve in the Garden of Eden. There is a free will
choice between the snake of self-deception and the apple of the tree
of self-knowledge. Many religious, philosophical, psychological, and
institutional systems of thought have recognized this duality, which
suggests that it is a widespread understanding of human nature.

CHART 4:

Human Nature

SYSTEM OF THOUGHT	INJURED SELF	CREATIVE SELF
Alcohol Recovery Movement:	Wounded Child	Wonder Child
Mental Health Movement:	Narcissistic Wound	Healthy Personality
New Age Movement:	False Self	True Self
Developmental Psychology:	Low Self-Esteem	High Self-Esteem
Freudian Psychoanalysis:	Death Instinct	Life Instinct
Kleinian Psychoanalysis:	Bad-Breast/ Bad-Mother	Good-Breast/ Good-Mother
Jungian Psychoanalysis: (Analytic Psychology)	Shadow Self	Self
A Course in Miracles:	Ego/Projection	God/Christ/Love
Buddhism:	Lower Self	Higher Self
Christianity:	Devil/Satan	Soul/Spirit
Hinduism:	Shiva/Maya	Brahma/Vishnu
Islam:	Shaytan	Allah
Judaism:	Yetzer Ha-Ra	Neshama
Karate Martial Arts:	Jishin Soo Shitsu	Chi
United States Military:	Wrong Stuff	Right Stuff
Star Wars Trilogy:	Darth Vader/ Evil Empire	Jedi Knights/ Rebel Alliance

Numerous authors in the history of the behavioral sciences have considered conflict between the "biological" and "social," or "primitive" and "civilized" side of humans, to be "natural law." Similarly, according to contemporary theory in the natural sciences, matter is composed of positive and negative dimensions. This is reflected in the designation of elementary particles into protons (positive charges) and electrons (negative charges) in the nucleus of the atom. (There are also neutrons, which are neutral.)

The inner self tends to wear either of two faces, one of laughter or one of tears. The dramatic masks of comedy and tragedy from theater are also illustrations. The line between self-love and self-hate distinguishes the two. A student once remarked, "Some days I am a mature woman and other days I am my mother's lost child." To the same mind the world is either heaven or hell. (Emerson: "To different minds, the same world is a hell and a heaven.")

There are countless dualities in literature: Beowolf and Grendel, Dr. Jekyll and Mr. Hyde, Dr. Frankenstein and Dr. Frankenstein's Monster, Beauty and the Beast, Batman and the Joker, Peter Pan and Captain Hook, Scar and Mufasa.

The dark side of the mind derives its influence entirely from its concealment. In being kept hidden, it appears deceptively smart and powerful. Its first and foremost trick is its illusion of existence. In the light of consciousness, however, it is rendered dumb and helpless because it is not real. Dracula withers in the daylight, Mr. Hyde is undone in public, and Darth Vader is kept at bay with a "light saber."

Chart 4 provides names for the two faces of the self in various systems of thought. As primary experience of good and bad, there are many names to refer to the Injured and Creative Selves. As only approximate descriptions of basal experience, however, words are bound to be inadequate in comparison to the vivid rawness of physiological sensation. Words are much less precise in identifying feelings in the psychical world than in labeling objects in the physical world.

Below let us look at these three components of the self using *Career Star System* terminology. The Rational and Creative Selves are covered in this chapter, "Bright Stars," and the Injured Self in the next chapter, "Dark Stars."

RATIONAL SELF

The Rational Self is the intelligent and conscious part of the mind represented by the smaller part of the circle, unfortunately. Child development experts disagree about the beginning and earliest forms of thinking, but most agree that thinking is acquired after birth through learning language and develops in stages over childhood.

Technically, there is no "thinking" without words, which are symbols in our mind for "things" that exist in the world. The intelligent part of the mind is contained in the cerebral cortex, especially the left hemisphere. The cerebral cortex is also called the neocortex, or the new brain, and is considered the "higher" or "adult" self. Rational thinking arises with the development of the ego through the socialization process.

The larger, lower circle represents the emotional part of the mind, associated with functions of the right hemisphere of the brain. Emotionally based thinking is present from the very beginning of life in the form of images or fantasies. We do not remember the earliest years of thinking in this way and the ability tends to remain mostly unconscious to many adults.

While thinking with images exists preverbally in the imagination, its content is also influenced by personal, social, and environmental circumstances. Because the emotional part of the mind is the first and oldest part of the mind, it is often considered the "child" part. Based on the same reasoning, you may also hear it referred to as the "animal" or "reptilian," as distinct from the "human" or "civilized" portion of the mind.

In the diagram, a thick line called the "Bar to Consciousness," is drawn between the rational and emotional circles. Although this barline might be lowered slightly to show that we are aware sometimes of our more superficial feelings, the fact is that most are deeply hidden from awareness. Age and experience may allow us to become more insightful about our emotions. Trite but true, most of our feelings are "unconscious."

This conception of the Three Selves is based on the work of Freud. Most Americans are familiar with the three-part division of "id," "ego," and "superego." This model was revised in Freud's later work into an unconscious divided between "Eros" and "Thanatos," or life and death "instincts." Consciousness, the third component, remained "ego." The earlier model was set aside in preference for the later model. The Three Selves model is also influenced by Jung's tripartite division of the mind into Eros, Logos, and the Self.

Freudians also refer to emotionally based thinking as "primary process thinking." It is primary not only because it is first and fundamental, but because feelings are linked to our bodies through our senses via the central nervous system. It is "primary," therefore, because it is biologically rooted. While intellectually based thinking tends to be cerebral, emotionally based thinking tends to be much more viscerally charged.

CREATIVE SELF

The Creative, or the Gifted Child Self, lies in the undamaged area of the unconscious and is the source of all our spontaneously creative ideas and actions. Every individual has inherent capacities and special abilities that make him or her an absolutely unique individual who is distinct from all others. The Creative Self is probably a genetic given although learning can greatly modify and enhance it.

Potentials are unrecognized and unrealized abilities; the beginning of their fulfillment is this awareness. Everyone has different natural talents, potentials, and powers, but unless they are acknowledged by conscious and rational action, the gifts remain dormant and the individual appears to be undifferentiated from the masses of others. To actually become a creative person, you must follow impulses and inspirations with disciplined action so that the gifts become manifest.

It is this special linking of intelligence with creativity through action that distinguishes one unique individual from another. "You can wait, delay, paralyze, or reduce your creativity almost to nothing. But you cannot abolish it," according to *A Course in Miracles*. The Injured Self, to be discussed fully in the next chapter, can become so great that it causes almost a total eclipse of the Creative Self.

The Creative Self also interfaces with the Injured Self, so that being creative simultaneously activates and fuels self-destructive tendencies. The more creative an individual, or the more emphasis an individual puts on creative activity, the more aroused the Injured Self becomes. It is unfortunately true that our damaged side, which generates resistance, described in Chapter 3, fights individual differentiation and specialization of talent.

Whenever you begin to think about or actively engage in development, like giving up bad habits and acquiring good ones, the Injured Self is aroused and appears in consciousness in the form of anxiety, fear, and doubt. Ordinarily, these emotions are signs of danger and there *is* danger if you undertake the development without an awareness of its impact on the Injured Self.

Potentials are unrealized abilities.

Without consciousness there is a delay in development due to an intolerance for developmental anxiety known as "procrastination."

People are frequently misled and act on the anxiety rather than utilizing it for creative purposes. Acting on the anxiety instead of the creativity will further aggravate the injury because it reinforces a negative view of the self that impedes the developmental process.

Being blessed with creative abilities usually means being cursed with a large measure of self-doubt and self-destructive inclinations. In becoming creative one must overcome these self-destructive tendencies, which everyone holds in common, to become original and unique, which makes each of us different.

A very creative client, not financially disciplined, once confessed, "I'm always afraid that if I really get into creativity, I'll lose touch with the practical side of life and not pay my bills or take care of myself."

Human nature thus seems two-sided in its creative and destructive dimensions. It is the triumph over the negative and the expression of the positive that makes true talent so greatly admired and rewarded. Of course, it is also true that talent can be overrated or underrated and overpaid or underpaid.

The Creative and Injured sides of our emotional life are inversely related and constantly in conflict. Specifically, self-destructive activity is anticreative; or conversely, creative activity is directly opposed to self-destructiveness.

The struggle with drug addiction among all types of artists and performers is legendary. One of the most self-destructive ideas in the creative community is that talent diminishes without chemical enhancement. This view sees addiction as a prerequisite to creative success. It is contradicted by the demise of many famous drug dependent careers.

EXERCISE 8:
STAR SELF A TO Z

Your calling is a part of your natural gifts and talents that lie dormant on the plane of the unconscious part of your mind, especially when they are not recognized and cultivated. Whether you have an intuitive hunch about your calling or no hint whatsoever, the following exercise will stir up the developmental anxiety described above.

This exercise will also bring to the surface some of your natural interests and characteristics of your true self. These need to be recognized first in order for your calling to be discovered. Follow the instructions without judging anything your mind produces nor expecting immediate and impressive results.

For each letter of the alphabet listed below, provide three words that capture your positive characteristics. You may think you do not have an alphabet of positive attributes. Try anyway to use words that are honestly accurate and that come readily to mind. Avoid using a dictionary. If you let the words come from your heart rather than a book they will be more authentic.

You may learn that you need to improve your vocabulary in order to do an adequate job of describing yourself. Do not be concerned if the words you pick resemble one another, because we are seeking underlying qualities that are characteristic of you.

The hardest letter is X. You may need to draw on words that sound like they start with X, such as "expressive," "exciting," and "exotic." If you come up with three valid X terms without consulting a dictionary, you are exonerated; that is, you are "X Honor-Rated."

Do not agonize over Y and Z either. If descriptive terms that start with these letters do not come readily to mind, just continue the exercise. Some individuals complain about the difficulty of the "Alphabet Exercise," but usually the results are revealing.

A few individuals may find it difficult to control the impulse to describe themselves in incredible terms. Almost everyone else, however, finds it easier to come up with negative terms.

For example, you probably exclaimed "X-ed out" or "X-rated" when unable to think of positive X-terms above. There is a litany of terms students spontaneously recite, a kind of catechism of self-criticism. All around campus you hear: "A is for Awful, B is for Bad, C is for Crazy, D is for Dumb, F is for Failure, all of which I am."

Since our objective is to identify positive, not negative, characteristics there is no need to recite the entire alphabet. The persistence of a negative recitation over a positive one is truly remarkable, however. If you get stuck on certain letters filling in the chart, you may want to first brainstorm for a minute or two on a separate sheet of paper. Then plug the positive words into the alphabetical blanks on the chart. Begin now to fill in the blanks with positive and accurate terms about yourself that cover the entire alphabet.

I AM A TO Z

A:_____ , _____ & _____
B:_____ , _____ & _____
C:_____ , _____ & _____
D:_____ , _____ & _____
E:_____ , _____ & _____
F:_____ , _____ & _____
G:_____ , _____ & _____
H:_____ , _____ & _____
I:_____ , _____ & _____
J:_____ , _____ & _____
K:_____ , _____ & _____
L:_____ , _____ & _____
M:_____ , _____ & _____
N:_____ , _____ & _____
O:_____ , _____ & _____
P:_____ , _____ & _____
Q:_____ , _____ & _____
R:_____ , _____ & _____
S:_____ , _____ & _____
T:_____ , _____ & _____
U:_____ , _____ & _____
V:_____ , _____ & _____
W:_____ , _____ & _____
X:_____ , _____ & _____
Y:_____ , _____ & _____
Z:_____ , _____ & _____

CLUSTER ANALYSIS

With a list of three adjectives for each letter of the alphabet, you will have a total of seventy-eight terms. Some will have common meanings. Review the whole list and look for words that are similar or synonymous in meaning. For example, if you have used "bright," "alert," and "keen," you are acknowledging your intelligence.

Group all similar words together in clusters. This is hard work but do it anyway and try to enjoy it. After you have listed all the words that resemble one another into a cluster, pick the one word from the list, or come up with an altogether new word, that summarizes this dimension. Try to identify at least five different dimensions. Write each dimension down on the line beside the large numbers on page 132.

The results of this exercise are a preliminary sketch of the characteristics of your core Creative Self.

Cluster 1

_____
_____
_____   Dimension 1:
_____   I am _____
_____
_____
_____

Cluster 2

_____
_____   Dimension 2:
_____   I am _____
_____
_____
_____

Cluster 3

_____
_____   Dimension 3:
_____   I am _____
_____
_____
_____

Cluster 4

_____
_____   Dimension 4:
_____   I am _____
_____
_____
_____

Cluster 5

_____
_____   Dimension 5:
_____   I am _____
_____
_____
_____

Cluster 6

_____

_____

_____   Dimension 6:

_____   I am _____

_____

_____

_____

Connect the dots on page 132 to define your Gifted Self and to draw out your star. Along the rays of the star, the center of which represents the core of your Gifted Star Self, write out the dimensions you have uncovered through your cluster analysis.

These dimensions are some of the essential facets of your Gifted Self and need to be recorded and remembered. When your star has been drawn out, paint or color it. If it will not diminish your regard for its importance, you may glue rice, macaroni, sequins, and glitter to it.

Take a moment to notice the whole list of adjectives that describe you. Then reflect on the names of the specific dimensions that define your core Gifted Self. Take a little time to think about the kind of work you might do with these gifts, or how you might use these gifts more fully in your present occupation.

Appreciate the way your Career Star looks and notice the qualities that are expressed in each word that identifies a ray. After a moment of reflection repeat the words aloud to hear how they sound when spoken about you. If you feel self-conscious, or if the words seem hollow, you continue to doubt these are _your_ key qualities. Nevertheless this exercise has helped document "for the record" the basic attributes of your core Gifted Self.

Below write your thoughts about these particular dimensions of your self. That is, tell yourself in writing what you think about the fact that these qualities are _yours_ and that they are at the center of your being.

_____

_____

_____

_____

_____

_____

_____

With these dimensions of your Core Gifted Self what career or calling is suggested to you? Release and record your thoughts about the possibilities.

_____

_____

_____

_____

_____

_____

_____

1. _____

1. ●

2. _____

5. _____

9. ●   10. ●   2. ●   ●3.

Core
Gifted 4. ●
Self

8. ●

●
6.

7. ●   ●5.

4. _____

3. _____

DARK STARS:
Overcoming Doubt and Fear

He grapples with his evil star.

Alfred Tennyson,
In Memoriam, 1850

PRIMAL INJURY

How an original emotional insult comes to be a common feature of human psychology takes us briefly into the subjects of infant and child development. The concept of "Primal Injury" is a difficult and abstract concept about what takes place in the early mental life of children.

In terms of the model of "Three Selves," Diagram 5, page 122, a newborn baby has only the larger, lower circle of feeling. The intellect and ego have not yet formed and there is no focus on the objective world. As yet there is no bar to consciousness. A baby is a sensate organism without awareness of its own feelings or reality.

In Greek mythology, Narcissus was a handsome young man who fell in love with his reflection in a pool of water. Like Narcissus, infants are self-centered and lack the ability to differentiate themselves from their surroundings. Babies perceive reality, feel sensations and emotions without any differentiation in their mind between external and internal worlds. In their view it is obvious that the two worlds are one and that they are the center of both.

Being at the focal point, infants take for granted that what goes on about them is a manifestation of their own constructive powers. The most primitive, unsocialized image of ourselves, therefore, tends to be one of grand omnipotence. Overcoming the influence of this earliest state of mind in stages over childhood and in adulthood is the basis of maturation. Gradually, albeit reluctantly, narcissism diminishes. There is nothing quite like being tired, wet, dirty, hungry, and alone, however, to reduce a mature adult to the mentality of a child.

If an infant is well cared for by loving parents, this narcissistic view of the self as ruler of the cosmos is initially reinforced by parental attention and affection.

Held, fed, cleaned, coddled, fondled, and cuddled, all are tribute proper to the baby's eminence. But inevitably this perspective is transformed; control over one's parents, and over pleasure, is not sustainable indefinitely.

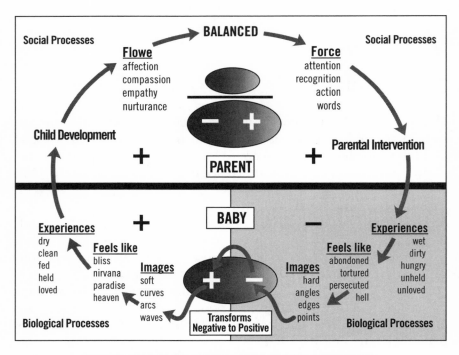

DIAGRAM 6: TRANSFORMATION OF NEGATIVE TO POSITIVE EXPERIENCES

No matter how excellent the parental care, a baby unavoidably becomes wet, soiled, hungry, and alone at times. Because of this experience, which may be for longer or shorter periods, depending upon the quality of care and environmental circumstances, the original wonder of infant power is contradicted by the awful pain characteristic of infant reality.

If there is neglect by parents, then sociological processes compound the biological ones. Social mistreatment makes it more than twice as difficult to develop psychologically even while physical growth proceeds naturally. The cycle of parental social intervention into the biological process is illustrated in Diagram 6.

The pain that accompanies the biological events of infancy are natural physiological processes that operate twenty-four hours a day in the body of a baby. This process is outside both infant and parental control. The presence of pain and the loss of control over pleasure, are experienced together as a double insult, a "Primal Injury," that razes the grandiose dignity of the infant personality.

Everyone experiences this trauma in infancy, which is preceded by the trauma of birth and together constitute the original Injured Child Self. The "Primal Insult," is often mistaken for something like "original sin." Subsequent socialization can aggravate or assuage the basic wound. The intervention of parental caregiving transforms the negative into positive experience and mitigates, but never eliminates, the extent of the Primal Injury.

Because of the ongoing impact of biological processes, even extraordinary parental care cannot prevent an Injured Self. At best, parenting can only balance the negative of biological with the positive of social forces. Inadequate parenting, however, can aggravate the injury and interfere with the acquisition of intelligence, because emotional issues can override cognitive development.

The fact that you have an Injured Child Self as a result of a Primal Insult does not mean there is something abnormal about you. It only means that you have had an experience shared by all humanity that is carried in the psyche.

The Injured Child Self is usually an unconscious part of the personality, which gives rise to negative feelings and thoughts in the adult self. The Injured Child Self is often concealed from the self and others through deceit and denial. This does not mean that the injury becomes insignificant or disappears. Its effects are real but often unrecognized.

The Injured Child Self is the source of most of our bad feelings and self-critical thoughts; it continues to show up in the impairment of our rational functioning as adults and causes us to make illogical decisions that throw off the natural course of our life. The Injured Child Self also blocks contact with our Creative Self, and prevents us from reaching our potentials.

INJURED CHILD SELF

"Everyone is a moon and has a dark side that he never shows to anybody," wrote Mark Twain. Jungian psychoanalysts refer to a "shadow side" of the personality. The beings in Dante's *Inferno* were called "Shades." "Dark," "Shadow," and "Shade" are all names for the Injured Self. Acquired from experiences in infancy and childhood, no child escapes the primal wounding though the breadth and depth varies greatly according to experience.

Generally, people who were physically abused or emotionally neglected as infants or young children have larger Injured Child Selves. The earlier and more harsh the mistreatment, the more severe the injury. A client with many tragedies in her life once told me she had suffered much torment as a child and summed it up saying she was "abnegored" (abandoned + neglected + ignored).

Children born with genetic defects or deficits, especially if these are physically painful, suffer a correspondingly enlarged emotional injury. If an individual is both abused by parents and physically handicapped, there may be a great magnification of the core Injured Self (see Diagram 7).

Because the core injury occurs before a child is verbal, it usually remains unconscious in adulthood. Rooted in primitive experience, any name seems a remote and imprecise abstraction. "The empty lump of myself" was one student's expression of the core feeling. In an individual this part comes to consciousness as "obsessions" and "addictions" and it appears in society as "enemies" and "criminals."

The Injured Self is a primitive emotional experience that is really beyond words to describe. Nevertheless, Chart 4 presents the array of names used in many different systems of thought. The terms are all negative and make the mistake of conceiving of the innocent and faultless child part of the self as a deeply malevolent figure.

This mistake must be recognized if there is to be development in the present. The adult must take responsibility to nurture the faultless Injured Child Self. With this change of mind the child will be seen as cooperative and benefit by the development. Without compassion, the adult will see his own cruelty in what appears to be the child's stubborn opposition and will continue to practice self-attacks disguised in the expectation of self-improvement.

Ongoing attacks may be exactly what the person experienced from adults as a child. The attacks are a continuation of the past and in this way passes on adult scapegoating of children over guilt for earlier failures. The old war within the psyche is prolonged and personal change is preempted for the same historical battle scenes.

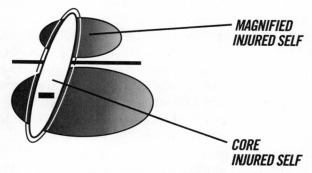

MAGNIFIED
INJURED SELF

CORE
INJURED SELF

Diagram 7: Core and Magnified Injured Self

An ignored and misunderstood Injured Child Self is frightened by the prospect of developmental career work because it means greater sacrifice, pain, and hardship. The child is correct, of course, if we proceed in the old way by repeating past mistakes without a new consciousness. Based on previous experience, there is no reason to believe that career transitions will be undertaken with his best interests in mind.

Career development imposes an added burden on the child part of the self already suffering from years of neglect and abuse. Because we do not readily believe in the value of the child we do not see that the changes can be accomplished successfully only through communication and cooperation with the child.

INJURED ADULT SELF

In our functioning as adults, the full use of our intellect is often restricted by the intrusion of hurts and wrongs suffered in infancy and childhood. Originally the capacity to learn was impaired and encased in feelings of self-doubt. Consequently we came to believe something is wrong with us that the mistreatment communicated and corroborated and this view of ourselves was subsequently internalized.

To a greater or lesser degree, depending upon the amount of emotional mistreatment and overt physical abuse in a person's background, the ability to have self-trust and act with self-interest in adulthood continues to be sacrificed. The unseen Injured Child Self burdens and impairs all later learning and development.

The injury has ramifications for every aspect of adult life. If you think of the original injury as causing a "misalignment" in the self-relationship, a "gap" shows up in adulthood in work, relationships, and the physical body, among other places. That is, you find dissatisfaction in each of these areas of life that replicate the underlying missing link to the self. The misalignment began before your memory began.

Alienation in work, estrangement in relationships, and physiological symptoms in the form of injuries and illness are by-products of fundamental psychological misunderstandings, specifically, the feeling that there is something "bad" or "wrong" about your self. You cannot pick accurately what you want in life because the original injury prevents you from learning who you are and what is right for you.

Some events are beyond our control: illness, deaths, layoffs, and unemployment, for example. These incidents can aggravate the original injuries, and reinforce our self-image as "victims" of a great "tragedy." As we did when we were children we feel helpless and it prolongs the trauma.

When the core Injured Child Self is enlarged in this way by losses in adulthood, the damaged part of the mind intrudes further into consciousness and interferes with rational thought processes. Healing rights the mind to see correctly the positive self. A damaged mind sees in reverse the same way a *camera obscura* shoots the world upside down. It is common, therefore, to engage in more self-destructive activities under the influence of an aggravated Injured Self than under the ordinary core injury.

Because of the injuries to the self in childhood many adults continue to regard themselves as victims. Both Starphires and Starphades seeing in reverse perspective, seek in the outer world to acquire the value overlooked within. Starphires, for example, want power, or the representations of power: money, status, and possessions. They believe power attained in the material world will change the way they feel about themselves.

Starphades, on the other hand, want attention, affection, and admiration. Both types of stars are correct about needing to feel better but are mistaken about its source. They both need to love themselves directly instead of cutting off its internal source through external preoccupations. They are deprived of self-esteem by mistakenly seeking it where it does not exist.

CASE ILLUSTRATION

James, a man in his early forties, laid off work as a tour guide in the travel business, became increasingly despondent over his situation. In his depressed state of mind he was reminded of events in his childhood when he experienced similar kinds of feelings. For example, he recalled that he was considered the "outcast" and "black sheep" of his family.

James never understood that he always felt bad about what had happened. With the free time his unemployment forced on him, he began to discuss the circumstances of his birth with relatives. He suspected that he was an illegitimate child and thought this was the basis of his mistreatment, an unresolved issue in his life.

Everyone he contacted in the small town where he grew up refused to talk with James or answered him curtly or evasively. Their common reaction aroused his suspicion all the more that a "conspiracy" existed about his parentage. Finally he was able to confirm that he was the product of an extramarital affair by his mother with a man known as "Blackie." These events were apparently well known in the community.

James already suspected that he was illegitimate as a child and its confirmation as an adult only made him feel worse. The prime emotion of feeling unwanted was apparently reality based and a final explanation to him for the scorn and humiliation he felt in his treatment as a child.

Coupled with his current unemployment this news caused James to become very depressed. Now he had another misfortune upon which to dwell. The collection of incidents, both from the present and the past, reinforced his feelings of exclusion and worthlessness. Accordingly, he was lethargic about involvement in his recovery, both from the depression and the unemployment.

When childhood and adulthood injuries double up, it is usually more than twice as difficult to escape their impact. As adults we often lock-on to external events as proof of a prior conviction we hold about ourselves. The reinforcement of learned malice for the self in James's thinking is common among Starphades.

To the extent that James continued to believe that these unresolved wrongs from the past had meaning in the present he was prevented from starting afresh now. As a result of counseling this individual began to understand that the way he was treated originally as a child and subsequently as an adult were not valid indicators of his real self-worth.

With support and insight he was able to let both incidents pass and to concentrate instead on constructive activities in the present. By focusing on issues such as exercise, establishing friendships, and job searching, he was relieved of the weight of the past and began to build a future.

Toxic Thoughts

A formerly abused child can become so obsessed with morbidly negative thoughts as an adult that physical and emotional pain seem to be desirable and death can even appear inviting as an escape. A person with a severely Injured Self can continuously manufacture and sustain thoughts so toxic that long-term emotional and physical well-being are precluded.

The focus on the negative in the form of undeserved loathing and self-contempt can become so compulsively repetitive that it amounts to an addiction. A full addiction to negative thoughts means that an individual believes self-hatred is a valid self-appraisal. The way you feel is a reaction to the way you think but you can feel so awful that it is hard to shift to a positive point of view.

Dwelling on losses in this way serves to keep the emotional wound open and unhealed. Some examples are: ruminating on past traumas, reliving previous failures, dwelling on the breakup of a relationship or marriage, resenting the aging process, bemoaning a decline in appearance, fantasies of revenge, blaming others and circumstances for setbacks, and regretting financial decisions.

A perceptive client once noted that the Injured Self "runs straight through" the other two parts of the Self. That is, it eclipses the Creative and the Rational Selves as shown in Diagram 5, "Model of the Three Selves," page 122, and Diagram 7, "Core and Magnified Injured Self," page 137.

Systems of Denial

There are two basic ways that the Injured and Creative Child parts of the self are denied attention and care. These are identified in the *Career Star System* as the Rational and the Irrational Systems of Denial.

That is, individuals either rationally or irrationally deny the existence of these two sides of their personality. The two denial systems correspond to being left- or right-brained. Diagram 9, page 152 and Diagram 11, page 165, provide illustrations of these two circular types of thought systems.

The Denial Systems are ways individuals learn to cope with their Injured Child Self. Right-brained Starphades are prone to the Irrational Denial System: body rushes and psychological highs as remedies for an underlying emotional injury. Starphires, or left-brained individuals, are inclined to the Rational Denial System, goal-oriented pursuits like the acquisition of money, power, and property.

Left-brained individuals, who focus exclusively on external goal achievement, locate what matters as outside themselves. Right-brained individuals, on the other hand, adopt a focus on sensate body states and physical pleasure. (See Diagrams 9 and 11.)

The idea that there are Injured and Creative Children within us is figural, not a literal truth, even though all too often we may act as if we are good or bad kids. People learn from experience that children are considered a bother and a burden, and to regard the child part of our mind as a great hindrance. We try to get rid of it by "being grown up" and "not being a baby."

But to develop successfully we need the adult part of our mind to perform child care, just as we needed our parents' care to develop into adults. Both Injured and Gifted Child require conscious recognition of their existence by breaking the habit of the System of Denial. That denial habitually reinjures us emotionally in exactly the same way we were originally injured as a child. At the same time, the Gifted Child is ignored, in the same way this part was ignored during childhood.

Forging a link between the Rational and Creative Selves is the goal of developmental change. You should be prepared for the opposition of your Injured Self. Being anxious is a warning in consciousness that the developmental thoughts or actions are a threat to the Injured Child Self.

Children as children do not realize that they are engaged in denial, because they lack the capacity of insight. The acquisition of insight, therefore, stands at the center of the transition from childhood to adulthood. And the insight at the heart of human development is the recognition that there is an Injured Child part of the self being disavowed by either rational or irrational means.

In Chapter 10, "Star Force," we will look more closely at the Ra-

---

CHART 5:

Characteristics of Starphades and Starphires II

STARPHIRES	STARPHADES
Left-Brain Lateralization	Right-Brain Lateralization
Rational/Outer Adaptation	Emotional/Inner Adaptation
Thinks and Acts	Senses and Feels
Rational Denial System	Irrational Denial System
Goal Achievements	Body Rushes
Blocks Feelings	Blocks Logic
Workaholism	Addictions
Uses Force	Uses Flowe
Bright Stars	Dark Stars

---

tional Denial System and the consequences of workaholism and burnout. In Chapter 11, "Star Flowe," we turn to the Irrational Denial System and the option of creativity in place of addiction. In the meantime the exercise below, Injured Child Meditation, initiates the process of nurturing the Injured Child Self.

 EXERCISE 9:
INJURED CHILD MEDITATION

In this exercise the idea of "special time" is borrowed from the field of child development and applied to the subject of the Injured Child. "Special time" is the notion of giving a child an exclusive ten minutes or more for an activity entirely of his own choosing. In the Injured Child Meditation you are asked to devote special attention to the injured child part of you through a meditative visit.

The Injured Child Meditation is a way of making you more conscious of a child part of you that actually exists. Because the child part probably mistrusts your interest, it will take several meditations to get a clear picture of the child. If you are consistent in your meditative practice it will be easier to get into the mood each time.

This meditation asks you to remember yourself as a child. If you are not able to remember your childhood, call to mind a photograph of yourself as a child. The photograph will help you picture yourself and enable you to get started with the meditation. Please note that even though you are being asked to remember yourself from the past, *this meditation is about your current relationship with your child self.*

Some people are wary of this exercise because they are afraid feelings suffered in childhood, like feeling abused, may be stirred up or relived. If you feel strongly about this you may skip the exercise.

However, remember that this is not about your childhood but your current child-self relationship. It is important to become aware of your current self-mistreatment so that it can be corrected. If at all possible, therefore, do this exercise.

Begin with the "Progressive Relaxation Meditation" found in Appendix 3, to help ease your mind and body as preparation. It might be beneficial to have both the "Progressive Relaxation Meditation" and your "Injured Child Meditation" read onto your own audiocassette so that you can be guided by hearing instead of reading.

Once you have relaxed, try to remember yourself as a child of any age in a place where you once lived. You can see yourself indoors or outdoors. Do not anticipate seeing anything or seeing nothing. Relax and appreciate what comes to mind. Take a few minutes to notice from a distance your appearance and your activities as a child.

When you have taken in the scene, imagine walking closer to the child and noticing her or his eyes and facial expression and any other features or facts that may catch your attention. Of course, give attention to what the child appears to be feeling, doing, and wearing.

If the child ignores you, or acts too busy to give you any attention, remember this is how the child feels treated by the adult part of you, suspicious and mistrustful that you genuinely care. Is this valid? (One client visualized her Injured Child searching unsuccessfully for a Mother's Day card.) If you are sincere, let the child know by saying something like, "I really do care about you" even though you may not be believed or answered for a while.

After a time, the child will respond, usually by paying more attention to you. He or she may act angry in the beginning. The anger tends to pass quickly; Injured Children rarely hold a grudge or retaliate. You might add, "I know that I have not given you very much attention in the past but I really do care. I will try to visit you more often in the future." Try to mean what you say!

Ask the child to look at you, and you look at the child. Ask, "How are you doing?" Try to hold a dialogue. If he or she will not speak, then say that you recognize that "you are the child part of me, and I know that you are feeling hurt," or "angry," or "sad." If the child appears to be smiling and playful, say, "I know underneath your happy appearance there really is a hurt child."

Sometimes people doing this meditation persistently see an adult rather than a child. If your inner child has the size and appearance of an adult, taking care of you as her child may be a way to be cared for. Real children often learn to give care as a way of trying to receive it, although the strategy does not usually succeed. If you get the image of an adult say, "I know you are trying to be big and grown-up for me. I know you are the Injured Child part of me, and I am interested in knowing you and taking better care of you."

Ask the child for his name to help you remember to come back for another meditation. Say you will be back and mean it sincerely. Then say "goodbye" for now. Meditate with the Injured Child four times in the next week, taking approximately twenty minutes for each meditation. Write up your experience after each meditation below and use more space if necessary. Again, do not try to force an appearance of the child, just let the image come to the surface of your mind freely "out of the blue."

Describe what takes place between the two of you—what you visualized and experienced and what the child said and did in the meditation. If you have other images instead, describe them as graphically as possible—even if it is just the back of your eyelids. Note also the day, time, and conditions of your meditation. In the future, try to make the child one of your best friends by giving more generous and consistent portions of time to the Injured Child in your meditations and in your life.

INJURED CHILD MEDITATIONS

Meditation One: *Date:* _____.

_____
_____
_____
_____
_____
_____

Meditation Two: *Date:* _____.

_____
_____
_____
_____
_____
_____

Meditation Three: *Date:* _____.

_____
_____
_____
_____
_____
_____

Meditation Four: *Date:* _____.

_____
_____
_____
_____
_____
_____

STAR FORCE:
Relinquishing Power

Every man will fail who,
though born a man
proudly presumes to be
a superman.

Sophocles, 495–406 B.C.

FORCE

You have made an assessment of your "brain lateralization," a measure of the extent of your right- or left-brainedness. We have also looked at how the lateralization came about.

Because psychological change is accompanied by the resistance of the Injured Self, the next step is not a discussion of how to overcome the lateralization, as you might guess, but the nature of the Injured Self and the two modes of adaptation to it. The short-term and long-term goals are to establish rapport and *amour* between the rational and emotional sides of yourself.

The Rational Denial System relies on "Force"; it seeks to repair the Injured Self by controlling the external world through goal-oriented behavior. The technique of Force assumes that if the outer world can be managed, this proves that the individual is powerful. This is the way of Starphires; they use Force.

The emotional, Irrational Denial System relies on "Flowe"; it seeks to repair the Injured Self by turning away from the external world. It tries to fill the mind and body with pleasurable experiences that deny the outer world's influence.

The external world is assumed to be irrational and impervious to control by any kind of action, mental or behavioral. And without any kind of cause-and-effect relationship between thinking, acting, and reality, the outside world is written off as incomprehensibly beyond control. This is the way of Starphades; they use Flowe.

Whereas Flowe disconnects, the Force overconnects the relationship between the external and internal worlds. Will Durant referred to the phenomenon of Force and Flowe as the "systole and diastole of history." One approach tries to alter the mind as an adaptation to the world; the other tries to alter the world as an adaptation to the mind. Both deny the Creative and Injured Child sides of their nature and the possibility of mutual interaction that balances the inner and outer spheres.

Force is uptight with might.
Flowe is loose and slow.

There is another possible connection between the external and internal realities. With an appreciation of the Force and Flowe comes a third way of coping that is not reducible to one or the other. This third way is learning when to weave the Force and Flowe and when to use them separately. This is a lifelong task of knowing when to differentiate and when to integrate.

The Serenity Prayer below, adopted by the alcohol recovery movement, captures beautifully the nature of the task. It suggests changing the things that can be changed, accepting the things that cannot be changed, and discerning the difference between the two.

> God, give us grace to accept with serenity
>   the things that cannot be changed,
>   courage to change the things which should be changed,
>   and the wisdom to distinguish the one from the other.
>   Reinhold Niebuhr, *The Serenity Prayer*, 1934

Force and Flowe are the two primary ways of responding to the world that originally injured you and are also the two ways the world responds to you. Left- and right-brain orientations are two exactly op-

posite modes of adaptation children use in response to the emotional
injuries of childhood. Both modes involve different ways of denying
the Injured and Creative Selves as a means of trying to cope with them.
Starphades tend to live as the Injured Child, while Starphires tend to
deny its existence.

PERFECTIONISM

Starphires want to preserve the external world as a perfect representation of themselves. In theology perfectionism is the doctrine that
you can live without sin. In secular practice it is the belief that you
can survive without ever making mistakes. Those who think they are
imperfect endeavor to become perfect. Starphires strive to be mistake-
proof; they want to be what Milton called real stars, "living sapphires."

"Sapphire Stars," perfectionistic Starphires, tend to think there is
something uniquely wrong with them for not being able to accomplish the impossible quickly. Frightened casualties under the siege of
constant self-attacks, they expect omniscience and omnipotence of
themselves. "No mistakes and never failure," is their motto.

Two Starphire clients confided to each other in the waiting room.
"It's true, I'm a perfectionist," said one, "but I'm not really very good
at it." "Well," said the other jokingly, "then I'm a better perfectionist
than you are." Another perfectionist once told me, "Perfectionism
Flats is located on the wrong side of the *Career Star Map.*" She went
on to explain that in her opinion it should be nearer the Desert of
Isolation than the Gully of Guilt where it is.

Guilt is an underlying motivation for deviations from the center
path on both the circular and angular pathways but guilt is nearer the
surface of Starphades and buried more deeply in Starphires. The
map perhaps should read, "Gullies of Guilt," to reflect the true
amount of guilt felt by a Starphade. Because of perfectionism, this section on perfectionism was the hardest to write.

Perfectionism is found at all career levels, in both men and women.
Starphires are reluctant to regard perfectionism as a flaw because it
"looks good." Ironically, the underlying assumption of imperfection
is the mistake that gives rise to the need for perfection. Starphires wish
to represent themselves as polished and well-rounded while judging
themselves as blemished and jagged. The false assumption is an unrecognized "fault," which is self-inflicted and hidden from themselves
and others.

Perfectionism

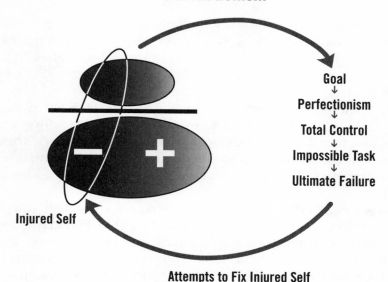

Goal
↓
Perfectionism
↓
Total Control
↓
Impossible Task
↓
Ultimate Failure

Injured Self

Attempts to Fix Injured Self

Diagram 8: Perfectionism is a Form of Self-hate

Perfectionism is a cover for perceived defectiveness of the self. It replaces hidden self-deflation with an attempted demonstration of greatness. If you unwittingly demean yourself, you will want to be exalted by others. Debased in their own mind, perfectionists are easily offended by what is regarded as others' curtness or rudeness. Arrogance is a pretense that hides self-abuse that is then blamed on others.

Perfectionism is also an attempt to conceal false defects that creates and exposes the exact opposite, true defects. As illustrated in Diagram 8, perfectionism aggravates the Injured Self and stimulates self-hate. Perfectionism is a way of competing with yourself and losing when you need not be in the race in the first place!

Judging yourself as someone who needs perfecting is the perfectionist's first mistake. Forgetting that the judgment was made is a second mistake. When you come to realize this you might say, "Damn, I'm failing again" and this is a third mistake. Accusing yourself of "three mistakes" makes the count four.

There is one mistake made over and over and all mistakes are just one size. Even the sum total of mistakes is still just one mistake. But counting every little mistake is nothing more than a way to avoid real change; it assures that you are always starting over, and never have to get where you say you are going.

Learning makes a perfectionist feel little and vulnerable since it means an imperfect lack of control. It is difficult for a Starphire to learn something new because he figures he should already have known! When learning is not facile, a Starphire says, "See there, I was right all along about not being capable."

Perfectionists try to overcome a − self by being a ✚ self in the external world. Efforts to appear perfect to others only reaffirm a presumption that the self is lacking. Perfectionism is a mental trick in which self-denigration poses as a protective service. Being "imperfect," however, is perfectly natural; self-denigration is not. Humans are God but in mortal form.

As you plan and try to control your image of perfection, you reinforce a view that something is wrong with yourself. You may then become angry at yourself for having a plan that does not work. And, if you do not make a plan, you believe you are not safely in control. Perhaps you are determined to make a plan that does not work, in order to reinforce the view of yourself as imperfect.

Starphires strive to organize and control the external environment with an expectation that it follow the law of their command. When this strategy works, the results are proof positive to the individual and others as witnesses that their flaws are imaginary, or at least adequately covered up. If this strategy falters, the ego is deflated and it confirms a sense of incompetence.

If perfectionism is a characteristic of your personality, look over the suggestions below and pick a few to do:

✿ Leave some task undone.
✿ Leave a mess messy.
✿ Dirty something clean.
✿ Waste some time and money.
✿ Give a gift unwrapped without a bow and card.
✿ Throw away all your extra boxes, wrapping paper, and ribbons.
✿ Wear nonmatching colors and outfits shamelessly.
✿ Break your routine habits irregularly.
✿ Forgive yourself habitually.
✿ Try not to take all these steps perfectly at once.
✿ Tolerate imperfections in this list and in this book.
✿ Accept imperfections and you are perfect.

RATIONAL DENIAL SYSTEM

The Rational Denial System relies on the use of the cognitive powers of the mind: concentration, logic, will, decision-making, and determination to govern conduct. The "rational" approach stresses purpose and attempts to organize actions and resources so that there can be no deviation from a central goal. Some of the more popular external goals are money, power, material objects, and fame. There is nothing wrong with goals per se, but if you focus on them to the exclusion of feelings, your approach is imbalanced.

If the purpose is achieved and the Starphire experiences progress and a sense of power, his self-esteem is usually bolstered. Because it is a denial system, he will not necessarily have an awareness of this personal motive. A diagram of the Rational Denial System is provided on page 152.

The Starphire thought system is future-oriented. As children Starphires claim that they will be happy when they become grown-ups. As adults, they successively assert that they will be happy when they are graduated, married, promoted, successful, wealthy, and retired.

When control fails to achieve the desired results, a Starphire knows only to repeatedly try harder, through the perseverance of Force. Rather than concluding that the method is flawed, he tries to regain stricter control over means and ends in order to produce the expected outcome. There always seems to be some rational explanation, such as insufficient effort, for why happiness is elusive in the present.

But the authentically logical approach would be to stop and look at why the approach failed. Instead, Starphires become locked into a cycle that can ultimately lead to physiological burnout and psychological meltdown. Lao-tzu also said, "To yield is to be preserved whole."

The Rational Denial System often works throughout childhood and early adulthood; Starphires often persist with the use of Force until changes outside of their control start to break down their mighty fortress of defenses. Births, aging, illness, separation, divorce, unemployment, and death are a few examples.

The collision with Force is depicted by the walls, boulders, blockades, and mountains on the right-hand side of the *Career Star Map*. Repeatedly hitting these the rugged individualist becomes a ragged individual. In a subsequent stage, in their early thirties, at an age corresponding to the beginning of middle age, maturing adults begin to recognize that something is awry in the Force field.

That is, because of repeated "failures" in work and/or love, Starphires may finally reevaluate their adaptive mode of functioning. "The only conquests that are permanent and leave no regrets are our conquests over ourselves," said Napoleon, even though he was not an exemplar of the principle in practice.

Rational Denial System

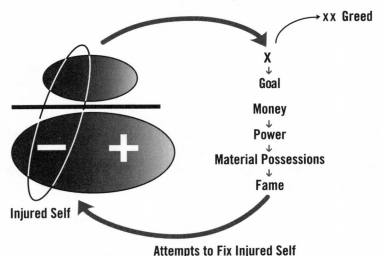

Diagram 9: The Rational Denial System

WORKAHOLISM

The ultimate outcome of the Rational Denial System is workaholism. For the workaholic constant work activity reinforces the bar to consciousness, prevents awareness of anxiety and depression in the Injured Self and constructs a facade of self-importance. Leisure time endangers a workaholic in much the same way that work threatens an addict and workaholics experience "withdrawal," physiological symptoms, and a panic reaction, when unable to bind their feelings by a structured activity.

Workaholics tend to treat their minds and bodies without compassion, as if they were machines and that needing to slow down, rest, sleep, or stop was a malfunction. They act as if they believe the German proverb, "When I rest I rust." In always trying to get ahead they usually wind up where they already were. Living by deadlines can be lethal (Diagram 10).

While concentrating on external goals protects you for a time from internal emotional pain, it sacrifices a connection with your Creative Self. Although not necessarily a conscious decision, you are trading off contact with good feelings in exchange for protection from bad ones. If you are cut off from the Creative Self, you have no guide to meaning in work or play and life may seem bland and boring.

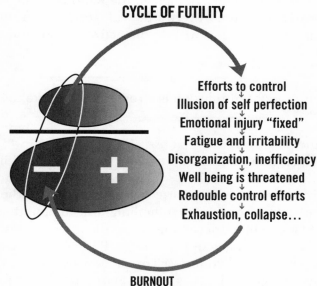

CYCLE OF FUTILITY

Efforts to control
↓
Illusion of self perfection
↓
Emotional injury "fixed"
↓
Fatigue and irritability
↓
Disorganization, inefficeincy
↓
Well being is threatened
↓
Redouble control efforts
↓
Exhaustion, collapse...

BURNOUT

Diagram 10: Cycle of Futility and Burnout

Workaholism is an extreme form of being left-brained or an "ultimate Starphire." Workaholics present an air of indifference to the world to mask disappointment with its perceived meaninglessness. Seeing a harsh world outside which mirrors the one they have created in their relationship with themselves, Starphires develop a tough, "calloused" exterior in order to endure. They follow the Tyrant Archetype and are a tyrannous rex to themselves and others.

In workaholism, goal-oriented activity becomes an obsession, the hidden motive being to prevent the intrusion of the experience of the Injured Self. Attempting to take care of an emotional injury by attending to business, trying to fix *things* as a way of repairing *feelings,* the rearrangement of physical objects to improve your mind, are behavioral non-sequitors.

The workaholic addresses external goals rather than internal changes and remains unaware that his efforts to accomplish something on the outside are misguided by inner feelings. As with a classical compulsion, his "dirty hands" can never be scrubbed clean since his work never washes his soul. A client once confided that he realized that labor-saving devices had been invented so that he could work harder, longer, and take fewer vacations.

In that neither internal nor external problems are actually ever solved, the underlying lack of logic in the Rational Denial System is evident. Workaholics report very little real satisfaction from their accomplishments, which means that the activity barely touches their inner self.

The thought of relaxing is stressful to a workaholic.

Since the purpose is to keep busy, almost any activity will serve the fetish for distractions. The intellect, under the influence of the injured mind, finds all tasks equivalent. Without a link between intelligence and creativity, tasks cannot be sorted and ranked, and in the void one experiences a desire only to do something instead of nothing.

At the first sign of job accomplishment the threat of unstructured time and the dread of inactivity reappear. Rather than a sense of satisfaction over a job well done, task completion arouses anxiety about not having enough to do. As a result, Starphires hoard projects to make sure they have more than enough and, as a result of overwork, their efforts become late and shoddy.

A rush of adrenaline and the urgency to block the anxiety emerge in place of relaxation and free time. Starphires' system of security is threatened and goal activity and efforts at control are doubled and tripled, further compounding the condition. Disorganization and inefficiency increasingly set in. Starphires hate this condition, but it persists until they are overdosed with work and burned out with exhaustion (Diagram 10).

BURNOUT

Burnout is the final phase of a stress reaction to work overload. It is a state of mental and physical exhaustion that results when work no longer serves as an emotional fix. If the issue literally is survival, work cannot be considered an addiction. Therefore, it is the motive for the work, not the quantity, that determines its nature.

Like most alcoholics, a lot of burned-out people deny that they are workaholics. Burnout, with its attendant feelings of depression and depletion, may be compared with the breakdown that inevitably occurs with chemical forms of dependency, but it is also a special state of mind.

True burnout takes the form of a mental "seizure" or "fit" similar to what occurs when a muscle cramps from overuse and fatigue. Prior to a full-scale work stoppage, there are usually minor periods, beginning ordinarily with weekends, when one is immobilized and unable to will oneself into action.

For example, a client once called me from her bed at home, paralyzed on a Monday morning, having worked all weekend as well as the week before. She was unable to get to work at the start of the work week, because for her the week's work had never ceased. Her own nervous system actually intervened to protect her from further self-abuse.

A workaholic needs a vacation from himself.

Workaholics are usually impelled to a greater work effort as soon as there is the slightest recovery and, as a result, they tend to ensure an eventual burnout. They misunderstand their needs and speed up when they need to rest. You can go on a work overload in an emergency, but if you make it a way of life, you will inevitably invite the crisis of burnout.

The burned-out mind, distressed by stress, becomes tense from the work overload and continues to tighten until it locks. The mental system on overload automatically shuts down in the same way muscles refuse to function when cramped or workers go out on strike. Trying to force more mental work under these circumstances only intensifies the reaction and tightens the shutdown.

When burnout occurs, the emotional part of the mind takes over and seizes the intellect to stop further thinking and acting. A built-in system of protection overrides the individual's determination to physically abuse himself further. An autonomous survival instinct prevents more serious and permanent stress reactions, such as brain strokes and heart attacks, as a result of the mismanagement of workloads and emotions.

CHART 6:
Flowe(r)ing

1. Rest and relax.
2. Be open, receptive, and cooperative.
3. Be patient, quiet, and still.
4. Suspend expectations, desires, and decisions.
5. Do not judge, censor, or criticize yourself.
6. Let go of rational controls and results.
7. There is nothing to do or change.
8. Let be and be.

Starphires engaged in the tedium of workaholism within the Rational Denial System can learn to flourish by immersion in Flowe. (See Chart 6: "Flowe" and practice "Flowering.") New knowledge appears in unexpected forms and therefore may not be recognizable at first. You will interfere with learning if you let lack of control bother you. The task is to unlearn control, or to learn to surrender to the natural process of Flowe. Try to master surrender and surrender mastery.

FLOWE

Water is the epitome of Flowe. It flows in different ways but water always flows. As sprinkles and torrents, it rains on earth and according to the shape of the landscape, forms puddles, pools and lakes. In streams and rivers, water rushes or meanders down mountains, hills, and valleys to the sea. It vaporizes as clouds and gushes out of the ground as fountains. Water loves to flow.

In its course water penetrates, spills over, and avoids fixed objects such as rocks, boulders, and dams: downward, onward, upward, around, and beyond. Even standing bodies of water circulate in the process of hydration. Evaporated by heat into the atmosphere, water comes full circle by condensing back into earthbound rain and repeating its rounds. Stagnant or cascading, water flows in unchanging circularity, returning to its origin in the vast ocean or great sky.

Life is like water and water is like life. In the long-distance journey, you may think you have a rational plan to follow a course to achieve your ambition. If the outcome is not in accord with your will, you may set up a barrier with angry disappointment. Your reaction reflects a conflict because it opposes a greater ecology. "We work, we scheme, we plan one way," wrote the French dramatist Beaumarchais. "Fate finishes it all off in another."

Let the Flowe be with you.

You establish an obstacle by believing your life should go one way, when you have been sent already along another channel. Your reaction impedes the natural Flowe and opposes a greater plan. Going with the Flowe involves giving up a conviction that your life-course is to follow your solitary plan. "Since we are driven by fate, let us yield to it," wrote Seneca, one of Nero's tutors.

At first, going with the Flowe may involve the awkward frustration of being put out of your element. If change is too abrupt, the waters can be choppy on the surface or with strong undercurrents beneath. Going with the Flowe may at first feel like being swept away but the water will settle your fears and doubts in time. Flowe refreshes your mind, which bubbles up with creative ideas. This idea is simple and true, not convoluted like a brain.

EXERCISE 10
STAR FLOWER

Writing with your nondominant hand is a simple introduction to the experience of going with the Flowe. Your dominant hand is the hand that is within the control of your will and ordinarily does what you ask of it. Your nondominant hand is usually not within your control. It acts as if it has a will of its own and rebels against efforts at manipulation.

If you are ambidextrous you may be ambivalent about the following exercise because you are already skilled at doing things two-handedly. But do you have bilateral symmetry mentally? If you are ambidextrous try an exercise that uses your mind either logically or creatively according to the weaker side revealed in your star-type assessment in Chapter 5.

Writing with your nondominant hand often evokes many old feelings that are disliked and forgotten, chief among them frustration, irritation, and helplessness. Students practicing this exercise often report that they feel like a child again and remember how they felt when they first learned to write. Others are struck by how painful it must be to have suffered an incapacitating disease or illness such as a stroke.

Appreciating the Flowe teaches us tolerance for the experience of not being in control. It takes patience to comprehend what you do not understand. Bearing frustration and helplessness are usually viewed as undesirable. But it is actually an achievement when learning to adapt to forces that are outside our control, forces such as the weather and the will of other people.

If you overcome the desire for control you cannot be disappointed by being powerless. The more you put up with the experience of feeling powerless, the easier it becomes to bear in reality. This is not to say that you capitulate or grovel in surrender. You appreciate when you are totally helpless against the magnitude of the opposition.

Es mano no es fuerza.
It's technique, not force.

With the Flowe you give up control over the outcome of events without feeling like a victim. Fighting the Flowe, like a salmon swimming upstream, instead of going with it, takes longer and only makes life harder to endure. Herodotus said, "Force has no place where there is need of skill." The idea is finesse in place of muscle.

Allow yourself to be in control of your inner world by not demanding that it give you the power to change the outer world, especially when this is not a realistic possibility. If you can learn to stand not having enough control you will eventually be able to tolerate feeling completely helpless, which actually gives you some control. The flexibility of this option is essential when something really is beyond your control. "The softest things in the world overcome the hardest things in the world," said Lao-tzu.

A very left-brained engineering professional once reported, after practicing this exercise a few times, that he had a dream in which he saw himself in neon swimming trunks ready to dive into a pool of water. He interpreted the dream to mean that, "If you dive in and go with the Flowe, the Flowe will glow with you, like neon trunks."

Learning to Flowe requires patience because natural and social forces are more powerful than you. Patience, however, is the very trait you need to acquire. Since you have no choice but to adapt, try to submerge yourself in the waters of unknown outcomes until you become buoyant and fluent in the stream that carries you along a course of life that is just right for you. Water has been everywhere, done everything, and knows all.

Dominant Hand:
Write a paragraph in your own words of your understanding of the concept of "Flowe." What is the essence of the idea? Writing this paragraph will give you the experience of being in control, especially if you know the answer.

_____
_____
_____

Nondominant Hand:
Now continue to spell out your understanding of the idea of Flowe but write this time with your nondominant hand. Provide at least one full paragraph in this way.

_____
_____
_____

Experiential Feelings:
Continue to write with your nondominant hand in the space below but now change the subject you are writing about and focus on the experience of your feelings. Note as you continue to write what it feels like to be writing with your nondominant hand. Allowing yourself to have this experience by actively doing this exercise is an achievement in itself.

_____
_____
_____
_____

Sleight of Hands

Following is an example of this exercise as written by a clever client, a banker by profession. You still can see traces of her not letting go of control in her thought that you have to work hard and practice every day rather than just letting go and being the star that you are. She tries to control surrender before she surrenders control. Is a change of hands the same as a change of mind?

This poem is written with my left hand
Because I'm trying to take a stand.
And show myself that I can grow
By doing something I don't know.
I'm trying hard to do it right
Although it really is a sight
But then again I'm almost through
So why don't I not continue?
Now the pencil's in my right hand
And I'm trying to understand
Why some things seem so hard to do
When the only thing is that they're new
You can't expect to get it right away
You have to practice it day by day!

STAR FLOWE:
Developing Self-Trust

If you have a wounded heart,
touch it as little as you would
an injured eye.

Pythagoras, 582–500 B.C.

CHILD ABUSE

Addiction in this chapter and workaholism in the previous chapter are two outcomes of extreme left- and right-brain lateralization. Right-brained Starphades usually have Injured Selves larger than Starphires, which explains why they often act more self-destructive and appear more "half-witted." Being an *extreme* Starphade is a sign that abuse was severe emotionally and possibly physical during childhood. The harsher the mistreatment, the greater the right-brain lateralization typically.

Left-brained individuals who are also injured in childhood on the other hand learn to focus their attention on learning and achievement and thereby gain some mastery over their emotions, behavior, and environment. In dealing with the world, Starphires rely almost exclusively on Force, which gives them a sense of well-being so long as it is effective. Starphades rely almost entirely on Flowe, which ultimately engenders a sense of helplessness and depression with no illusion of control if they turn to substances and addictions take over.

When the trauma to the child is early and severe, it occurs before logical functioning begins and it interferes with the acquisition of cognitive skills. As a result, the injury mars and scars thinking, usually for the rest of life, especially if there is no subsequent intervention from caring adults. Although the process is complicated, basically it is correct to say that the ability to be respectful of oneself is not acquired because there is no rational, consistent treatment by grown-ups.

Mistreatment does not mean you are worthless, although it is almost impossible for a child not to think so. Children define themselves by their experience; they know only to take mistreatment literally. They believe they are identified by the heaping criticism or praise bestowed by others. Even as an adult, it is extremely difficult to transcend a literal point of view and differentiate the self from the treatment received from others.

Usually the more hateful the mistreatment the worse you feel about yourself—just when you need to feel better so that you can cope with the mistreatment. There is no correlation between external treatment and internal self-worth except an imputed cause-and-effect connection children assume. To link the two is understandable for a child; to overcome this view is the challenge of adulthood. "That my love was not good enough means I was not good enough to be loved," is the way a client explained it to me.

As adults, formerly abused children have great difficulty in acquiring and retaining a lasting sense of their distinct basic goodness. They regard themselves as "primordially evil" and treat themselves with unconditional positive disregard. A deep-seated sense of presumptive guilt is the foundation of their thinking and behavior. Often they seek the approval and affection of others to palliate their incessant self-contempt.

Without the experience of having been loved it is almost impossible to learn to love yourself. Children raised by parents who are desperately insecure learn to be insecurely desperate. Treated badly, they come to believe they are "bad" and they actually feel bad as a result, emotionally and physically. Like the endless cycle of a feedback loop, their bad feelings in turn reinforce their poor self-concept, and their poor self-concept increases their bad feelings. They become to themselves like the authority who has tortured them.

Feeling badly often justifies more self-attacks and may be considered "punishment" for being a "worthless person." Over time, maltreatment is incorporated into their identity and personality and is taken literally as an appraisal of their self-worth. That is, the customary feeling of worthlessness becomes ingrained as a fixed state of mind.

=====
Adults abused as children often mistake their parents' limitations for their own and their children for their parents.
=====

The mistreatment is meaningless, originally and currently, when you are regarded positively in your self-perceptions. A client from an abusive family once told me frankly, "I don't fear failure, I'm accustomed to it." Based on experience, a right-brained person's self-relationship tends to be overwhelmingly negative. Another client remarked contemptuously about her mother, "For all she was, she did the best she could," which was a mirror of the daughter's self-regard.

Adults abused as children tend to think their mistreatment is deserved. How hard it is to overcome self-doubt when so little faith has been shown to you by so many others for so long. A student once wrote, "If love hurts, I am definitely loved."

Formerly abused children usually try harder and harder to be recognized as "good" by others. Their lack of success means to them that they are not good enough or have not tried hard enough. Consequently, they try harder yet again. Their insistence on receiving recognition for their efforts may be misinterpreted by others as an "unreasonable demand."

The original premise, "not good enough," is followed by the idea "I will never be accepted as okay." In striving to give, in order to receive, they become martyrish in relationships. Martyrs are left-brained about themselves but right-brained about others. That is, extreme Starphades are Martyrish to others but tyrannical to themselves and are depleted of the self-love they need.

Whereas left-brained Starphires tend to be more isolated and alone, a Starphade's relationship with others tends to be one of fusion, where distinctions are merged and blurred. The tendency to fuse makes right-brained people highly sensitive to the external world and their creative contribution often is to express their unique vision of it, whether as an artist, teacher, clergyman, or chef. Starphades are extremely sensitive and vulnerable to indifference and rejection, and the execution of their work is undermined. The vigilance with which they scrutinize and ruminate on how they are mistreated by others is a form of their own self-abuse. The guilt felt unconsciously shows up in the wrongs others do apparently to them so intentionally.

A gifted client from an abusive family background once concluded a counseling session saying, "I know that I have a sado-masochistic relationship with myself." Another complained, "My reputation with myself is awful."

Right-brained individuals as children are not afforded the option of learning as a means to relieve and compensate for the pain of their emotional injury. In their confusion they may lose the distinction between responsibilities and obsessions on the one hand and relaxation and distractions on the other. Their pain may be so great that learning is unable to overcome it, or they may lack the intellectual capacity necessary to make a leap forward developmentally, or both.

Almost certainly they lack role models who accomplished this developmental step in their own lives, probably because of their own ancestral wounds. Just as there are resilient children who adapt to mistreatment, there are vulnerable children who succumb to it. In turn, their injuries are passed on to their children, as they mistake their parents' limitations for their own and mistake their children for their parents.

THE IRRATIONAL DENIAL SYSTEM

The Irrational Denial System is an attempt to repair the Injured Self through reliance on a variety of substances and activities that stimulate physical rushes in the body and elevate your mood. Because of the connection between the brain and the body through the central nervous system, activities and chemicals that cause a physical rush bring about a temporary improvement in your sense of well-being.

The most obvious examples are the "medicinal" use of substances but there are nonchemical methods of stimulation that work just as effectively—and addictively. The excitement in the body takes attention away from the mental anguish, a diversion similar to the distraction that obsessive work provides for left-brained individuals. (Diagram 11, page 165, illustrates the process of the Irrational Denial System.) Chart 7, "Sources of Body Rushes," contains an incomplete list of common ways of obtaining physiological twinges. Each technique depends upon a pharmacologically induced psychophysiological reaction classified according to chemical source. In the first grouping, the chemical substances are ingested and therefore have a source external to the person.

Irrational Denial System

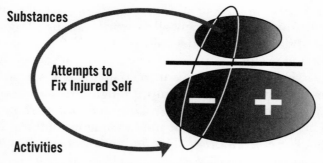

Diagram 11: The Irrational Denial System

CHART 7:
Sources of Body Rushes

SUBSTANCES   ACTIVITIES

❏ Alcohol   ❏ Exercising
❏ Drugs   ❏ Gambling
❏ Sugar   ❏ Sex
❏ Chocolate   ❏ Shopping
❏ Food   ❏ Arguing
❏ Tobacco   ❏ Fighting
❏ Caffeine   ❏ Romantic
❏   ❏ Physical
❏   ❏ Risk Taking/Death Defiance
❏   ❏ Sky Diving
                                    ❏ Bungee Cord Jumping
                                    ❏ Mountain Climbing
                                    ❏ Hang Gliding
                                    ❏ Speeding
                                    ❏ Crimes
                                    ❏ Violence
                                    ❏
                                    ❏

The second grouping is of a variety of activities that stimulate secretion of chemicals internally to cause the rush; adrenaline and endorphins, for example. The word endorphin in fact is a contraction of "endogenous morphine," in other words a painkilling and tranquilizing substance produced within the body.

Almost any prolonged physical activity can cause a body to rush: running, swimming, pumping iron, dancing, or spinning like a dervisher. In the nineteenth century religion-related body rushes, known as "the quickening," were evoked by ecstatic spiritual practices like prolonged chanting, singing, and talking in tongues. The body-engine can be revved more quickly and fully if the activity is dangerous and life threatening like diving, climbing, and racing.

Most of these activities are harmless when used in moderation. The problem arises when you employ them to repair a personal problem; they may work temporarily, but when the effect wears off you will find you need ever greater dosages to recapture the feeling. All the techniques have in common the quality of diminishing returns.

With substances you need to consume greater quantities for the same effect; with activities, the element of risk has to be increased continuously. Both lead ultimately to addiction if the motivation is psychological, an attempt to cure the mind by altering the body. Look over the two lists and check (✓) the boxes that apply to you.

The Injured Self of right-brained individuals presents itself to consciousness literally in the form of physical needs, such as cravings for food, drugs, and sugar. These spices to the body substantiate the fantasy that satisfaction exists in a physical form. Used habitually to repair an emotional injury the physical sensation of an orgasm, excitement, or a high are substitutes for developmental learning.

Instead of facing tasks on the left-brain side of life, compulsive shopping, chain smoking, and other short-term forms of hedonism blot out the pain of the right-brain. Multiple addictions are a measure of the extent of childhood abuse. As a rule, the graver the emotional injury, the greater the number and variety of addictive behaviors.

Addictions are obsessive attempts to be comforted by objects irrelevant to the real need. If comfort resided in the substances or activities, the obsession would not be insatiable. The arousal of the body as a way to calm the mind only whets the base appetites.

If physical cravings are not correctly perceived as symbolic of an "emotional hunger," the misunderstanding will lead to the ingestion of what is not needed. The calories, crystals, and powder—actually, the warm and exciting feelings stimulated by their use—are associated in our minds with the experience of being loved. And that is what we truly crave: self-love and love by others.

"We symbolically seek outside of ourselves qualities that we feel we are lacking within," wrote Eugene Pascal. Almost anything can serve as a misrepresentation of real needs. Chocolate, caffeine, and nicotine are but ersatz forms of your true self. Why pale and paltry witnesses to your fame? Why pick a surrogate for yourself when you can give up your bad habits and have "the real thing"?

You need to be aware that the injury is emotional and not physical. You must now become the parent who knows and cares for your real needs and cease treating yourself like the parentless child you once were, or thought you were. Without the intervention of intelligence and compassion, damaged feelings can only repeat an obsessive lie that sensate gratification brings psychic peace.

The basic needs of the wounded adult, listed in Chart 8, are much more expensive to purchase and maintain than the basic need of self-love of the Injured Child, which is freely available with a mere change in self-perception. But the latter is reluctantly given. Children of inner poverty are we even while we possess enormous material wealth.

ADDICTION

Individuals find many reasons for the psychological use of drugs. Addictions are obvious illustrations of the power of the Irrational Denial System. Alcoholism is the most common form of addiction.

Initially, alcohol stimulates the central nervous system causing a temporary physiological and a psychological high. Used in moderation, when there are no severe emotional problems, it can bring about relaxation and euphoria. Used to treat a psychological problem, however, alcohol causes complications because its long-term effects are physical and mental depression.

The Injured Self in an extremely right-brained person already exists in a depressed state, except during the throes and shock of reinjury. Mood goes up and down to the alternation of stimulation and depletion. A major reason to continue, or to return to a habit, is to

---

CHART 8:

Basic Needs of the Wounded Adult

1. a Prestigious Profession
2. a Fabulous Income
3. a Perfect Mate
4. an Ideal Child or Two
5. a Sizable Residential Estate
6. a Natural Setting with an Ocean View
7. a Cool Wine Cellar
8. Cellular Telephones
9. Luxury and Sports Cars
10. a Wise Stockbroker
11. a Gorgeous Personal Trainer
12. a Golden Retriever
13. a Golden Suntan (if applicable)
14. near a Golden Sunset
15. on a Golden Pond

---

ward off the onset of a depression through the provocation of rein-jury. Shocked and reshocked, the Injured Self is excited, alarmed, and engaged in an emergency response.

Eventually, the mind and body wear thin and shut down as an emergency becomes an ongoing crisis. Though the body reacts autonomously, some permanent damage may occur before a stop is fully engaged. Time between reinjuries becomes shorter and ultimately disappears and the Injured Self comes to exist in a perman-ent state of immobilized depletion known as "burnout" (Chapter 10).

The Rational and Irrational Denial Systems are both circular thought forms that lead to the dead end of burnout. They both cause a similar kind of breakdown in the nervous system, with common symptoms of exhaustion, depression, and motor paralysis.

As the Injured Self is aggravated, more of the emotionally damaged part of the mind takes over the intellect. Clouds of Depression and the Sea of Addictions, on the left-hand side of the *Career Star Map,* become common scenes. Accordingly, radically right-brained individuals often lack a capacity to comprehend the problem and support themselves financially.

Under these circumstances, the negative self is usually regarded as positive and vice versa. For example, the injured mind may tell you convincingly and urgently that what you really need is more of a substance or activity. The irrational mind claims the quantity was insufficient rather than the prescription. Addiction is "malchemy" instead of alchemy.

In the meantime, because the relief of a high itself is lost, suffering increases. The cycle goes about its infernal rounds as we are repeatedly drawn to self-destruct. The physical body defensively adjusts and becomes habituated to the abuse, requiring greater quantities for diminished results, and ultimately the degradation of psychological dependency.

The Irrational Denial System usually involves substances that alter body chemistry and create a physiological rush that brings about a temporary sense of well-being. This mode works for as long as a change in body state serves as a mood elevator. Because nerve endings have only short-term memory, the duration of irritation, satisfaction from synthetic sources is as transient as a hobo. Depleted by addictive overstimulation, even the physiological capacity ultimately gives way.

Addiction is an execution by self-hate carried out against the body.

The bodily approach is fundamentally self-defeating, because the injury is mental, not physical, imaginary, not organic, at least in origin. The problem remains unsolved because the remedy does not address the source. With enough substance and physical abuse there can eventually be permanent physiological damage; the culmination of a self-fulfilling prophecy. Addiction is like a slow execution by self-hate carried out against the body.

You may convince yourself that your disorder is "organic" because it has been around so long and is repetitive. This point of view justifies feeling more futile about recovery. Therefore, you may dismiss notions that your physical and psychological ailments are consequences of your abusive lifestyle and potentially within your control. Altering your body state to feel better emotionally is like fixing a fender when your automobile needs mechanical repairs.

If you are starving and, instead of eating, you read a book or watch television with the expectation of satisfaction, you are confused about the link between cause and effect. Just as you will remain hungry while reading or watching television, even though distracted, the Injured Self continues to feel deprived and depraved. It craves nourishment all the more, as bodily appetites arouse psychological greed.

The Injured Self cannot differentiate between injuries that are emotional and those that are physical. It responds to bodily stimulation, but as sensational arousal diminishes, you begin to experience a double loss: the temporary relief and the option of permanent well-being.

Once the chemical process is initiated, the losses, both physiological and psychological, are outside your control, and further your sense of powerlessness, a primary motivation in the addiction. The irrational solution always fails because it is a short-term treatment of the body for a long-term injury of the mind.

RESILIENCE

Self-esteem is a prerequisite to a successful Career Star quest. Chart 9, "Logical Activities," contains a list of techniques for right-brained Starphades to help build and maintain self-confidence. These rational activities are derived from crisis-intervention work with psychotherapy clients in clinical and private practice settings.

The idea is to exercise, not exorcise, the rational self. These tools are most effective when used in combination with one another rather than singly. Self-esteem cannot be improved solely by exercising, for example.

The techniques presented in Chart 9 are classified into categories of "cognition" and "action." The division is not always clear-cut; for example, journal writing has elements in both the cognitive and behavioral spheres. For this reason, journal writing is a very powerful tool. Keeping a journal is taken up again in Chapter 13, "Star Wheel." More logical activities are listed in Chapter 13, "Star Strategies." Most of the techniques in Chart 9 are self-explanatory, except perhaps "naming" the Injured and Creative Selves. "Naming" is a way of giving recognition to a person or an object; it also helps keep that person or object in your awareness, and that's what we want to do with the Injured and Creative Selves. In naming you want to try to capture some specific characteristic of each of your positive and negative sides. Therefore, a specific name is more effective than a generic name.

CHART 9:
Logical Activities

COGNITION

❑ Name Injured Self
❑ Name Creative Self
❑ Acquire Adaptive-
   Change Attitude
❑ Welcome Discomfort
❑ Contain Impulse to Quit
❑ Delay Gratification
❑ Hardest Step First
❑ Know First Step is Hardest
❑ Chant Goal to Focus
❑ Change Process is the Goal
❑ Remember Progress is Spiral
   (forward and backward)
❑
❑
❑

ACTION

❑ Physical Exercise
❑ Title and Start Journal
❑ List Expectations/Compare
   with Experience
❑ Record Practices and
   Achievements
❑ Give Self Credits and
   Take Rewards
❑ Pursue Active Objective
   Career Exercises
❑ Acquire Education
   and Skills
❑ Find Interests and Hobbies
❑ Attend Social Functions
❑ Cultivate Friendships
❑ Commit to a Support Group
❑ Use Faith Object of Choice
❑ Start Creative Project
❑ Volunteer for Community
   Service
❑ Build Personal Prayer/
   Meditative Space
❑ Pray/Meditate
❑ Attend Place of Worship
❑ Add to this List
❑
❑
❑

It is important to remember that the Injured Child Self often may be angry about its previous maltreatment and act like a "monster child" who wants to destroy you on account of it. I once heard a client remark to another, "Your Injured Child must be kicking and scream-ing!" On the positive side, the anger means that the Injured Child is still healthy enough to fight for decent treatment and has not suc-cumbed to depression and defeat.

Historically the Injured Child has been misunderstood and dis-credited, as the cast of characters in Chart 4, page 123, reveals. In re-ality the child is innocent and blameless and its destructiveness is totally illusory.

The mistake of equating the Injured Child with negativity reveals how readily we collude with our self-hate and lend it corroboration. Names clients of mine have given their Injured Children are Dog, Sneaky Billy, Pussy Hunter, Princess Perfect, Terrified Terry, Hell Cat, Baglady, Shamster, Cujo, Worthless Penny, and La Destructora. A name that expresses the essential goodness of the Injured Child is preferable.

Ironically, there is no corresponding set of positive names because people find it much more difficult to name the Gifted than the In-jured Self. Frequently by default, their own first name, or a diminu-tive, is given to the Gifted Child. This name then gets confused with the name of the real adult self. Try to find a distinct and unique name for your Gifted Self.

❈ EXERCISE 11
FOUR LITTLE STARS

To go with the Flowe means among other things to give up control and be less self-occupied. In this way you can take more of an inter-est in other people and activities. If you believe you are personally in distress, however, it is difficult to pay attention to anything but your-self. When you go with the Flowe you see others either thrashing about or floating in the stream of life. Jerry Garcia, of The Grateful Dead, said, "To forget yourself is to see everything."

Accordingly, think of someone who is close to you, someone you care about, a "significant other." Next, make a list in order of impor-tance of five things you know he or she wants. The gift can be an ob-ject, a service, or a task you accomplish for them. Try to make the gift something tangible rather than an abstraction such as love, trust, and honesty. Time, space, and practical help, for example, are more con-crete.

If you have any friends or relatives, you no doubt already know what they want from you by their repeated requests and complaints. If you are convinced that you do not know, or do not know exactly, you are welcome to interview the person as to what he or she wants.

The basic rule, however, is not to reveal that you have been put up to this as an assignment in the *Career Star System*. People may be curious or suspicious about your sudden interest in fulfilling their wishes. Particularly if you give gifts that are extravagant, you can stimulate paranoia. If this idea appeals to you, perhaps you do not feel like giving a gift at all. Are you feeling angry and vindictive toward your significant other? If so, give the gift of a conversation to try to resolve it.

Do not go overboard with the giving. You do not have to clean the whole house, wash all the laundry, dress up, prepare a delicious dinner, and invite all his or her relatives. Reassure your friend or family member that you just want to know him or her better and to understand what he wants from you.

For example, he may want your attention, as expressed by saying "hello" or "goodbye" whenever you arrive or leave home. Or there may be a desire for a conversation now and again. Perhaps you are asked to take out the trash regularly, or bring a cup of coffee in the morning, or provide a back rub in the evening. *Pick the least important gift and give it to your "target-subject" freely at least four times during the next week.*

Give the same little gift four times in one week. If you must change the gift, make it the same level of importance. The emphasis is on the giving, not the gift. Do not pick the most important gift, because it is probably impossible for you to give this one. Marriage, graduation, and finding employment, for example, are usually difficult orders to fill.

Act as if you are doing this because you know it is exactly what he or she wants and discount that it is out of the ordinary. Reassure him or her that you are not going to subsequently spring a secret major request of your own in exchange. Appear to truly enjoy giving the gift and try to mean it. If comments are made about overt or covert motives, reassure him or her that it is just part of your routine, that it's your love and that there will be no surprise announcements later on.

Try to give the gift with a spirit of generosity, without hesitation or reservation. A true gift is given unconditionally with no expectation of gratitude or exchange payment. Giving to receive is a business deal, not a present. Being resentful is not only ungenerous but a disguised form of retribution. Let control go and allow the recipient to do whatever she wishes with the gift, including disparaging you, devaluing it, and failing to be grateful. It is easier to be generous when you are not expecting anything in exchange.

The recipient can always change his or her mind later and reaccept the gift and become appreciative. If you behave angrily because of thanklessness, you establish a barrier that prevents a later change of mind. Give freely so the other person has space to change his or her mind. Until given without expectation of reciprocation the beneficial effects of the giving of the gift are delayed for both parties.

We are often in power struggles with people with whom we are close and we withhold affection and kindness because we believe it is withheld from us. If you are not able to enter into the spirit of this exercise, you are probably engaged in a power struggle.

In giving we are sending a message to ourselves that we are beyond the power struggle and have more than enough to share, which strengthens how we feel about ourselves as well as our bond with others. Our unconscious mind, unable to differentiate between ourselves and others, is grateful for the generosity that has been bestowed on ourselves, just as others are grateful to us for the gifts.

Further, what is requested of you to do may be some practical skill that you really need to learn, beyond being generous, such as cooking, sewing, or repairing things. You may be concerned that your "significant other" will become accustomed to your contributions and begin to regard them as their right and your regular duty. It is not hard for them to become accustomed to the gift because their desire for fulfillment is so great.

You may initially think that incurring an obligation like this is giving up power. Since the gift is also really to you, perhaps you will be struck with your own desire to receive some special treatment yourself. Perhaps you will become really generous and adopt the practice of nurturing yourself regularly through generosity to others. Be a hero for the day and feel delighted and overwhelmed by your goodness.

In the space provided, record each incident of giving. Try to go beyond saying "she freaked out" or "he thought it was cool." Describe what takes place between the two of you socially and emotionally and write it up. What did she or he do and say and what did you say and do? Discuss how the giving made you feel. Be giving about this information below.

Rationale for the Choice of Person:

_____

_____

_____

_____

_____

_____

Type of Relationship:

_____

_____

_____

_____

_____

Rank Order of Gifts (what the other party wants):

1. _____.
2. _____.
3. _____.
4. _____.
5. _____.

First Giving   Date:_____.

_____

_____

_____

_____

_____

_____

_____

Second Giving Date:_____.

_____
_____
_____
_____
_____
_____
_____
_____

Third Giving Date:_____.

_____
_____
_____
_____
_____
_____
_____

Fourth Giving Date:_____.

_____
_____
_____
_____
_____
_____
_____

STAR DREAMS:
Waking Up

I have therefore made it a rule to put dreams
on a plane with physiological fact.

C. G. Jung, *Modern Man in Search of a Soul*, 1933

PRINCIPLES

That the answer to your calling lies hidden within the unconscious
portion of your mind is the theme throughout this book. One way to
access your unconscious is through dreams. Freud called dreams the
"royal road" to the unconscious and he was a pioneer in dream interpretation. Other routes include meditation, visualization, guided-
visualization, hypnosis, and free association.

There are many definitive and contradictory ideas about the purpose and meaning of dreams. Historically dreams were revered as spiritual vision. This idea was replaced during the scientific and industrial
revolutions of the nineteenth century with the modern view that
dreams are just bizarre and incomprehensible imaginings. In the *Old
Testament* dreams are referred to as *"Visions of the Night."*

This chapter introduces the reader to the principles used in the
Career Star System to understand dreams. (Robert L. Van De Castle's,
Our Dreaming Mind, provides a comprehensive review of the entire

subject.) Both references encourage you to wake up to the importance of your dreams. Applying the principles will help you make sense of your dreams. Dreams are crucial because they offer a depiction and a solution to core life-problems.

Dreams help pinpoint the nature of our unconscious relationship with ourselves and are indispensable in this respect. A dream fragment can save hours of trying to identify the problem through verbal discussion in counseling. Dreams, correctly interpreted, are the single most important source of information for you to understand your basic self-conflict.

Star dreamer wake up!

Below are the "Rules of Dream Interpretation" in the *Career Star System*. These are guidelines derived from the practice of reading dreams and will help you understand the meaning of your night visions. None of these principles is original to the *Career Star System*— all have been stated previously by a variety of authors. But the combination of principles and the particular emphasis may be different or unique.

Starphires often claim not to dream at all, or at least not to remember their dreams. Starphades, on the other hand, report dream activity frequently. In fact, occasionally you must pinch Starphades to see if they are awake. Actually, Starphades do not dream more than Starphires, they just remember them more. A separation from feelings and their preoccupation with goals block Starphires' memory of dreams.

Starphires who join the *Career Star System* and practice their subjective exercises (Chapter 13), usually report a significant dream fragment within a matter of weeks which when interpreted, yields important information relevant to understanding their core life-problems. When you rest and dream you may think you are wasting your time but you are actually establishing the conditions for fixing your direction.

Because they communicate more with their feelings, Starphades usually have elaborate dreams and remember them in great detail. Dreams of Starphades are close to the surface of consciousness. In the narration of their dreams often they will "slide over" without a sense of contradiction into a depiction of some related or identical incident in reality. This means that the dream is about reality and also that reality is about the dream in the life of a Starphade. That is, the incident in reality is a product of the dream and vice versa.

Starphades are living their dream and dreaming their lives to such an extent that the difference is blurred. The connection between reality and dreaming is so transparent in light of their behavior that the meaning of their dreams sometimes requires little interpretation.

I have been entertained and awed by Starphades as they casually told me some fantastic account of a dream. On occasion, these descriptions may only need to be recorded and edited to become unique contributions to child or adult literature. More often than not, however, Starphades' self-doubt interferes at the creative point of follow-through. Rarely will they commit to paper what they saw in their dreams. It is unfortunately true that they do not believe in their gift, a tragic loss to them and to us.

Below is one example of a creative dream, *The Songbird and the Owl,* which a client wrote in the third person. It is a dream within a dream, written all in one sitting, a day later. The dreamer composed it as a gift to his son on the occasion of his second birthday a few days away.

However, you will see that the author did not finish the story. He broke off his writing, did not read nor give it to his child. It evokes vivid imagery. As you read, use the colors of your own imagination to visualize the pages of a prospective book. If you are talented in this respect, draw and finish writing the story.

The Songbird and the Owl

As dawn was breaking early one morning Daniel lay sleeping in his bed, covered with his blue blanket and surrounded by his friends, the stuffed animals who sleep with him every night. The sounds of whistling began to fill the air.

Tweet—tweet—tweet—tweet . . .

A bird was singing outside of Daniel's bedroom window. Daddy heard the sounds as he had many mornings before, when the sun began lighting up the sky. Something was a little different this time though; it was as if the bird was trying to tell Daddy something.

But Daniel was still deep asleep with Oso the Bear and the two ducks by his side.

The whistling continued and while little Daniel did not awake, Daddy could not fall back to sleep. And what about Mommy? Like Daniel she was fast asleep, although without any stuffed toys next to her and soon not even Daddy.

Promptly, the bird's sounds got the best of Daddy and he crawled out of bed, put on his thick gray robe, the one with the stripes that he wore every morning when he looked like a big bird himself. He slipped on his slippers and walked quietly over to Daniel's bedroom.

Daddy leaned over Daniel and gave him a kiss softly enough not to disturb him. The whistling was still going on, so Daddy tiptoed over to the window, drew open the white blinds that had been closed the night before, and looked out to see what was making the pretty sound. As the blinds slowly parted, Daddy could see a tiny, lime-green songbird perched on a tree branch.

Tweet—tweet—tweet went the bird.

Tweet—tweet—tweet . . .

The bird noticed Daddy peering through the window but did not fly away. It kept right on whistling.

Tweet—tweet—tweet

Tweet—tweet—tweet . . .

The cute bird craned its neck to look right at Daddy while it was whistling. Usually when a bird is surprised at seeing a person suddenly, it rapidly flies away, even when there is something between them like a window. But not this time. It was almost as if the song-bird was waiting for Daddy to come up to it.

Daddy stood at the window looking at the bird, listening to the beautiful melody that was being played. Daniel had a contented look on his face, as if he, too, were enjoying the rhapsody during his sleep.

As Daddy was peering out the window, he noticed a nestlike basket on the ground near the tree. The basket was made of twigs, leaves, and fine needles; things that were found in the area. How had the basket gotten there? It wasn't there yesterday. And its construction was so neat, someone must have taken great care to put it together . . .

At this point the author broke off the story where it remained unfinished. It stops exactly at the recognition of the content of the basket. What is in the basket and why is the author compelled to stop the narration? What about the owl mentioned in the title? Write below what you think Daddy's dream means.

First Interpretation:

_____

_____

_____

Jot down your speculation about the meaning of the "Story of Daddy and Daniel." Take a minute now before you read the principles of interpretation of the *Career Star System*. This will help you see by the end of the chapter how much you learned about understanding dreams. An interpretation is provided following the principles later in this chapter.

As a clue, think about what the songbird might be trying to say to Daddy. Is the songbird singing a message? Another hint that might help solve the riddle are the parallels: father is to child, tree is to bird as spirit is to a person. After you have read this chapter try a second interpretation and you will see the growth in your understanding of the meaning of dreams.

Here is another example. The fantasy below came to this client through a meditation instead of a dream. She found meditation an easy and effective way of receiving scenes and dialogues that were ongoing in the theater of her unconscious mind.

The Parrot and the Drapes

Once upon a time there was a family who had a parrot in their living room and every time someone came in the door the parrot said "hello." One day, the parrot stopped talking and no one could figure out why until the housekeeper came to work one day. She opened the drapes and then the parrot began talking again because the sun shone in the window.

Try your hand at deciphering the meaning of this visualization.

First Interpretation:

_____

_____

_____

_____

WE DREAM ALL THE TIME

Dreams parallel our conscious experience of life so we are dreaming all the time. We do not need to be asleep; we are dreaming also while we are awake. We do not realize that we are dreaming when we are awake because the dream is not powerful enough to break through consciousness to take attention away from our focus on reality. Unconscious dreams lack the force to impress or distract us while awake.

Our dreams influence our rational thinking and behavior even though we may not know it. If you study your dreams you will become more acquainted with their influence. As you learn more about your self through your dreams you can begin to facilitate or impede their realization in reality.

You are in a dream and a dream is in you while you are both awake and asleep. When you sleep, however, your logical mind rests and your creative mind continues to function. Dreams, like respiration, circulation, and digestion, are involuntary; they are outside your conscious control. As part of the unconscious mind, dreams function autonomously.

Parts of your dream may be remembered when you awaken, before your logical mind regains control. Dreams usually fade during the course of the day as the external world commands more rational attention. If you record your dream you are much more likely to remember it later in the day than if you do not. But some clients have had the strange experience of later reading about a dream they do not remember having!

Usually, the visual component of a dream is most prominent. Dreams are often like stories told in pictures. Emphasizing the visual allows us to describe dreams as "images," "scenes," and "visions." Or, if the sequence is more elaborate, we can call them "fantasies," "myths," or "stories." Painted visions of the night, dreams can help you see yourself more clearly in the daylight. People also have tastes, smells, sounds, physical sensations, and emotional feelings in their dreams.

Dreams are like plays or films about unconscious feelings and thoughts playing in the late-night theater of your mind. You are the star of the production but without an awareness that there is a projector, a screen, a director, and a script. Dreams are often remembered in fragments, just bits and pieces of the whole performance. That they are remembered at all is a clue that a particular scene is crucial to your self-understanding.

In dreams you are given important information about yourself that is otherwise hidden from your awareness. Since dreams are influenced by the senses of the physical body, you learn exactly how you feel. If interpreted correctly, you will have an understanding of how you feel about your current life situation in the present moment. This knowledge can be used to take charge and direct your life course. As you begin to know your true feelings more fully, you will be able to really live your dreams.

THE DREAM IS YOU

A major principle of dream interpretation is that the dream is you and you are the dream. Every person and every object in the dream is a reflection of the dreamer. For example, in *The Songbird and the Owl*, Daddy and Daniel, songbird and owl, are all aspects of the dreamer, as are Mommy, the house, the window, the basket and the stuffed toys.

People usually think dreams are about the people they see in the dream. If you dream about your mother, for instance, you might think the dream is about your relationship with your mother. Certainly when you think of your mother consciously, your thoughts are of her life, her personality, your relationship with her.

But dreams are not *logical*, about you and some external object, but *psychological*, about you and your relationship with yourself. They are "logical" only within the domain of the psyche. So a dream about your mother is really a message about the mother part of you, not your actual mother.

The dream makes use of your real mother to symbolize the mothering part of your self. The mother is in this case a symbol that represents your self-mother, because the mothering part of ourselves is usually modeled on our experience with our original caregiver.

Often, the dream is communicating the idea that you are mothering yourself in the present in some particular way. This may be the same way in which you were mothered in the past by your real mother, nevertheless, the dream is understood in the *Career Star System* to be about the self-mother instead of the real mother.

Dreams may be related to experiences you have had during the day or in the past but they are overtly and directly about you and particularly about your relationship to yourself in the present moment. Dreams are 100 percent narcissistic.

A dream is a portrait of the self-relationship.

A dream about your mother is a dream about a mothering part of you that is not conscious to you. Since dream work takes place largely in terms of images, the dream uses the image of the mother to represent an unseen mother part of you.

All the characters in the dream are symbols of the self because a dream is entirely a subjective dialogue between the conscious and unconscious division in you. A "mother dream" usually carries a message from the hidden self that hopes you will realize how you are treating yourself.

Symbolically, you may be present in someone else's dream because in reality they see in you what they do not see in themselves. Their dream presents your image to them as a reminder to them to see the "you part of them" that is denied. They do not recognize consciously that the you they see in reality is really also within them.

Their dream makes use of your image to show them a part of themselves that is unseen by them in real life. If the dream is interpreted to be about reality, this insightful self-understanding is missed. You need to know that the meaning is subjective, or the message will remain unconscious. Using this principle of interpretation, look inward instead of outward, because the dream is a mirror rather than a window.

Your dream offers you an opportunity to see within you what you see more readily in someone else. People are symbols of aspects of you in your dreams. You are symbolic of aspects of them in their dreams. Your dream tells you that you recognize these qualities in others so why not wake up and see them consciously within you?

To reiterate, everyone and everything in a dream is an aspect of the person doing the dreaming, not a representation of a real person nor objects in the outer world. The dream is a rendition of how you feel about you in your current life situation. Jung quoted the *Talmud* that, "The dream is its own interpretation."

A dream is like a dynamic self-portrait. If you understand this principle, that the dream is you and you are the dream, you will be able to see the relationship you have with yourself much more clearly. And if you understand your self-relationship you possess the key to career and human development.

TRANSPORT VEHICLES

When I first began working in the field of careers, I was struck by the number of clients who had dreams about automobiles. Puzzled, I gradually began to hypothesize that the meaning of "car" had to do with career.

In time I thought that perhaps the explanation went something like this: because a career carries you through life, your career is often represented as a vehicle of some sort. Of course, the real "transport vehicle" in the Star Quest is your mind and body. There are many ways of traveling, of course, so your career, or life-course, can turn up in dreams as almost any means of transportation but often it appears as an automobile.

The word "career" is derived from the Latin word for road and has the same root in Spanish: *carerra*. Notice that "car" is composed of the first three letters of career and that the word automobile also suggests self-mobility. Careers can also be symbolized in dreams in more grounded ways like walking and running. If you are not taking much action on your Career Star, it may be depicted as a parked car.

Here is an example.

A middle-aged flight attendant, dissatisfied with her work, had been unable to decide on an alternative career for many years. Gloria felt hopeless, afraid that she had procrastinated too long, and in the meantime she had completely burned out. She reported two recurring dreams.

In Gloria's first dream she saw herself jumping out of an airliner in midflight. This seemed to indicate a desire to "bail out" of her flight attendant career; even though she had not found an alternative, she could just take the plunge and quit her job, and then when she recovered from her burnout maybe she would be able to find more meaningful work. But giving up steady income, seniority, benefits, and the security of working for a major airline seemed risky, dangerous, and perhaps even fatal.

In her second dream Gloria's car stalled at an intersection. In other words, she was at a crossroads and having difficulty making a decision. While she waited in her car at the intersection, several shadowy men in a car behind her begin to honk, bump, and push her forward into the traffic against her will. These men, who represent the logical side in the background of her mind, are forcing her to take some action.

That is, back on the ground Gloria is still stuck, fearful at the prospect of taking another wrong road but forced to move forward by the logical side of her mind that just keeps urging and pushing her uncaringly onward. Up in the air she jumps with great fear and at risk of being killed. These are the two sides of her; one extreme wants to wait no longer and leap while the other extreme wants to park and wait some more. ("Polar Stars" Chapter 6, discusses cases that alternate between extremes.)

Reason without compassion can be cruel.

The second dream perhaps reflects how Gloria felt about making no decisions and taking no risks in changing career direction, namely, stuck, paralyzed. It was a terrible feeling. Now well into midlife, she was beginning to panic and was trying to force herself to bail out of her flight attendant position and make a new choice even though she still was unsure about what meaningful choice to make.

As we have discussed, giving yourself a deadline to choose a new career is risky because without an inner source of guidance it is very likely that you will simply repeat previous mistakes. My proposal to Gloria was that she take a moderate course, a compromise between the two extreme actions. That is, that she not quit (bail out of) her present position nor make an arbitrary decision based solely on logic.

A middle way would be for her to continue her employment and initiate inner work to help locate her Career Star and find her proper course. Not only would it prepare her for a successful transition, but just knowing she was doing something productive would also help soothe her frazzled feelings.

Here is a second example. Jennifer, a student, had recently decided to buckle down, give up extracurricular activities, and devote herself to her studies and future. She was trying to "reform" by quitting her social life entirely. She dreamt she was driving a big truck in circles, sometimes injuring people and animals who scattered out of her way and at other times flying out the window herself.

This dream perhaps shows how she really felt about making the decision to get control of her life by relying exclusively on external goals and logical means. In her head she thought this was the right decision, and it was reinforced by her family and teachers. But in her dream it was clear that she felt as if she was just going in circles, causing chaos, hurting herself and others, and getting nowhere fast.

This is what she had been afraid would happen in reality if she did not get more strict with herself. But ironically, it was happening precisely because she was too strict. Her true feelings about her decision to reform were unconscious. Because she thought that she was being "bad" she thought she had to deny her true feelings in order to be logical and get ahead in life. She really felt, but was unaware that she felt, that the decision to develop herself by being only rational was hurtful.

This is suggested by the number and variety of frightened animals and flying herself out the window, a symbol of vision. Her decision really put her in mad circles communicating that reason untempered by compassion is rude and rough. She felt run over by her own decision and thrown out by her own logical self-disregard. Jennifer's dream helped her to understand more clearly how decisions without tender mercies for her own feelings left her with no true reference point for her life course.

Here is another automobile dream reported by a young man analyzed by Jung:

> My father is driving away from the house in his new car. He drives very clumsily, and I get very excited about his apparent stupidity. He goes this way and that, forward and backward, repeatedly getting the car into a tight place. Finally he runs into a wall and badly damages the car. I shout at him in a perfect rage, telling him he ought to behave himself. My father only laughs, and then I see that he is dead drunk.

Following the principle outlined above, you can guess that this dream is about the young man's relationship with himself, not about his actual relationship with his father, who Jung says was not at all like the one in the dream.

He appears to be extremely angry with the father part of himself because he has lost control, gets him into difficult places, and damages his car. Just as the mother in our dreams tends to represent our nurturing side, the father in dreams often represents our logical or rational side. Thus, this young man seems to be attacking himself for having feelings that interfere with control over his life direction.

Like Jennifer, he is furious that his reliance on strict logic yields illogical outcomes—as if it is perfectly logical not to have feelings. His emotions, however, are apparently so strong that the father side of himself appears completely overwhelmed, disorganized, and impaired by the decision, suggested by the incompetent driving and being drunk.

This interpretation suggests there is an unconscious struggle in reaction to his attempts to be conscious only in a logical way. The young man is apparently enraged with himself, and completely illogical, for not being able to dispense with the emotional side of his personality. Fortunately, he is not in control of his unconscious, which keeps sending him communications about the importance of feelings even though he disregards them as being irrational.

Here is one final car dream transcribed from a career counseling session with a male architect in his early thirties.

> **SD:** I was driving in a small car in a parking lot. I was going around in circles. There was a woman in another small car following me. When I would speed up there would be a larger gap between us. Or, she would slow down a little bit and there would be a bigger gap between us. The space between us widened and closed up.
>
> **JS:** Do you have an interpretation?
>
> **SD:** It is some part of me that I'm getting closer to realizing. Maybe I'm not constantly aware of it so it gets farther away and at some point I come close to it.
>
> **JS:** What were your feelings in the dream?
>
> **SD:** Curiosity and also some uneasiness. Wondering, what is this car doing following me? Why am I going around in a circle. A frustrated feeling because I kept driving around slowing and speeding up and I wasn't getting anywhere and she kept following me.
>
> **JS:** The woman represents the creative side of you. She speeds up to try to get you to come closer to her by slowing down your logical, circular left-brain ways. She is doing what she can to try

to get your attention and attract you to her but you are in control of the relationship with your conscious intentions.

She can't do anything but try to stick with you and wait for you to relax your decision about going ahead and appreciate that she is there waiting to connect. She also slows down to try to entice your interest. Since you are in a parking lot you may decide to park, which would give her an opportunity to park beside you. It's true that you've been thinking about letting yourself slow down.

I am not saying that you must dream about transport vehicles in order to be dreaming about your career or that automobiles have no other possible meaning in dreams. The point is simply that people who are working on career discovery and development often do dream about transportation because it is symbolic of the journey of the career quest.

The symbolism of the "career car" or "transport vehicle" may seem more valid in southern California where we tend to think of automobiles as extensions of our personalities. There is no comparative data to know whether this symbolism is true for other parts of the country or elsewhere in the world where they have no cars. In any case, you can follow your Career Star in a career car or by hiking, canoeing, taxiing, taking a camel, an airplane, or any other way you dream.

Exercise 12: Dream Journal

In Chapter 2 you were encouraged to start a *Dream Journal* from the back to the front of your *Career Star Notebook*. Do this now if you have not already done so. Put a name of your own invention at the top of the last page of your notebook (now the first page of your *Dream Journal*). If you cannot think of a unique name just use "Dream Journal," but actually write it down.

It is important to write down your dreams as soon after they occur as possible. You will not be able to prevent their disappearance but your effort will usually help with retention. When you go to sleep you can ask to have more cooperation with yourself to remember your dreams. A pencil and paper, or a voice-activated tape recorder placed on your night table will indicate that you are sincere about the request. Also, practice the Starphire exercises in this manual, or begin any kind of creative endeavor, and dream activity will be stimulated.

Recording your dreams does involve waking up in the middle of the night to write them down. If you tell yourself at night that you will write your dreams down in the morning when you wake up, you may be fooling yourself into getting more sleep. Rest assured that you are going to lose some sleep over the project of recording and analyzing your dreams. The results are usually worth the effort, however, and it is less sleep than you will lose in the long run if you do not wake up to the importance of your dreams.

1. As soon after the dream as possible write it down with all the detail you can muster and in the sequence it occurred. Make a note of where there are lapses in your recollection.

2. Record the feelings you had in the dream and now that you are awake.

3. Just as you might state the theme of a play or a film, try to interpret your dream. Keep in mind the basic principle that everything and everyone are aspects of you. Therefore, the dream is about your relationship with yourself. So, what is the story?

4. Write down any speculations or associations you may have to the dream.

5. Note any themes in your dreams that parallel events in your waking life.

6. Ask others to tell you what they think your dream may mean. If necessary teach them the *Career Star System* principle that the dream is a manifestation of your self relationship. Then, ask them again to give you an interpretation. Others often have insights about our dreams that we find difficult to see and vice versa.

7. Remember, as with all learning, your ability to record and interpret your dreams will improve with practice over time.

8. Now write down your second interpretation of *The Songbird and the Owl* and *The Parrot and the Drapes* based on the principles of interpretation we have covered. Do not read the interpretations below until you have done so.

INTERPRETATIONS

The Songbird and the Owl: Waking up to the dream in the dream is analogous to waking up to your dreams in life. The meaning is contained in the whole of the dream not just its discreet elements. The dream is about the dreamer waking up to the existence of his real creativity. The songbird and the child are symbolic of artistic aspects of the dreamer about which he is sleepily unaware.

"Daddy," wakes up in the dream to a songbird singing in his dream. He says that he knows the singing has happened many times before but this morning it is a "little different." He senses that the bird wants him "to come up to it." The bird must have a meaning to Daddy since he is the only one in the dream reacting to it. The bird has a message for him to wake up to his own dormant creativity. All that happy whistling is an attempt to awaken Daddy to the beautiful vision of his ability.

Classically, birds are spiritual symbols, common in literature and folklore around the world. For instance, the dove descending from heaven in Christianity refers to the arrival of the holy spirit. The song-bird therefore represents the spiritual part of Daddy trying to wake him to his real creative ability. His creativity sleeps in his unconscious mind the way his wife and child lie asleep in the house in his dream.

Within Daddy are the creative child and mommy parts that he has forgotten because of his worldly preoccupations. The bird attracts him to the window of his inner house and shows him that there is caring there—represented by the careful construction of the basket—and knowledge—represented by the owl. "How did it get there?" is really a question about the origin of his creativity. The realistic lime green color of the bird communicates that Daddy's artistic ability is not just fanciful.

Through his son Daniel in real life, Daddy is connected to toys and play. But Daddy does not realize that the dream tries to communicate what is also true within him. The dream tells the story of the rela-tionship between the creative child and the rational adult in Daddy's mind. The songbird outside the house, however, suggests that Daddy considers creativity to be beyond him.

Daddy says he is surprised that the songbird is not afraid of him peering through the window. But, of course, Daddy's spirit is not afraid of Daddy. It is really Daddy who is afraid of his creative spirit. Daddy usually protects himself by being the busy preoccupied adult who keeps the creative child and feminine parts of himself asleep.

The basket in the dream represents the importance of conscious recognition of this Creative Self. "The owl is in the basket," Daddy later told me. An owl, common symbol of wisdom, is also suggested by the word kn-*owl*-edge. Can Daddy hold the truth in his mind in the same way the basket holds the owl? Thoughtfully, the father minds his child, the basket holds the owl, and the holy spirit contains a per-son. This knowledge is hidden in the basket of the mind.

The owl who never shows up in the story represents the knowledge that never comes to stay in Daddy's consciousness. While Daddy wakes up to his dream in the dream, he did not wake up to the knowledge contained in the dream in his real life. His ability to write this story did not convince him either. If he truly believed in his creative ability he would awaken and know the dream is true and that he genuinely is an artist.

The Parrot and the Drapes: This visualization has essentially the same message as the dream above but with some minor differences. All the action takes place within the house (mind) and the image of a parrot is perhaps more sociable and playful than the image of the songbird, which is more aesthetic.

Houses and buildings of all kinds in dreams usually represent the structure of the mind. The "housekeeper" is suggestive of the disciplined part that organizes a person's mind. This dream, therefore, seems to suggest that without a thoughtful housekeeper in the mind, the friendly, outgoing, talkative, social, fun-loving part of the self (the parrot) shuts up. The dreamer can choose to let this knowledge (sunlight) stream into her mind (house), by opening her eyes (drapes), to escape dark confinement and restore spontaneous aliveness.

Two years later, on the eve of his son's fourth birthday, the author of *The Songbird and the Owl* finished the story and read it to a gathering of children and parents the next day. As a perfectionistic Starphire, he had stopped short of completion to protect it from his own scrutiny as a finished product. The author had continued counseling over this period and was often urged to render the conclusion. He used the deadline of yet another birthday to force his hand to spell out what he had originally seen in the dream:

> Daddy was so curious about this basket that he went outside to get a closer look. Approaching it, he saw that something was inside. Stepping softly toward the basket he could see what appeared to be an animal curled up inside. Then, ever so slowly the creature began to stir and Daddy could see that it was an owl. A brown owl with white markings. The owl unfurled its wings as it gradually arose from the basket.
>
> Daddy stopped in his tracks to watch the great owl emerge from the basket. Awakening from hibernation the owl's eyes focused on his surroundings and cocked his head to make out Daddy's figure. Standing up in the basket and extending his wings, the owl took off into the air, not very high, only slightly higher than

Daddy. It swooped around the backyard, first in one direction and then in another. Daddy followed the bird's flight with smooth turns of his head.

The owl flew gracefully back and forth, passing just over Daddy's head. Whoosh! Whoosh! Daddy felt the breeze from the flapping of the bird's wings. And as the owl continued to glide through the air, Daddy felt just like the bird. The feeling of awakening turned into caution, which gave way to curiosity and finally to excitement. The owl confidently swooped through the air and Daddy too felt a sense of flight, the feeling one gets when beginning a new and exciting journey.

Though this story ends on an upbeat note, suggesting that Daddy was about to embark on an artistic pilgrimage to make creative work a part of his life based on his knowledge of faith, he did not come to really believe in his talent nor to act on it even after he had further proof in the completion and in the meaning of this story. The Songbird is still singing and the Owl is still hiding in the basket while Daddy's creativity is still sleeping.

STAR STRATEGIES:
Taking Action

Though my soul may set in darkness,
It will rise in perfect light;
I have loved the stars too fondly
To be fearful of the night.

Unknown

CAREER STAR WHEEL

In this chapter we introduce the Career Star Wheel, a model of how to get started on the path of your Career Star. The purpose of the Career Star Wheel is to help you actually begin the career discovery and development process by practicing exercises relevant to the assessment of your star type. The appropriate kind of action will get the wheel moving and ascending your Career Star.

There are two basic Career Star Strategies depending upon whether you are a right-brained Starphade or a left-brained Starphire. For your Career Star to rise and shine it is important to function on both hemispheres. You need a "right-brain" to communicate a calling and a "left-brain" to devise a plan of action. Strengthen intuition or logic, whichever is weaker; the former to discover and the latter to develop your career. If you are a mixed star, both types of strategies are recommended.

Starphires, who control their emotions, need to practice insight meditations and inner work of all kinds. Activating your inward faculties will open the channel of intuition and connect you with your Creative Self. Starphades, on the other hand, who tend not to control their emotions, need to practice logical activities to bolster their rational capacities to advance their calling.

Starphires tend to think and act more than they sense and feel and Starphades feel and sense more than they think and act. The basic split between Starphires and Starphades is illustrated in Diagram 12. For Starphades feelings interfere with thinking and for Starphires thinking interferes with feelings. Each star type finds it more difficult to do what comes naturally to the other type and each is biased against half the spectrum of the Career Star Wheel.

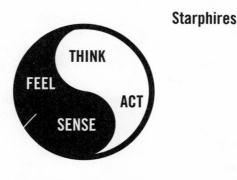

Diagram 12: Starphire/Starphade Split

Starphades typically oppose logical career activities and Starphires eschew creative impulses. Starphires usually love to work and hate relaxation. Starphades tend to hate work and love relaxation. Starphades would rather relax and "thank God it's Friday." Starphires prefer to work and "thank God it's Monday." Each type is cursed by wanting more of what is already possessed in excess. Your potentials are enhanced by exercising the less dominant side, however, and success is achieved through flexibility and balance.

The Career Star Wheel is illustrated in Diagram 13. Notice the hub of the wheel is split between the thinking and acting preferences of the Starphire and the sensing and feeling proclivities of the Starphade. For development to occur each star type must become acquainted with the other dimension of the wheel. Therefore,

Starphires are to explore, experience, and observe sensing and feeling, and Starphades to describe, reflect on, and conceptualize action. Chapter 14, "Star Dawn," contains subjective exercises for Starphires and objective exercises for Starphades.

Refer to the diagram again and this time pay special attention to the outer circle of the wheel. You will see it is divided into two sets of three activities, as follows:

Exploration—Experience—Observation
Description—Reflection—Conception

The first three activities, "Exploration," "Experience," and "Observation" are experiential in nature while the second three, "Description," "Reflection," and "Conception" involve abstract thinking. Starphires will work the behavioral half of the wheel to become familiar with inner feelings and creative urges. Starphades will work the thinking side to implement logical plans to actually promote their art in the real world. The first three activities take action without concern for results while the other three are evaluative and involve journal writing as a way of gaining greater conceptual understanding.

Notice the sequence of all six areas in relation to one another. That is, at this point just take step 1, "Exploration," and review the wheel. Do not expect yourself to figure out how the whole wheel turns, which is the equivalent to an instantaneous accomplishment of step 6, "Conception." You will get there but not by leaping over the middle ground.

Below we will discuss each of these six areas of acting and thinking before looking at their application with the wheel. The Career Star Wheel is more reliable than roulette and less complicated than the zodiac. So, be patient with yourself as you learn how to make the wheel spin and find your fortune.

Exploration and Experience:
Again, we want Starphires and Starphades to do the opposite: sensing and feeling for Starphires and logical thinking and acting for Starphades. Exploration is an initial phase of any searching when you suspend any desire or expectation of finding a result. Your focus is placed instead on following the steps that allow you to take in as much data as possible. In the beginning you concentrate just on absorbing all the information with sense perceptions, in this case,

the inner world for Starphires and the outer world for Starphades.

In order to explore, you have to face the fear of the unknown and tolerate, even appreciate, being lost. If you try to control the outcome you already have obscured your Career Star. Optimally, exploration is the procedure for getting lost in order to find your way. True research is totally nongoal oriented except in a general sense to find the truth.

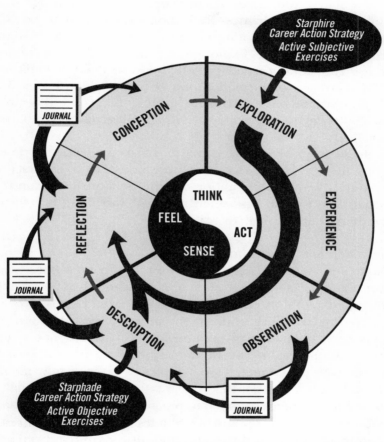

Diagram 13: Career Star Wheel

In pure exploration there are no mistakes because each "misstep" is a part of the procedure of discovery. When you think you are "wandering" you are actually engaging in an essential part of the trip. The early stages of research are investigations in an unplanned way. "Exploration" is the active, initiative side, while "experience" is the passive and receptive side of the first phase of learning about senses and feelings (Starphires) and logical thoughts and actions (Starphades).

The exploration is registered consciously and unconsciously while the mass of sensory impressions are being input. At this point you want as much data as possible. Therefore, suspend all conceptions and preconceptions and open all your senses to the experience. Do not judge that any idea, feeling, or insight is trivial or insignificant. Try not to organize or interpret the meaning of any image. Conceptual steps follow exploratory steps. It is premature now to draw conclusions.

Also, do not be concerned with whether you will remember the important discoveries of the exploration. Worry also interferes with discovery by blocking out experience. Just trust that you will be able to recall all that you need to know so you can allow yourself to have the experience.

In the next phase you are going to be asked to record a description of your experience in written observations. So, in this first phase allow yourself sensory exploration of either left- or right-brain activities according to your assessment. Be thankful there is a stage in where there is no thinking or writing.

Observation and Description:
In Observation and Description you enter the second phase of career discovery and development by first observing and then describing in words your exploratory experience. You write your experience down in your journal from beginning to end in sequence with as much detail as possible on the same day if possible. (Do not take notes during the observation because this will be a distraction.) At first you may think that your experience is too complex to describe in writing.

Our education is often theoretical rather than experiential. Accordingly, we are unaccustomed to practice-based methods of learning. You may also think you will not remember the salient details. Keep in mind, however, that the important lessons return voluntarily to consciousness even though at first you may not recall them easily. Also, your facility with description improves considerably as you practice this technique.

After you have written several depictions of your experience you will begin to notice that the same issues show up time and again. With a sufficient number of observations these basic patterns will become obvious. When this happens it amounts to a conceptual leap in your understanding, a topic covered in the third phase below.

When the patterns emerge you will know that you have had sufficient experience; and you will have had sufficient experience when patterns emerge. The identifications of patterns comes naturally and unexpectedly to mind of their own accord. You do not make or create the patterns.

That is, the patterns will be presented to you as a result of the synthesizing function of your unconscious mind that is operating in your own interest and outside your control. When the patterns come to impress you with their consistency, write them down in a separate section of your journal. That is, reserve a special section just for noting "identifications of patterns" through experiential exploration.

Again, do not worry if you do not see common patterns right away. If you are in a hurry to obtain results, you are trying to exercise control over the outcome instead of letting the news come in naturally. That will only interfere with the acquisition of knowledge. The insights about patterns are yielded up to consciousness when there has been sufficient time, relaxation, and self-trust to allow the experience to be absorbed, synthesized and interpreted.

Reflection and Conception

In moving from observations and descriptions to reflections and conceptions, you are going from the particulars of the experience to a general pattern or "theory." Another way of saying this is that you are learning to practice inductive, as opposed to deductive, reasoning. You are trying to arrive at general theoretical understandings based on the repetition of a particular set of observations as outlined above.

Reflection is exploration at a mental level and resembles exploration at a behavioral level. You now allow yourself to move among the descriptions and observations in your mind to see what is discovered. You mull over the issues that float to the surface of consciousness. You may worry that you are wasting time again but reflection is necessary, because processing information yields understanding in the form of new concepts.

Concepts are the summary of all the raw data formed into an abstract principle, usually concisely identifiable in a name or phrase. For example, "Follow Your Career Star" is the name for the concept that summarizes all the descriptive details of this book. "Career Star

Wheel" is the name of the concept described in this section. Concepts are complex and have many aspects, the way gems have facets and stars have rays.

Usually concepts leap out of reflections in the same way that observations jump out of explorations. There must be sufficient time and adequate relaxation, however, for the unconscious to decipher the meaning and present it to consciousness. Concepts are a quantum leap above description because they sumarize a mass of material into a concise idea that can be named, remembered, and applied. The *Career Star Map* is a pictorial conception of the five major life-paths.

When concepts emerge record them in your journal. Try not to judge their quality. Keep in mind that you are writing a draft or sketch, not a final declaration on the subject. The concept will evolve as you understand it more fully and the final version will come forth over time.

ACCELERATION

The diagram of the Career Star Wheel is not able to show progression. As the arrows around the circle of the wheel indicate, the outer six areas are linked. Concluding one area leads to the unfolding of another. That is, the next stage begins to appear out of the completion of the previous stage in an evolutionary way. You need only focus on one stage at a time and trust that the subsequent stage will emerge as you are ready for a transition.

The links or interconnections between stages also occur within the inner circle. That is, thought leads to action and action leads to sensation, which impinges on feeling and eventually gives way to new thoughts. Further, working on the outer circle will move the inner circle and working on the inner circle will rotate the outer ring. Diagram 14, "The Dynamic Career Star Wheel," illustrates the idea of the progression of the whole wheel.

Diagram 14: Dynamic Career Star Wheel

If Starphires practice sensing and feeling exercises, their thoughts and actions will be influenced by experience. These thoughts and actions in turn will modify their sensations and emotions, and stimulate new thoughts and actions and continue the rotation of the developmental wheel. The same interactive process is valid for the outer circle of the wheel. Forward movement leads to new conceptions for Starphades and new sensual experiences for Starphires.

INTEGRATION

In the previous chapters you have learned to understand the nature of the left- and right-brain division of the mind, performed a self-assessment, practiced a variety of useful and creative exercises, and accumulated much technical psychological information. These activities have been preparation for arrival at the present destination, Star Strategies. The wheel condenses all the previous principles into an integrated whole.

Caution: Thinking Area.

The Career Star Wheel is the platform for the action component of the *Career Star System.* There are two action strategies, one for Starphires and one for Starphades. Each star type practices the capacities of the opposite type to strengthen their weaker side and become more balanced. Practice is the impetus that overcomes the inertia of the Career Star Wheel. As the wheel begins to move, perhaps undetectably at first, your star ascends. Trust that both are in motion even though you may think not.

The next chapter provides a rational plan of *active objective exercises* for Starphades to become more logically minded. Starphires, on the other hand, are given an experiential plan of *active subjective exercises* to acquaint them with their senses and feelings and activate their intuitive potential. Once knowledge of a calling is secured, a goal-oriented Starphire will also need a logical plan of career development, the same as a Starphade.

For left-brained Starphires the purpose of the exercises is to give up rational control and to put up with the awkwardness of exploration. The insecurity of not knowing the absolute right step, and the ultimate outcome, are the challenge. Permission to explore lets happen whatever happens with tolerance for not being in charge of knowing and achieving.

When you curtail the hurry of life, abandon the drive to organize all its chaotic elements, and trust in the moment, something new and exciting begins to happen in your mind. An urge to play or create surfaces, two forms of flowering. There are many different types of play, some competitive where the objective is to score and win, like board games and sports, but pure play is a joyful fun, an end in itself.

For Starphires, the objective is subjective (Exercise 13A: "Sensual Meditation") and for Starphades the objective is objective (Exercise 13B: "Action Plans for Employee and Entrepreneurs"). Mastering a rational plan to apply Force is to the Sharphade what bathing in the Flowe is to the Starphire. Starphires need a step-by-step plan to discover, and both Starphires and Starphades need a step-by-step plan to develop, their calling.

For right-brained Starphades the purpose of the exercises is to take rational control over their career choice by following a logical plan of action. In undertaking this process you begin to accept reasonable risks and acquaint yourself with the idea that anxiety within limits can be mastered.

First, anxiety is managed, second, emotional reactions are mastered, and third, positive outcomes are achieved. Once you start exercising the logical side, the success of the process becomes a reinforcing dynamic of its own. This is not to suggest that Starphades must abandon creative pursuits but only that a logical plan supplements a creative plan of action.

Starphades usually have a hunch about the nature of their calling and need only a logical plan of action to develop it. Our strategy offers procedure, structure, discipline, and direction.

Both action plans stir up resistance. To counteract resistance, the *Career Star System* emphasizes a step-by-step approach that makes each action step an end in itself without a concern for final results. Both action plans include specific, practical activities and exercises that take you through an incremental process. Process is the goal and the goal is the process. The emphasis on the steps instead of the outcome is called a Strategy of Incremental Action.

Still, be prepared to feel resistance and reluctance to practice your action plan. Starphires can be incinerated by their anger and Starphades overwhelmed by the magnitude of the developmental task. Starphires collide, Starphades miss and neither really communicates with a Career Star.

Starphades may actually feel anxious and overwhelmed by the prospect of change. Starphires may not feel anything in particular but find something else more compelling to do instead. Starphires usually dislike anything that diverts them from their preoccupation with rational control. Starphades, on the other hand, resent the way thinking interrupts more pleasurable pursuits. They may decide to discharge their discomfort by not taking any action, returning to familiar diversions.

In summary, discovering and developing your Career Star is a product of combining logical and intuitive functions and activities (✖ + ✚ = ❄). Starphires are to explore sensing and feeling, while Starphades try thinking and acting on their respective Career Star Strategies. Starphires and Starphades have a need for a consistency of practice but with emphasis on the opposite hemisphere of their respective preference. Both types are reluctant to implement their plans for contrary reasons.

You may very well find the assignments of the opposite star type both more appealing and more feasible. But those are not what you need to work on. Do practice the exercises appropriate to your development.

Exercise 13A is designed especially for Starphires to enhance their intuitive and creative abilities. Exercise 13B is designed for Starphades to strengthen their logical ability. Practice the exercise appropriate to your assessment as a Starphire or Starphade. If your assessment is mixed or scattered, practice the two together.

EXERCISE 13A:
SENSUAL MEDITATION

The Sensual Meditation focuses on career discovery and begins with an exercise that connects the Rational Self with the Creative Self via intuition. As a result, the Starphire is informed of a career choice from an inner source. Relaxation and stress-reduction techniques are emphasized which left-brained stars need to practice for physical and mental health. (Exercise 13A can also be used by Starphades to stimulate creativity.)

In Chapter 2, intuition was defined as the use of bodily senses in an inward way. Combining the five senses inwardly yields a surprising intuitive sixth sense. In this exercise begin very simply using just one sense at a time, by taking any one of the five bodily senses and concentrating it on some activity.

Chart 10 provides a list of sensual activities and objects from which to choose. First pick an activity and then a sense to combine with it. As an example, you might try "to see deep breathing." In this case, you relax and pay attention to the images that come to mind while you breathe deeply. If an objective thought intrudes, push it out of the way to focus on seeing your breathing.

Instead of an activity, you can do the same exercise with an object. For example, you can feel, hear, taste, or smell a sunset. Of course, you can watch a sunset but because it is a common activity, this combination will not be as effective in arousing your intuitive ability. Finger painting (touching paints and colors) is one of the simpler activities and frequently chosen. You might also see, hear, taste, and smell the paints inwardly as well as outwardly.

A more advanced form of Exercise 13 is to combine activities, objects, and senses. Listening to your deep breathing and feeling rocking, for example, can be combined with watching a sunset. There are no limits to how you mix and match the choices, but while you're still a novice try to keep it simple. Later on, warm baths can be taken with incense, perfume, bubbles, candles, and many kinds of sensations may follow. Try not to make the Sensual Meditation too complicated at the start, however.

Reading fiction or "faction," however, is out of the question, because there is a goal in both, even if it is a low level one. Viewing television, for instance, is either a distraction or entertainment, depending upon the channel and level of concentration. Many forms of entertainment are passive diversions that require little mental effort. Television and alcohol are a popular mix that block feelings. Cocaine and marijuana, two other prevalent drugs, also inhibit imaging.

Start now by picking one sense to link with one activity from Chart 10. There are other possible choices, and if you decide to be really creative, you can find your own combination of sensing and acting activities to practice. The goal of the Sensual Meditation is to connect the rational mind with the creative mind for no purpose other than the pure experience of the sensation itself. If you allow your body to send sense impressions to your rational mind you will be amazed at your artistry.

CHART 10:
Sensual Objects and Activities

Activities	See	Feel/Touch	Hear	Taste	Smell
Sitting					
Breathing	✓				
Rocking					✓
Meditating					
Talking					
Walking			✓		
Jogging					
Playing				✓	
Laughing					
Floating			✓		
Painting		✓			
Messaging	✓				
Doodling					
Dancing					
Singing	✓				
Showering					
Bathing					
Eating					✓

Objects	See	Feel/Touch	Hear	Taste	Smell
Breeze					
Beach					✓
Waves					
Sunset		✓			
Nature					
Music					
Plants					
Stars	✓				
Garden				✓	
Clay			✓		
Toys					
Animals					
Children					

If the combination of sense and activity are unfamiliar, all the better. Use uncommon sense for a change. For example, because we frequently go "sightseeing," why not try "hearing walking" instead? Maybe we should call it "Aimless wandering," to emphasize the pointlessness of the activity, since "walking" can be turned into a destination or exercise. "Learn to pause," wrote journalist Dorothy Ballard, "or nothing worthwhile can catch up with you." Slowing down can also help to refocus your goal.

**Workaholics sweat at the thought of relaxation.
Addicts panic at the thought of work.**

Concentrate your attention on one sense during an activity for at least twenty minutes daily. Like any learning, your skill will grow more quickly if you practice twenty minutes twice a day. Practice at least four days per week. This way you are practicing one more day than you are not practicing per week. If you can practice five or six times a week, all the better. Also, give yourself a break and do not practice every day.

Rationally oriented people find it extremely difficult to have unstructured time in which to do something pointless. Workaholics, for example, break out in a sweat at the prospect of relaxation, just as addicts panic at the thought of work. A Starphire may approve of leisure time if it can be construed as goal-related. For example, social occasions may be "networking opportunities," art galleries may have "investment potential," reading is "staying informed."

It is really you, however, who is irrational for not allowing yourself to do something pleasurably purposeless. You may carry this to extremes by avoiding rests and vacations altogether. As a novelty, give yourself permission to become "pointlessly preoccupied." If you do not try, you will continue to do what you have been doing for years, and that is *thinking,* under the guise of achieving in the future something to prevent *feeling* in the present.

Take the risk of giving up control over your body and allow your body to take control of you for *at least a few minutes a day.* What you imagine will happen if you relax is much worse than what will actually happen. And what will really happen if you do not relax is much worse than what you imagine. If you are addicted to work, your body will be much kinder to you in this exchange than you have been to it.

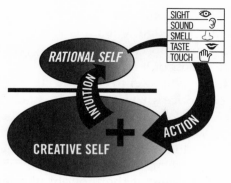

Diagram 15: IQ-Sensory-Intuition Process

If you are a typical left-brained star you may scrutinize Chart 10 looking for the most "logical" illogical task to select. Do not bother. When you realize that a particular choice does not matter, that all choices are equal, you are freed from enormous frustration and actually may enjoy doing these things.

At first, you will find that your intellect flies off the assignment because "it's not rational." The point of the meditation for a change is that there is no point. You will think of countless chores you have postponed and now suddenly are eager to perform. In fact, whenever you cannot remember what tasks you have assigned yourself on a given day, meditate. As you begin to relax, the list will appear on your "mental screen" in order of importance.

For example, as you try to meditate, you will remember that after running to the store, you promised yourself to lie down in front of the television to relieve a splitting headache. Or, perhaps you have a more upbeat plan to bond with a friend, work in the garden, and read an encyclopedia. Having a list of chores is a way to wash the cloak of self-hate with which we traditionally robe and rob ourselves. That the motive is hidden is why we rarely feel fresh and clean, even when the wash-job was well done.

Your senses remember what your mind forgets.

Starphires will prefer to classify and graph the exercises before they are moved to carry them out. Persevere, however, by continuing to concentrate your attention on whatever sense you have chosen. Fear of relaxation, "higher duties," "not enough time" sabotage your effort to change. With a preoccupation or two you can spend the whole meditative period sitting on edge, watching the clock, thinking about what to do next. Then you can turn to your planned work unrefreshed and make a mess of it as well.

You will have to use willpower to concentrate your attention on the sensory experience. Notice what it feels, looks, smells, tastes, or sounds like to do whatever you have selected. Absorb the experience for twenty minutes, allowing nothing else to enter your mind or to matter. Just study the activity completely and repeatedly with one particular sense. *You can change the sense or the activity, or both, daily, but not the senselessness.*

At a later time, and it need not be the same day, write up your experience of the Sensual Meditation in your journal. As you reflect on what took place, record whatever comes to mind spontaneously in a stream-of-consciousness fashion. If you find that you are thinking about what you are going to write while you are having the experience, temporarily suspend the writing requirement.

Writing introduces a rational element that can corrupt the sensual quality of the exercise. However, if you suspend logical analysis and permit yourself to be immersed in the writing process, you will be exposed to another creative medium that will also help open the unconscious pathway to your calling. Write up your experience of the exercise at least four times each week.

Diagram 15, IQ-Sensory-Intuition Process, illustrates the rationale for the Sensual Meditation. Notice that the process is actually circular. You can begin with any component and feel confident that you are going nowhere. For example, if you concentrate your senses, your mind can only be in the present. The intuitive and creative side will be connected unavoidably and when practiced regularly, images and ideas break through conspicuously.

It is important to schedule a time for your Sensual Exercise and when the specific time comes, just to do it. Thinking of doing can take the place of doing. For instance, you can listen to self-help tapes all day, but without action, no benefit. *Stop thinking about feeling and start feeling about thinking,* by connecting your intellect to your senses. Be truly sensible for a change by being sensate and you will find it is really sensational.

Like any learning, your skill with this exercise will improve over time. Practice at least four days per week. Change can only occur when you practice at least one more day weekly than you do not practice. It may take a day or several weeks for your "homework" to begin to pay off. Be ready to record night dreams—they are an indication that the process is working.

SENSUAL MEDITATIONS

Meditation One: Date:_____.

_____
_____
_____
_____
_____
_____

Meditation Two: Date:_____.

_____
_____
_____
_____
_____
_____

Meditation Three: Date:_____.

_____
_____
_____
_____
_____
_____

Meditation Four: Date:_____.

_____
_____
_____
_____
_____
_____

EXERCISE 13B:

ACTION PLANS FOR EMPLOYEES AND ENTREPRENUERS

Starphades have a choice of strategies: Employee versus Entrepreneur. The first is for those who intend to work as an employee within an organizational setting and the other is for those seeking to become self-employed entrepreneurs or consultants. The two plans parallel each other but the content varies according to whether the career ojective is dependent or independent of an organization. You can also devise and practice your own set of relevant exercises.

You may find both of these two plans useful at different times in your career, because an individual who has worked for years in an organization may want a midlife transition to working autonomously. Others may begin directly with an entrepreneurial venture and never pass through the employee phase. It is much less common for a person to move from entrepreneurship back to organizational employment, however.

Both employee and entrepreneur plans for Starphades present lists of acting and thinking exercises designed to strengthen left-brain functioning. At this stage the task is not to find the job or the entrepreneurial niche but to engage in the objective activity for its own sake. The process of incremental actions—not the outcome—is the goal, to achieve the primary purpose of becoming more logically minded. The trip is the destination.

Employee Plan

1. Résumé
Starting or revising your résumé is a good way to begin to find employment, so fill in the blanks of the following outline. This can be a draft résumé that you revise and actually use in your job/career search.
a) *Name, Address, Telephone Number*

_____

_____

_____

b) *Specify Your Career Objective*

_____

_____

_____

You must specify your job or career objective. Ordinarily this is the first and most important entry on your résumé and often the first question asked in an interview. Do not omit, or let this crucial data, be vague or general. You can have several résumés with different job/career objectives if this will help you be specific.

If you fail to include this information, the recipient will have no clue about the purpose of your résumé, and not knowing what else to do with it, may put it aside or in the trash. Your career objective needs to be specified on your résumé even when you mention it in a cover letter because the two documents are often separated. Customize the objective in the cover letter if necessary for a specific job.

c) *Qualifications and Abilities*

_____

_____

_____

_____

_____

_____

_____

List no more than seven of your skills and abilities. Think of this segment as an advertisement for yourself. List six or seven of the major benefits to a prospective employer in hiring you. That is, state what services you have to offer and what makes you desirable as an employee.

d) *Experience*

_____

_____

_____

_____

_____

_____

List your work or professional experience. Begin with your most recent employment and cover all relevant and significant work history. Give the dates you were employed and include a brief description of the work that you performed and goals you accomplished.

e) *Education*

_____

_____

_____

List your educational accomplishments. Begin with the most recent and continue in descending order. Give the dates of degrees or certificates that you hold.

f) *Honors and Achievements*

_____

_____

_____

_____

List any honors, awards, or achievements that are noteworthy. It is not necessary to offer references.

2. Design a Business Card

Design your business card. This is a good exercise even if you do not have an immediate need for a business card or expect to have one printed. This task highlights the importance of having a specific career objective. You will find that it is difficult to design a business card without having an objective.

3. Job Search and Network

❊ Check newspaper advertisements and career center listings at colleges and universities.

❊ Network with friends, relatives, and acquaintances who may know personally about the "hidden job market," that is, jobs that are not listed in the classified advertisements.

❊ Pursue potential leads by making telephone calls and acquiring additional information.

4. Information Interviews

Seek out individuals in careers similar to the one you are considering and request an "information interview." Explain that you are thinking of entering the same field and seek their advice. What is the career like, how did they enter it, and what are future prospects in their opinion? Be clear that you are asking for information only and that you are not expecting a job interview. People usually are flattered to be asked for information and eager to help.

5. Research

Conduct research about your career field. Look in the consumer magazine section of bookstores to see if you can find current articles about your prospective field. Use the library to check out books and trade magazines in your potential career field.

6. Volunteer Work Experience

One of the best ways to determine whether a career field is suitable is to do volunteer work. You will gain valuable knowledge from the experience about whether the work is right for you and you will meet other people with similar career goals with whom you can exchange information about the career and its future.

7. Documentation

Document in your *Career Star Notebook and Journal* all the leads and factual information you acquire in the above process. Record dates, times, names, and other pertinent data. In this respect, the purpose of the journal is twofold: to reinforce consciousness of your Career Star Strategy and to provide a practical reference for future use.

Entrepreneur-Consultant Plan

1. Organize a Work Space

Organize a work space in your residence exclusively for use in building your business. Include the supplies and equipment that you need to begin actual work on your new enterprise. The space has two purposes: to keep you reminded of your commitment to your entrepreneur/consultantship and to make it physically possible to start work.

2. Name Your Profession, Business, or Service

Since you ordinarily have another person's attention for only a fraction of a second, the name of your business must communicate exactly what you offer or sell. A prospective customer or client must be able to know quickly whether your business is relevant to his needs and interests.

3. Design a Business Card and Logo
A logo is the name of your business in picture form. It communicates the product or service you offer in imagery and is as important as the name of your business. You and others will know that you know your business when you can name and draw it.

4. Write a Service Contract
Describe the product you will make or the services you will perform in writing as if you and the other party are going to sign on the bottom line. Include a list of benefits and features as explained in paragraph 1c) under "Résumé."

Working on this task will help clarify for you the nature of your business. The written word requires precision that will help to improve your oral presentation.

Test market your statement once it is drafted by sharing it with others and by analyzing their questions and reactions. Revise your product description and service contract based on this feedback. Your service contract document can become the basis of a brochure that you will also need in order to market your business and inform others about the nature of your work.

5. Background and Qualifications
Describe your professional experience and education. Explain what makes you an expert or an authority in this line of work.

6. Market Research
Informally, in conversations with others or more formally using simple sample surveys, find out the characteristics of your "target" market and study the reaction to your product or service presentations.

7. Information Interviews
Apply the same technique as described in paragraph 4 under "Résumé." Try to interview individuals in similar or related businesses.

8. Revisions
Continuously apply and revise steps two through seven above, based on your research and interview feedback and results.

9. Network
Develop leads and gather information from other professional business people.

10. Documentation
Record all the information you acquire and activities you undertake in your *Career Star Journal and Notebook.* Also, write up your experiences and reflections about your enterprise adventure. The two purposes of the journal, again, are to help keep you conscious of your Career Star goal and to provide you with a resource reference for future use.

11. Timetable
Starphades also need a specific timetable for their job or career search. It can start out very modest, for example, an hour a day five days a week. Of course, several hours a day is not unreasonable. A Starphade who thinks eight hours a day are required, as if it was a job, may be overwhelmed and never start. The point is to get moving with activities that logically develop talents. Eventually the timetable can be extended as confidence is increased.

STAR DAWN:
Envisioning the Future

Until the day star arises in your hearts.

2 Peter 1:19

THEORETICAL SUMMARY

Our society is organized as a "patriarchy." This means that fundamental decisions are made by an elite group of males. Among the most important of these decisions is that the measure of a person's worth is the possession of social power. Individual value is established by the rank of the father in the hierarchy of the social order, and according to whether you are a male or female.

This emphasis on social power causes the external world to be perceived as more important than the internal world. That is, individuals are socialized to be highly aware of the outer world where gender and gender identity are considered paramount. As a result, men and women are divided socially and differ psychologically. This includes an unconscious division, an area of mental life generally unrecognized in patriarchal social orders.

Men are trained to use their logical left brains to strive for social power and women are taught to use their intuitive right brains to attract men and to care for children. Both sexes learn that the inner world is relatively unimportant, even though women generally are more appreciative of, and hampered by, their emotional life (See Appendix 5, "Gender and Brain Laterialization").

Because social power is made salient, the outer universe is studied more thoroughly than the inner self, and we tend to overlook insights, feelings, images, myths, and spiritual knowledge. If the emphasis were reversed and placed on the inner world instead, our understanding of reality would be as dim and opaque as our dreams. Then, at least, as much would be known about ourselves, and each another, as we know now about outer space.

In terms of the physical universe, Niels Bohr discovered the structure of the atom in 1913 and described the sub-atomic system as a solar system in miniature. Earlier, Ernest Rutherford had found the atom to be composed almost entirely of empty space. In contradistinction to Spinoza, "nature abhors a vacuum," nature is a vacuum.

The inner and outer worlds of matter replicate one another as space-orbiting objects and objects orbiting space. If we see only the objects as real, and not the space in between, we miss the third unseen dimension betwixt, which holds the two together. The space between, and in, the objects, usually considered vacant, is not nothing but the presence of something.

Empty space is not unoccupied but busy with a binding force. Space, therefore, indicates a presence not an absence, a fullness not an emptiness, a bonding energy that unites all objects into one. Space holds everything in its place. The fixed stars remind us that something holds everything in a totality. Stars, therefore, represent the intangible in the sphere of the solids.

A star is an intangible object of light. Light, space and objects, are three crucial factors in the equation. Light occupies the space and objects occupy the light. Light is the third factor for without light, objects and space not only cannot be seen, but do not even exist. If you see the light, you see the objects and the space in between. If you cannot see the light, you miss all three. Light, space, and mass are three forms of One great thing.

See the light and in the light you see the object of your Career Star in both geographical and mental space. The light reveals your calling otherwise and heretofore concealed by pitch darkness. If you do not see the light, you will miss your calling. The inner light shows the connection to the outer light so that you see yourself as you are seen. Self-doubt is the black hole and dark matter of the psychological universe.

The light of consciousness is that part of your mind over which you have control. Consciousness is under your direction if you choose to remember and exercise your will. The choice of what intentions to make and keep conscious is inevitably selective. With the light you have the option to focus on outer objects or the inner self to form a relationship that denies the negative and affirms the positive. Through ignorance or indifference you can elect not to exercise the choice.

Consent to Serenity

A calling is your precious life-purpose generously given to you. This fact can be kept conscious and conspicuous or unconsciousness and inconspicuous.

Shift your gaze and ask to see the light of your Career Star within you. You can always shift back again to believing it is without you, or give up hope and return to your tenacious hold on a dark star. Try to contribute 1 percent to the belief that the star is in your inner self rather than 100 percent to the conviction that it has left you. To believe or not to believe in your Career Star is your prerogative.

To help you achieve Career Star awareness you are given a thoughtful and powerful mind, a grateful and kind heart, and a pair of creative hands. When the intuitive intelligence of your bodily senses (✚), is raised to consciousness and crossed with your rational intelligence (✖), your Calling Star surfaces in your psyche in the form of illumination (✿). It appears on your mind screen as a flash of insight light that infuses you with self-understanding.

If you conscientiously activate the linking of the two, (✖) and (✚), your auspicious Career Star bursts forth from its hidden dimension in the darkness of your inner universe to the conspicuous and spacious light of your conscious mind. If you continue to intentionally cross ✖ and ✚, your Career Star erupts to eliminate the darkness with a light show like an inner aurora borealis.

The formula is: ✖ combined with ✚ = ✿ . That is, the enlightenment of ✿ drives out the darkness of ▬ (self-doubt) when ✖ and ✚ are joined. If you do not cross ✖ and ✚, you get zero. That is, ✖ times

0 = 0. Or, **0** times ✚ = **0.** (And, of course, **0** times **0 = 0.**) Again, the basic law of "psychological astronomy" is: ✖ crossing ✚ makes ✿ , an eight-pointed star.

Your Career Star is the guiding light of your unique destiny written in the stars by the Star, a celestial sparkle entrusted only to you by the Divine. Your mind is rendered whole by the spirit, and with the body, enjoined to serve a higher purpose. You are irreplaceably, indivisibly, and irretrievably one holy spirit under God in a star-spangled universe.

Right-brained Starphades know their calling but lack self-esteem without which they cannot fulfill their destiny. Left-brained Starphires do not know their calling and lack insight into their life purpose, by default they cheat their true selves by picking a career that is dictated mainly by logical considerations such as salary, status, and geographical location.

Following your Career Star is a function of self-perception. A concept of self, as an Injured or Creative Self, either enables or impedes the course of personal development. You can see yourself as worthless and reactively never reach your human potential. You can see yourself spiritually with a mission and proactively act on your potential.

Our Creative Self is everything we know deep down inside about our basic goodness. The Creative Self is part of an unconscious mind, shared with the Injured Self. When the Injured Self is integrated consciously with the Creative Self, a star arises that leads us down a predestined path. When we deny the Creative Self, we allow the darkness of the Injured Self to gain superiority and overshadow thinking.

Self-doubt (━), constantly vies with Creative Self-perception (✚), to cause a person to challenge and resist constructive personal change. To see negatively means your life-mission is obscured as you overlook your creative function and seek compensation for the loss in achievement, bodily pleasures, leisure activities, and material possessions. The Creative Self is eclipsed via the repeated aggravation of the Injured Self (Diagram 7, page 137).

In the *Career Star System,* there is an Injured Child and Gifted Child. Right-brain Starphades and left-brain Starphires are the two main modes of adult adaptation to the injuries of childhood. Both adaptations renounce the child parts of the self in adulthood in the same way the well-being of children is sacrificed in society.

The Rational Denial System relies on the cognitive power of the mind and the Irrational Denial System relies on the emotional power of the body. Both systems neglect the Gifted Child Self. "Developmental anxiety" is the manifestation in the conscious mind of the apprehensions of the Injured Child who is fearful of being deprived further by contemplated and attempted developmental actions.

The inner conflict between Injured and Gifted Child is dealt with consciously by negotiations in which the left-brain allows the right-brain to engage in indulgences as a trade-off for permission to work without obstruction. The right-brain in turn allows the left-brain to work in order to pay for the cost of the rewards. It is an incessant altercation and alternation of excessive physical gratification as compensation for the sacrifice of alienated labor.

Finding your calling brings this self-estrangement to an end, emancipates you from the prison of self-spiteful labor, and acquits you of all the charges of which you have hitherto been convicted by yourself. The reassuring paradox is that there is no toil and sacrifice, only joy and service, in consenting to the serenity of your meaningful life-work.

You believe you are a scared and scarred creature when you are actually a sacred star of light. You stand under your Career Star when you understand that it stands for you. Majestic starlight will overcome your feelings of doubt and make over your self-perception if you give the star the chance of a glimpse. Then you will beam just like your star.

PRACTICAL REVIEW

You are now coming to the end of the *Career Star System*. Three lists of various exercises contained in the book are given below. Make a selection of a set of exercises to practice. The page number is given in case you find it necessary to review the actual exercise. Of course, base your choices on your assessment as a Starphire, Starphade, Scatter Star, or Polar Star.

❏ *Active Subjective Exercises for Starphires:*

❈ Exercise 3, "Career Star Meditation" page 48.
❈ Exercise 6, "Star Painting," page 99.
❈ Exercise 9, "Injured Child Meditation," page 142.
❈ Exercise 10, "Star Flower," page 157.
❈ Exercise 11, "Four Little Stars," page 172.
❈ Exercise 13A, "Sensual Meditation" page 203.

Again, as you practice these exercises *do not* try to figure out what feelings are "appropriate," because a theoretical preoccupation may interfere with the experience. Instead, just slide and glide with the Flowe and avoid the hitches and glitches caused by Force.

❏ *Active Objective Exercises for Starphades:*

❀ Exercise 1, "Job Satisfaction," page 13.
❀ Exercise 2, "Star Commission," page 27.
❀ Exercise 5, "Star Course," page 76.
❀ Exercise 7, "Star History," page 118.
❀ Exercise 8, "Star Self A to Z," page 127.
❀ Exercise 13B, "Action Plans," page 210.
❀ Chart 9, "Logical Activities" page 171.

Each of these exercises involves a logical activity for Starphades. In addition, learning the principles of any objective system of knowledge, e.g., music, foreign language, technology, science, will also help you become more informed and skilled in the field while simultaneously strengthening logical thinking.

❏ *Scatter Star: (Starphire and Starphade)*

❀ Exercise 1, "Job Satisfaction Assessment," page 13.
❀ Exercise 2, "Star Commission," page 27.
❀ Exercise 3, "Star Meditation," page 48.
❀ Exercise 4, "Star Burst Mandala," page 67.
❀ Exercise 5, "Star Course," page 76.
❀ Exercise 6, "Star Painting," page 99.
❀ Exercise 7, "Star History," page 118.
❀ Exercise 8, "Star Self A to Z," page 127.
❀ Exercise 9, "Injured Child Meditation," page 142.
❀ Exercise 12, "Dream Journal," page 189.
❀ Exercise 13A, "Sensual Meditation" page 203.
❀ Exercise 13B, "Action Plans," page 210.
❀ Chart 9, "Logical Activities," page 171.
❀ Chart 10, "Sensual Activities," page 205.

Once again, think about your calling, how right it is for you and how much you want to find it. Select the exercises you intend to practice and enter the names in the chart below. Pencil in the times and days you actually plan to follow-through with your strategy. This is your Career Star Action Strategy and Schedule, the implementation of the *Career Star System*. Rx: one exercise most days, no exercise at least one day.

CAREER STAR ACTION STRATEGY AND SCHEDULE

EXERCISES	DAY	TIME	COMMENT
1. _____	_____	_____	_____.
2. _____	_____	_____	_____.
3. _____	_____	_____	_____.
4. _____	_____	_____	_____.
5. _____	_____	_____	_____.
6. _____	_____	_____	_____.

CONCLUSION

Thank your lucky Career Star for the spectacular light show you have witnessed and for all your astral experiences. Be glad that you have a sacred and not a "man-made" Career Star, one that can budge and nudge you correctly toward your proper destiny.

Do not cast away your grasp, hide away your vision, nor stray away from the path of your splendid star. Vow that you will search and serve, strive and stretch to arrive at the true destination assigned to you by your exquisite Career Star. Continue to dream the impossible dream until you reach the unreachable and irresistible star.

May the mythical journey of your career quest please the Great Spirit by whom it has been decreed and may you be honored with the prosperity and serenity you deserve. Let your lofty and loyal Career Star lift you to the love of others' starlight so that all together shine their brightest as they reflect upon one another. Pray that your Calling Star also assists others as it has helped you and that it replenishes the source from which it has been drawn.

Bask now in the sunlight of your bright Career Star and let it flood, fill, and overflow your soul with the joy of the dawn of a bright new beginning. Dawn is but the awakening in your mind to the vision of the pristine star that is always there ready and waiting to shine away any shadow of self-doubt.

"A dark shadow is but the cast of a strong light," says an old proverb. You are born within a starry world with the mystery of a golden star. Be aware, therefore, of your inherent star nature and consummate your journey to Stardom. The dawn of your star shows the way to the Garden of Earth, the wonderful place of emotional peace and economic security in the here and now.

Thank you for having undertaken your mission-quest with the aid of the *Career Star System.* I hope the results have been delightful and enlightening. I am certain that the brilliance of your star will be seen again and again. You are in the advanced party of the bearers of starlight to those still hiding in fright in the Shadowlands.

The price of resistance is missing the peace, and the *pièce de résistance,* is meeting your destiny. Believing in your Career Star is entirely *up* to you and it will not let you *down.* With your eyes uplifted you are the leader of the procession as you march to the stars. It is your time "to come a light into the world."

APPENDIX 1

OVERVIEW FOR CAREER COUNSELING PROFESSIONALS

PURPOSE

The *Career Star System* is a new and unique theory and method for career discovery and development based on inner values. The system emphasizes finding a calling through gaining psychological insight into the inner self where individual values are hidden. Life's purpose is concealed in the darkness of the unconscious mind and is referred to as a "Career Star."

The client/student embarks on an inner quest through the use of intuition and imagination to discover the light of their particular star. Once a Calling Star based on inner values is uncovered, the *Career Star System* also helps the individual design a practical plan of action to make the new career actually begin to happen.

The *Career Star System* is designed for young adults who are just starting out in search of their career and for older adults in transition to new careers. It is valid for careers in the creative arts and humanities as well as the fields of business and science. The approach offers intuitive-spiritualism as a genuine alternative to the rational-materialism of traditional career counseling.

Since callings come in many varieties there is also a calling to help others find their calling. Professionals help others hear a calling when they voice their own. Self-doubt is ubiquitous, however, and exists also among career counselors. Career counselors sometimes act like shepherds fearful of their sheep. Find your calling and you will know how to help others find their calling.

PRACTICAL APPLICATION

The *Career Star System* uses an assessment tool that is a full-color map representational of five major career paths. A client is instructed in the use of the map and then, either under supervision by a Career Counseling Professional or following instructions individually, performs an assessment.

WHAT IS ASSESSED?

The assessment informs the client about the nature and extent of brain laterialization. That is, a client learns the degree to which his right- and/or left-brain is used in thinking, problem-solving, and decision-making. In the *Career Star System* this means basically whether they are a left-brain Starphire or right-brain Starphade.

HOW IS THIS INFORMATION USED?

Using the text of the *Career Star System* as a reference that accompanies the map, the career counseling professional informs the client about how brain lateralization affects life decisions and career selection. The book also explains how the client originally came to be brain laterialized.

THE CAREER STAR SYSTEM

The *Career Star System* text carries the client through a series of practical exercises designed to integrate right- and left-brain functioning. This integration opens a channel of communication to the unconscious mind, where a calling is concealed. The ensuing dialogue enables the client to begin to formulate a plan and act on a calling.

PROFESSIONAL APPLICATION

The *Career Star System* may be taught to groups or individuals and adopted as a program of study in a career counseling center. Led by a professional, the *Career Star System* program can be covered in a series of workshops or classes of approximately three hours each, once per week, for a total of six to ten weeks. The system can also be used as an individual self-help study program under the supervision of a career counseling professional.

BENEFITS TO THE COUNSELOR

Once the client begins to get a sense of a calling, the counselor can integrate this information with a program that incorporates other methodologies traditional to the profession of career counseling. Specialized training for the career counseling professional in the *Career Star System* is available from the author but is entirely optional. The optional training is an opportunity for self-renewal and recommitment to the ideals of the career counseling profession.

BENEFITS TO THE CLIENT

- ✸ Start or Change Careers
- ✸ Find Career Passion
- ✸ Determine Intellectual Strengths
- ✸ Assess Creative Potentials
- ✸ Overcome Self-Sabotage
- ✸ Interpret Dreams
- ✸ Design a Career Action Strategy

OUTCOME

The client will gain a new sense of a calling and be more passionately committed to its achievement because it arises from an inner source. In the process, he will have less anxiety, more patience about taking interim steps, and more ardor about attaining career goals. Most importantly, an individual will be on a career path that originates from inner knowledge of the self.

APPENDIX 2

STAR SYSTEM QUESTIONS

HOW LONG DOES THE PROCESS TAKE?

How long the process takes depends largely upon your initiative, effort, and persistence. There are no shortcuts and you cannot be casually committed to your Career Star. No one other than you can do it and it is you who must want self-knowledge.

Some people are literally pushed into asking for help with their careers by a crisis of stress and burnout. In this case, the problem that career difficulties represent has often been avoided for a long time and as a result, has grown to critical proportions. These are people identified in the text as extreme Starphires.

Starphires ordinarily do not want to enter a self-learning process because they feel they should know already and have wasted too much time, money, and effort to expend any more. They want no further delays and, as perfectionists, insist on a quick remedy. They do not realize that impatience prevents their entrance to a process of self-discovery. Usually they insist that a logical solution to their career choice has evaded them even though this is not necessarily a logical conclusion.

While the elusiveness of an answer may bother them, Starphires still believe all that is required is the input of more data. They want ready-made results in books, tapes, and experts. They may allow one or two irregular consultations with a counselor but quit in dismay when the outcome is not fast and easy. They really believe that their Inner Injured Self is insurmountable but do not want to acknowledge that this part of them exists.

Usually Starphires are too busy to have time to study the manual and practice the exercises. They lack the patience to trek and track an internal star quest even though they have been climbing mountains of aggravation, stumbling over hills of perfectionism, and slamming into barriers of frustration repeatedly (on the right-hand side of the *Career Star Map*).

Since your calling is tucked away in the unconscious part of your own mind, there is no predictable timetable for its discovery. The task involves giving up intellectual control and entering into a process that allows feelings and sensations, intuition and imagination, creation and construction to merge and emerge. This experience is a relinquishment, not an accomplishment; it is a surrender to relaxation, patience, acceptance, kindness, and openness. You will find it when you give up looking for it forcefully.

On the other hand, Starphades, the opposite of Starphires, are usually in an emotional crisis but procrastinate and avoid getting started. Procrastination is a choice on the side of fear and doubt. If they do start, they will often quit, as they become worried about how they will live up to the changes they expect rather than the mistakes they have made. These are the individuals we have designated in the text as right-brained Starphades.

Starphades become *more wary of the future than weary of the past.* As soon as they realize they have an option, they fear they will fail, and are not glad and relieved to have found an alternative. Previously they did not even know they had an option. Now that they see one, they are afraid they will not be able to attain it. Starphades orientation to life is based on an experience of loss, an attitude that sustains a self-fulfilling prophecy.

You already have a glowing Career Star within you but getting to it through self-doubt appears to be an impenetrable barrier to Starphires and a cloud of confusion to Starphades. (See Chapter 6, "Types," and the barriers and confusion drawn on the two sides of the

Career Star Map.) The doubt you have about the *Career Star System* may be your own displaced self-doubt. This is not to say that the system cannot be wrong or flawed. If you believe, however, that the star of destiny left you out, your self-doubt is cast onto the system and shows up in the world outside of you.

DOES IT WORK?

An intuitive approach to career choice works when intellectual control is released. It does not work as long as surrender is incomplete. You cannot fool your unconscious mind since it knows you better and quicker than you know yourself.

Your unconscious mind is not on a linear track that delivers answers on demand. When you relinquish control by allowing results to appear in unexpected form, then you are truly ready to accept whatever is given to you without judgment and censorship.

There is no agency, book, or expert who can find the answer for you about your career without your own active participation. If you are looking for someone to give you work that is interesting and meaningful, you are misunderstanding the problem and overlooking your own inner resources. Finding your calling is not like shopping for a product or hiring the services of a lawyer or doctor who provide you with information or advice.

The answer to your calling is tucked away inside you. You cannot just hire someone to find it for you. You can obtain guidance, information, principles, insight, exercises, and support, all based on experience and training, but you cannot be absolved of responsibility and exempted from initiative in the search. The issue is self-trust. No answer will come from outside without a change of self-acceptance from within.

The desire for a guarantee reflects a doubt that the answer is within you and a fantasy that someone else has the solution. You will have proof if you will give your Career Star the benefit of trust.

WHAT IS OUT THERE?

This question is asked when some left-brained individuals assume that they have not found their calling because of a logical alternative that they have overlooked. Their belief is not logical nor can any evidence be found to support it. Usually they are mistaken because logically minded people are thoroughly comprehensive in their screening and scrutinizing of what alternatives are available "out there." A logical possibility is that there is an emotional factor intruding into consciousness that interferes with finding the answer.

If you pose the above question you might consult the classified advertisements for employment in a Sunday metropolitan newspaper, or check out the Yellow Pages in a telephone directory. These are two fairly exhaustive lists of what is available "out there." Some logically minded people do not care for this answer because they usually have researched these sources and others and still think there is something they have overlooked when actually all the choices are already known.

There is something missing, but it is not in the realm of logic, which is a tool for exploring and examining the outer world. What is missing is in the realm of the self, where insight is the tool of exploration. Just as you cannot explore the outer world without logic, you cannot find the inner world without the free rein of your imagination, intuition, and sensation. There are no resources better than your own inner resources, strong enough and right enough, to guide you on your quest.

APPENDIX 3

PROGRESSIVE RELAXATION MEDITATION TEXT

Meditation, correctly and regularly practiced, enhances communication with your unconscious mind, which is the site of your internal Career Star. As a student of the *Career Star System* once put it, "Meditation helps bring you your calling." It also helps reduce stress, produce energy, enhance well-being, and improve an appetite for life.

Some claim also that it can strengthen the body's immune system, slow the biological process of aging, answer most of the basic mysteries of life, reform Christianity, and solve all the world's economic and environmental crises. But there are skeptics.

A Starphire client once remarked, "I'd believe more in meditation if I thought it would get me somewhere, but I'm afraid that while I'm relaxing everyone else is moving on." More than one client has told me in all sincerity that they can meditate while driving an automobile.

Occasionally I have students refuse to meditate because "it is against my religion" while other religions regard it as a form of prayer.

Meditation can make you more receptive to spiritual ideas and creative impulses if you open yourself inwardly.

Progressive Relaxation Meditation involves a sequential releasing of tension from the body beginning with the head and ending with the toes. It prepares you for other meditations and forms of inner-work in this book.

Try to give priority to this activity. There is no goal beyond relaxation of the body and clearing of the mind. The more stress in your life, the more tension in your body, the more you need to meditate.

Find a setting indoors or outdoors that is quiet, a place where you can be alone for about half an hour. Indoors, you might turn off the phone and make the room semidark. Sit on the floor or in a chair with your feet flat on the floor and with your back straight.

If you prefer, you can sit on the floor, folding your legs in front of you "Indian" style. Rest your hands in your lap. If you want to use a "lotus meditative posture," touch your index finger to the thumb of each hand.

Do not lie down, rest your head in your hands, or lean your body against anything because these positions may cause you to fall asleep. If you need to rest before you meditate, take a nap or go to bed, as part of the relaxation and preparation process.

Begin by taking a deep breath. Fill your lungs fully and then exhale gently. Let your mind and body unwind. Next, close your eyes. Turn off the outside noise and clear your mind. Look inwardly quietly. Trust yourself, and follow wherever you are led.

What do you see with your eyes closed? What do you hear within you in a quiet room? What can you touch in your body with your mind? With your eyes closed continue to repeat the process of deep breathing. Yawn and stretch if you feel like it. Just notice the sensation of breathing and appreciate the easy feeling of deep breathing and relaxing.

You may object to giving yourself air. If you do, realize that this is a form of "resistance" as discussed in Chapter 3. Notice it, and let go of it. Do not judge yourself for resisting relaxation. Gently try to override the resistance by remembering that you are asking only to give yourself some more air. You will be surprised at how good you feel when you have given your brain more oxygen. It is really a very simple and special treat.

As you breathe deeply, notice how the air feels as it enters your body and fills your lungs. Focus your attention on the physiological sensation of breathing. As you do, notice how nice it feels to be relaxing. You hardly ever allow yourself this opportunity.

Next, notice if there is tension anywhere in your head, at the top, at the back, or behind your eyes. Collect this tension in turn and exhale it back into the universe after each deep breath. Allow your face to relax and in sequence: forehead, eyes, nose, mouth, and jaw. Continue to breathe deeply and exhale fully.

Gently move your head back and forth and up and down, and release the tension in your neck. Notice how much tension you carry in this part of your body. Continue to relax your neck until most of the tension is gone. Do not stop deep breathing.

Relax in sequence your shoulders, upper arms, forearms, wrists, palms, and fingers. Close and then stretch your fingers. Let any tension that remains anywhere in the upper part of your body slide through your body and slip out through the tips of your fingers. Do not forget to keep breathing deeply.

Again, relax your shoulders. Let your chest relax. Relax your abdomen. Let all of your internal organs go, and allow them to sink into your body cavity. Feel the waves of relaxation washing over you.

Relax your hips, thighs, and buttocks. Notice that whatever you are sitting on supports you, so you can relax. Let yourself melt into the chair, the floor, or the ground. Continue to breathe deeply, and become one with the air.

Next, relax your calves and the front of your legs. Relax your ankles, feet, and toes. Then stretch your toes several times, and allow any tension that remains to pass through your body, enter your feet, exit your toes, and go back to the universe where it belongs.

Take a moment to notice how wonderful it feels to be relaxing. Again, focus on the sensation of breathing and the physical feeling of relaxing. Promise yourself that you will do this more often.

Enjoy this experience for a few more minutes and then count yourself back into your surroundings. That is, count from one to five and become conscious of the sounds and sights around you.

Appendix 4

Aptitude Testing

There are two basic approaches in the field of career education: the "rational," or the outer values approach and the "spiritual," or the inner values approach. The concern of the rational approach is to help individuals become gainfully employed while the inner values approach emphasizes finding a calling.

The rational approach is the prevailing viewpoint. Many publications in this perspective repackage a basic set of tenets drawn from a few classics and lack freshness and originality. The rational approach also typically addresses a middle-class audience of potential corporate employees. Fitting into corporate America really has little to do with finding meaningful life-work, however.

In the rational approach the focus is on job hunting and concerns a basic set of topics such as cover letters, résumés, interviewing techniques, networking strategies, and salary negotiations. The approach assumes that jobs are prevalent, if not abundant, and finding one is a matter of persistence. The reality of a shrinking job market and depressed economy are not addressed because this question undermines the whole perspective.

The goal is understood to be employment, at lower or higher levels, in the national or international corporate structure. To fit uniquely rounded humans into organizationally squared slots is a basic tenet. Consequently, people tend to be regarded as interchangeable units, cognitive pieces in a giant economic machine. There is a profound distrust of the autonomously creative individual who might not serve a hierarchical model.

Books in this genre tend to be totally aspiritual and use material success in the business world as the only conceivable lifetime aspiration. The rational approach to career discovery and development is based on the idea of testing. There are at least four kinds of tests commonly used in the field of career counseling: values, interests, aptitude, and personality. In its most elaborate form, you can be tested for several days on a variety of dimensions, from dexterity to personality.

Each type of test yields useful data, especially when the results are in the hands of an experienced interpreter. You can also explore with a career counselor how you fit into the job and entrepreneur markets. But, many people are frustrated by traditional testing and counseling because too much is expected of the tests.

Aptitude testing cannot tell you *how to employ* talents. It may tell you whether you are tone deaf, which is relevant if you are planning to become a musician. Or, you may test high for a certain field, such as law, even when it does not coincide with your personal value system. Neither test results nor counseling can solve the problem of what to do with your career, however.

An intelligence test can only tell you that you are more or less intelligent, not how to use intelligence. You are not using the intelligence you have if you expect more. A counselor can list your options but how your skills and goals fit in the world are ultimately and always an inner question. This dimension is most often missing in the interpretation of tests scores and counseling process.

Testing is often used to fit a client's aptitudes to existing jobs and professions. This externalized approach works only if it does not matter to you personally where you fit. In traditional career counseling, emphasis is placed on searching out what opportunities the world has to offer you instead of what opportunities you have to offer the world in the form of your calling.

The difference in approaches lies in perspectives—whether "the job" is seen as inside or outside the client. If the view is outward, according to either counselor or counselee, then neither party believes in the idea of a calling. An inner value approach to career selection has not been the heart and soul of the career counseling profession.

Aptitude testing offers you feedback about whether you have natural talents to work with people or objects, or both. If you do not already have this information about yourself, you may find it useful and intriguing to be tested. You may think that you should "do more" with the information you receive, because you still lack a decision about what to do with your aptitudes and personality.

Testing may be more useful to a younger person just beginning a career search than to an older worker who has already learned about himself or herself through experience. The more specific and physiological the test, the less results are open to interpretation. The more general and psychological the test, the more it depends on subjective factors in the client and counselor. For example, a dexterity test can give you a score that can be compared with others' scores on a scale and provide a measure of eye-and-hand coordination.

From this you may have an answer as to whether you have an aptitude to be a surgeon, but whether it matches your personality and reveals meaningful work in the world is yet another question entirely. You cannot have an aptitude for work that is not your calling but the question of purpose remains even when you have gathered more information about the nature of your aptitudes and personality.

Testing is a testament to the success of rational thinking about finding career direction. It is so widespread it is often considered the only route in a career search. The question, "Do you do testing?" presupposes a precise, logical, and objective answer to your life-purpose. As practiced, testing is the opposite of an insight-oriented approach.

There is no test, expert, nor agency that can give or sell you the answer, and there is no one you can hire to be you, or figure it out for you. No one is you but you, so be you and figure it out for you. The answer lies within, and you must find it to know yourself. You cannot be absolved from responsibility and exempted from initiative in the search for the illumination of your Career Star.

APPENDIX 5

GENDER AND BRAIN LATERALIZATION

The issues of gender and thinking style are easily distorted and misunderstood because our identities as men and women provide us with powerful feelings that are central to our personalities. Since we usually identify with one gender or the other, it is often difficult to appreciate the whole picture. A more precise vocabulary may help pave the way for greater understanding about brain lateralization and gender.

"Gender" is a term that refers to the biological sex of the person as "male" or "female." "Gender identity" is a term that refers to the personality of an individual as "masculine" or "feminine." "Sexuality" is a third term that refers to choice of sexual partner, as homosexual or heterosexual. All three often coincide but not always. There are many possible combinations. For example, males may be psychologically feminine and females may be psychologically masculine and they both can be either homosexual or heterosexual.

The fact that there are so many variations suggests that there is no link between the three phenomena. The preference to be masculine or feminine may be there from birth as a function of genetics and bio-chemistry. Or, the pressure of socialization placed upon an individual may go hand in hand with or against a genetic prescription or predisposition.

Gender is an objective, uncontroversial, and observable fact: a person has either internal or external organs of reproduction. Gender identity and sexuality are much more controversial because they involve only indirectly knowable and subjective states of mind. Whether gender identity and sexual orientation are genetically or socially determined is also controversial, whereas gender itself is an obvious biological given.

The normative expectation for men is left-brain lateralization (Starphire) and right-brain lateralization for women (Starphade). The societal ideal for men is to be left-brained, concerned with goals such as career, money, status, and power. The ideal for women is right-brained, concerned with feelings, children, family, and relationships. The societal ideal may also be the real norm in terms of statistical frequency.

The exact figures for the numbers who conform and do not conform to the cultural standard is unknown. The frequency of right-brained men and left-brained women is probably larger than other statistical minorities; left-handedness and homosexuality are both estimated at about 10 percent of the population. What is decidedly rare is to find men or women who are psychologically bilateral.

The important point to emphasize is that there is brain lateralization and that it does not necessarily coincide with gender. There are two basic styles of thinking, just as there are two types of Career Stars, two-handedness, two genders, two sexual orientations, two-party politics, and "double dealing." For a flood of reasons the same two do not go two-by-two despite all the efforts of Noah and his Ark.

STAR BIBLOGRAPHY

A Course in Miracles. Glen Ellen, CA: Foundation for Inner Peace, 1992.

Alcoholics Anonymous, *Twelve Steps and Twelve Traditions*. New York: Alcoholics Anonymous World Services, Inc., 1952.

Anderson, Nancy. *Work With Passion: How to Do What You Love for a Living*. New York: Carroll and Graf Publishers, Inc., 1984.

Argüelles, José and Miriam. *Mandala*. Boston: Shambhala Publications Inc., 1985.

Arraj, James. *St. John of the Cross and Dr. C G. Jung: Christian Mysticism in the Light of Jungian Psychology*. Chiloquin, OR: Inner Growth Books, 1986.

Arrien, Angeles. *Signs of Life: The Five Universal Shapes and How to Use Them*. Sonoma, CA: Arcus Publishing Co., 1992.

Bach, Richard. *Illusions: The Adventures of a Reluctant Messiah*. New York: Delacorte Press, 1977.

Berg, Astrid. *Finding the Work You Love: A Woman's Career Guide*. San Jose, CA: Resource Publications, Inc., 1994.

Boldt, Laurence G. *Zen and the Art of Making a Living.* New York: Penguin Books, 1992.

Bolles, Richard Nelson. *What Color is Your Parachute?* Berkeley: Ten Speed Press, 1993.

Bradshaw, John. *Creating Love: The Next Great Stage of Growth.* New York: Bantam Books, 1992.

Bradshaw, John. *Homecoming: Reclaiming and Championing Your Inner Child.* New York: Bantam Books, 1990.

Bunyan, John. *The Pilgrim's Progress.* New York: P. F. Collier & Sons, 1909.

Bunyan, John. *The Pilgrim's Progress.* Retold by Mary Godolphin, 1884. New York: Frederick A. Stokes, 1939.

Catford, Lorna and Michael Ray. *The Path of the Everyday Hero: Drawing on the Power of Myth to Meet Life's Everyday Challenges.* Los Angeles, CA: Jeremy P. Tarcher, Inc., 1991.

Cameron, Julia. *The Artist's Way: A Spiritual Path to Higher Creativity.* Los Angeles: Jeremy P. Tarcher Inc., 1992.

Campbell, Joseph. *The Inner Reaches of Outer Space.* New York: Harper and Row, 1988.

Capacchione, Lucia. *The Power of Your Other Hand: Channeling the Inner Wisdom of the Right Brain.* N. Hollywood, CA: Newcastle Publishing Co. Inc., 1988.

Chopra, Deepak. *The Seven Spiritual Laws of Success: A Practical Guide to the Fulfillment of Your Dreams.* San Rafael, CA: Amber-Allen Publishing, 1994.

Coren, Stanley. *The Left-Hander Syndrome: The Causes and Consequences of Left-Handedness.* New York: The Free Press, 1992.

Carle, Eric. *Draw Me a Star.* New York: Scholastic Inc., 1992.

Curtiss, Homer F. and Harriette A. *The Key to the Universe.* North Hollywood, CA: Newcastle Publishing Co. Inc., 1983.

Dail, Hilda Lee. *The Lotus and the Pool: How to Create Your Own Career.* Boston: Shambhala Publications, Inc., 1989.

DeMille, Agnes and Martha Graham. *Dance to the Piper.* Boston: Little Brown & Co., 1951.

Diaz, Adriana. *Freeing the Creative Spirit: Drawing on the Power of Art to Tap the Magic and Wisdom Within.* San Francisco, CA: HarperCollins, 1992.

Dossey, Larry. *Recovering the Soul: A Scientific and Spiritual Search.* New York: Bantam Books, 1989.

Edwards, Betty. *Drawing on the Right Side of the Brain.* Los Angeles: J.P. Tarcher, Inc., 1979.

Edinger, Edward F. *Ego and Archetype*. New York: Penguin Books, 1972.

Faraday, Ann. *Dream Power*. New York: Berkley Books, 1980.

Fincher, Susanne F. *Creating Mandalas*. Boston: Shambhala Publications, Inc., 1991.

Fox, Matthew. *The Reinvention of Work: A New Vision of Livelihood for Our Time*. San Francisco: HarperCollins Publishers, 1994.

Friedman M. and R. Rosenman. *Type A Behavior and Your Heart*. New York: Knopf, 1974.

Grof, Stanislav. *The Holotropic Mind: The Three Levels of Human Consciousness and How They Shape Our Lives*. San Francisco: HarperCollins, 1993.

Hagber, Janet and Richard Leider. *The Inventurers: Excursions in Life and Career Renewal*. New York: Addison-Wesley Publishing Co., 1982.

Harner, Michael. *The Way of the Shaman*. San Francisco: HarperCollins Publishers, 1990.

Hart, Michael H. *The 100: A Ranking of the Most Influencial Persons in History*. New York: Carol Publishing Group, 1993.

Hendrix, Harville. *Getting the Love You Want: A Guide for Couples*. New York: Harper & Row Publishers, 1988.

Ingerman, Sandra. *Soul Retrieval: Mending the Fragmented Self*. San Francisco: HarperCollins Publishers, 1991.

Johnson, Robert A. *Inner Work: Using Dreams and Active Imagination for Personal Growth*. New York: HarperCollins Publishers, 1986.

Jung, Carl G. *Memories, Dreams, Reflections*. Recorded and edited by Aniela Jaffé and translated by Richard and Clara Winston. Rev. Ed. New York: Vintage Books, 1989.

Jung, Carl G. *Modern Man in Search of a Soul*. New York: Harcourt Brace Jovanovich Publishers, 1933.

Jung, Carl G. *Aion: Researches into the Phenomenology of the Self*. Translated by R.F.C. Hull. In Collected Works of C.G. Jung. Bollingen Series XX, Vol 9. Princeton, N.J.: Princeton University Press, 1970, p. 42.

Larsen, Stephen and Robin. *A Fire in the Mind: The Life of Joseph Campbell*. New York: Anchor Books, 1991.

Luke, Helen M. *Dark Wood to White Rose: Journey and Transformation in Dante's Divine Comedy*. New York: Parabola Books, 1989.

Millman, Dan. *The Life You Were Born to Live*. Tiburon, CA: H.J. Kramer, Inc., 1992.

Moore, Thomas. *Care of the Soul: A Guide for Cultivating Depth and Sacredness in Everyday Life*. New York: HarperCollins Publishers, 1992.

Moore, Thomas, editor. *A Blue Fire: Selected Writings by James Hillman.* New York: Harper and Row Publishers, 1989.

Morse, Melvin. *Closer to the Light.* New York: Ballantine Books, 1990.

Mott, Michael. *The Seven Mountains of Thomas Merton.* New York: Harcourt Brace & Company, 1984.

Niehardt, John G. *Black Elk Speaks: The Life Story of a Holy Man of the Oglala Sioux.* Lincoln: University of Nebraska Press, 1932.

Osbon, Diane K., editor. *A Joseph Campbell Companion: Reflections on the Art of Living.* San Francisco, CA: Harper, 1993.

Pagels, Elaine. *The Gnostic Gospels.* New York: Random House, 1979.

Pascal, Eugene. *Jung to Live By.* New York: Warner Books, 1992.

Pearson, Carol S. *The Hero Within: Six Archetypes We Live By.* San Francisco, CA: HarperCollins, 1989.

Pinsky, Robert. *The Inferno of Dante: A New Verse Translation.* New York: Farrar, Straus, Giroux, 1994.

Redfied, James. *The Celestine Prophecy: An Adventure.* New York: Warner Books, 1993.

Regardie, Israel. *The Middle Pillar.* St. Paul, MN: Llewellyn Publications, 1970.

Sark, *A Creative Companion: How to Free Your Creative Spirit.* Berkeley, CA: Celestial Arts, 1991.

Sher, Barbara. *Wishcraft: How to Get What You Really Want.* New York: Ballantine Books, 1979.

Sinetar, Marsha. *Do What You Love: The Money Will Follow.* New York: Paulist Press, 1987.

St. John of the Cross. *Dark Night of the Soul.* Translated and Introduced by E. Peers, Allison. New York: Bantam Books, 1990.

Steinbrecher, Edwin C. *The Inner Guide Meditation: A Spiritual Technology for the 21st Century.* York Beach, ME: Samuel Weiser, Inc., 1989.

Van de Castle, Robert L. *Our Dreaming Mind.* New York: Ballantine Books, 1994.

Young, Arthur M. *The Reflexive Universe: Evolution of Consciousness.* Mill Valley, CA: Robert Briggs Associates, 1976.

Whitfield, Charles L. *Healing the Child Within: Discovery and Recovery for Adult Children of Dysfunctional Families.* Deerfield Beach, FL: Health Communications, Inc., 1989.

Zajonc, Arthur. *Catching the Light.* New York: Bantam Books, 1993.

STAR GLOSSARY

Bright Stars: see Starphires (Chapters 6 and 8).

Calling: meaningful work that we are "called" to accomplish in life. Also referred to as "Calling Star" and "Career Star" (Chapter 4).

Career Star: symbol of life-purpose; guiding light of a calling (Chapter 2 and 4).

Career Star Strategies: an extensive set of exercises designed to strengthen left- and/or right-brain functioning in order to enhance awareness of potentials and fulfill a calling (Chapter 13).

Career Star System: a theory and method contained for career discovery and development based on inner values.

Career Star Map: a terrain map used as an assessment instrument to determine the extent of left-brain or right-brain lateralization (Chapter 5).

Career Star Wheel: diagram of a conceptual model of the process of career discovery and development divided into six stages (Chapter 13).

Core Injured Self: center of the Injured Child Self caused by the trauma of birth and other painful experiences in infancy and childhood (Chapter 9).

Creative Self: talents such as linguistic and musical skills; powers such as charismatic leadership and psychic abilities; and special knowledge of all types that comprise unlimited individual potential. Often dormant due to lack of awareness and practice. See also Gifted Child (Chapters 4 and 8).

Dark Star: see Starphade (Chapters 6 and 9).

Dynamic Career Star Wheel: a diagram of the Career Star Wheel with the added illustration and explanation of the dimension of forward motion that represents how to actually move and make progress in the Career Star quest (Chapter 13).

External Opponent: the sum total of the injured selves of individuals in a group that makes its appearance in the form of opposition and conflict between individuals and factional subgroups (Chapter 3).

Flowe: exclusive focus on process, reliance on experiential activities, and concentration on sensation, with disregard for ends and results, as a way of being in the world. Also the acquiescence, or adaptation, to larger forces of nature and society by yielding to their influence and power. To "go with the Flowe" is to float with and not fight against the currents in life (Chapter 11).

Force: exclusive focus on results and the reliance solely on logic and willpower to achieve ends. Can be extended to the use of physical might and violent means to achieve goals such as political control and territorial acquisition (Chapter 10).

Gifted Child: the bundle of creative abilities, skills, and potentials that are located in the unconscious part of the mind. If cared for, acted upon, and enhanced, this part of the mind communicates with and directs an individual to his Calling Star. Considered a "child" because the gifts are contained in the part of the mind formed first (Chapter 8).

Incremental Action Strategy: a principle in career development for Starphades that involves breaking down a logical plan of action into interval steps that are an end in themselves in order to avoid the emotional reaction of being overwhelmed and immobilized by the prospect of the whole program (Chapter 13).

Injured Child (Self): the Gifted Child part of the mind that has been damaged by the trauma of birth and by early experiences in infancy and childhood known as the Primal Injury. The Injured Child Self is a natural and unavoidable consequence of birth and early childhood experiences. The extent of the damage may vary, depending on the quality of parenting, genetic givens, and the nature of later life experiences. There may be actual physiological damage if the maltreatment, or subsequent self-destructive behavior, is severe. Also known as the Injured Self and Core Injured Self (Chapter 9).

Internal Opponent: a side of the inner Injured Child Self that resists, objects to, and sabotages developmental work because it imposes more hardship and sacrifice, particularly when an individual is unaware of the child's presence and this effect (Chapters 3 and 9).

Irrational Denial System: unconscious system of thought that seeks to repair the Injured Self through the use of substances or activities that cause the body to rush physiologically. The system actually reinjures the Injured Child and denies the Gifted Child. Long-term effect is addiction and depression (Chapters 9 and 11).

Ketchon II: name of the "inner space craft" of intuition that conveys the Career Star Questar from the point of desire for personal change in consciousness to the point of an unconscious location of a Career Star. The name plays on the idea of "catch on to" your life purpose through the *Career Star System* (Chapter 1).

Magnified Injured Self: name for the Injured Child Self that is enlarged by emotional and/or physical abuse in infancy and childhood or by painful losses in adulthood, i.e., unemployment, death, and divorce. If the Injured Self is aggravated by abuse in childhood, the losses in adulthood will be experienced severely and recovery will be more difficult or impossible (Chapter 9).

Misery-Go-Round: Repetitious and futile actions of the Rational and Irrational Denial Systems that constitute the two big rides in the Whirly World.

Perfectionism: a doctrine that advocates that something must be uniquely and absolutely wrong with an individual for not easily accomplishing the impossible. Psychological reaction of frustration over the slightest of impediments. This doctrine is usually applied by a being who has prejudged himself as hopelessly flawed (Chapters 7 and 10).

Polar Star: individual who has converted mental functioning from right-brain Starphade to left-brain Starphire, or vice versa (Chapter 6).

Primal Injury: the core of the Injured Child Self, the result of traumas experienced in birth and infancy (Chapter 9).

Projection: unconsciously attributing your own mental states to objects and other people. Usually regarded as perceptions. Projection is greatest among individuals whose personal growth is stunted by the Injured Self. Commonly, a negative view of the self is projected and seen as a cruel world (Chapter 3).

Quest: name for the inner journey to self-discovery and self-knowledge. Also, the corresponding endeavor to return the acquisitions to humanity in gratitude and service for the privilege of endowment (Chapter 4).

Questar: quester + star = questar; an individual actively engaged in the search for the meaning of their Career Star (Chapters 2 and 4).

Rational Denial System: system of thought that seeks to compensate the Injured Self through constant achievement and management of the environment. Thought system of justification and repression of both Injured and Creative Selves. While the drive for rational control is usually conscious, the effect of continuous reinjury to the Injured Child Self and denial of Creative Self is not. Long-term consequences are workaholism and burnout (Chapter 10).

Resistance: anxiety, doubt, and fear that are felt when contemplating or acting on developmental goals in the career quest. These feelings interfere and obstruct follow-through actions, especially when an understanding of this reaction is not conscious (Chapter 3).

Scatter Star: a person who has both right- and left-brain mental capacities but instead of integration, the two sides react to each other in opposition causing scattered thinking. Random and arbitrary career development is a result. The diametric opposite of a Sun Star (Chapter 6).

Scintilla: initial spark of life; impact and ignition point of the conception of life and of the self; beginning of conscious human awareness (Chapter 1).

Shadowlands: the secular material world that dwells in the cast of the shadow of Sun Stars because of a block created by the Storm of Self-Doubt and Fear. Also known as the Whirly World (Chapter 3).

Stardom: kingdom or universe in the mind that one enters in resolving to become a Career Star Questar (Chapter 2).

Starphade: an individual who intuitively knows his calling but has substantial, undeserved self-doubt. Tends to be idealistic, has good intentions, wants rewards of affection, and offers peace and justice to the world. Ironically, engaged in the self-destructive activities of the Irrational Denial System that steadily erode talents, capacities, and abilities of their Gifted Child. Life outcome is often underachievement and psychological depression. Also known as Dark Stars (Chapters 5 and 9).

Starphire: an individual usually intensely angry with himself for not having been able to identify his calling. Often engaged in displaced pursuits in the outer world. Usually fully engaged in the Rational Denial System. Tends to ignore and neglect his Gifted and Injured Child Selves.

The anger is frequently intensified when the individual is unable to find meaning in the outer world. Anger is usually externalized and serves to interfere with the use of intuition, which otherwise could be relied upon to access a calling. Long-term life outcome often includes overachievement, burnout, and workaholism. Also known as Bright Stars (Chapters 5 and 8).

Star Storms: the many and often tricky forms of resistance that are aroused by self-doubt when thoughts and actions are directed toward the identification and pursuit of a Career Star (Chapter 3).

Super Star: a person who is naturally able, without training or practice, to employ both left- and right-brain functions. Balanced mental functioning in the identification and quest of a Career Star. An integrated and combined Starphade and Starphire (Chapter 6).

Starwork: any type of inner work, i. e., relaxation, meditation, and visualization, that allows an individual's Career Star to come forth into consciousness. Also frivolousness and silliness that allow for light-heartedness and creative expression (Chapters 1 and 13).

Sun Star: a person on the center path, or attempting to be on the center path, of the *Career Star Map* by studying, applying, and practicing the principles of the *Career Star System* (Chapter 3).

Whirly World: material world, secular reality (Chapter 3).

Available from the Author

Career Strategies Map & Guide©

Full color, poster-size map of the 5 major career paths (24″ x 24″) suitable for framing. An assessment tool to determine the extent of right- and left-brain functioning that reveals the career path you are on currently and potentially, and represents visually the consequences of your choices. Rated "Highly Recommended" by the American Counseling Association.

❋ *Printed Glossy Paper*

Quantity	Price	Shipping & Handling
1	$7.95	($2.00)
2	$13.95	($3.00)
3	$17.95	($4.00)
6	$32.95	($5.00)

❋ **Laminated** (6 mil) $14.95 ($6.00 S&H)

California residents add 8.25% sales tax. Send check or money order with name and address to:

CAREER STAR SYSTEM
P.O. BOX 3564
SOUTH PASADENA, CA 91031-6564
(818) 441-6957

If you are interested in individual counseling, or creating a seminar, workshop, lecture or class by Dr. Jon Snodgrass, use the above address and telephone number.